IT BEGAN WITH HUNTLEY DRINKLEY

A Journey Through Alcoholism and Bipolar Disorder

Janny Becker

DORRANCE
PUBLISHING CO
EST. 1920
PITTSBURGH, PENNSYLVANIA 15238

Dorrance Publishing Co
585 Alpha Drive
Pittsburgh, PA 15238
Visit our website at www.dorrancebookstore.com

ISBN: 978-1-6461-0072-9
eISBN: 978-1-6461-0899-2

ACKNOWLEDGEMENTS

Dr. Grant Haven, for suggesting and supporting the project.

Dr. David Dunner, for taking the time to vet validity related to bipolar disorder.

Susan V Meyers, Director of the Creative Writing Program at Seattle University, Instructor at Hugo House, Seattle, Editor for this writing.

Members of my writing group, for feedback and encouragement.

Frederick Becker Hay, a major inspiration so he would know my story.

Brent Stark, my roommate, for all those French Press cups of coffee.

IT BEGAN WITH HUNTLEY DRINKLEY

ONE EVENING MY PARENTS WERE HAVING THEIR USUAL COCKTAIL HOUR in the Living Kitchen in front of the TV watching the evening news. My father, Fred, was in his brown leather chair. My mother, Maxine, was in hers, also leather but yellow and smaller with a straight back to accommodate her back problems. The Living Kitchen was a pleasant room, large with the kitchen on one side and the sitting area on the other side. A dining table was toward the end of the room. There was a fire in the fireplace that was perpendicular to the couch where I was sitting, and it was pleasantly warming me.

My father, Fred said, "Janny, would you like a little vermouth? It is the light part of our martinis."

His offer was unexpected, but I answered that, "Yes. I would like that." I drank what they gave me and felt a little buzz. When it was done, I asked carefully, "Could I have another small glass?"

They gave it to me. I don't recall ever having only one drink.

I was in eighth grade. For some years they would let me have a tiny glass of sparkling burgundy at Christmas, but to have a drink with them like a grown-up was special. I also liked the little buzz. In that moment, I felt quite sophisticated. Happily, I took them up on their offer. Why wouldn't I? From then on, I was included in the ceremony while watching the evening news. Chet Huntley and David Brinkley were the news anchors on NBC television. At our house the cocktail hour was known as "Huntley Drinkley."

Carolyn, my sister, had joined the cocktail hour a few minutes later, though she was a little upset.

"Janny is one year younger than I was when I got my first drink," she pointed out.

We were a bit competitive, and it was true: she was allowed to join this ceremony when she was a freshman in high school. As always, she was four years older and often blazed the trail for me for when we were allowed to do certain things. I looked at my parents to see if they were going to respond but they didn't.

My parents' philosophy was if we could drink with them, we would not feel a need to experiment away from home where we might get into trouble. This theory turned out to be only somewhat true for me. Soon after that first "Huntley Drinkley" evening, I was home alone while my parents were out for the evening and would be getting back late. I got a chair to get into the liquor cabinet that was higher than I could reach and proceeded to taste test the various kinds of liquor there.

This was a cautious project, as I was very careful not to take too much out of any one bottle. Still I got quite drunk and threw up not long after I'd cleaned up any evidence of my experiment. Even so, it all felt worth it. My high was amazing, like nothing I had ever experienced before. I felt a little like I was floating and had trouble navigating around the furniture. Although I had to be careful not to fall, I enjoyed the feeling of freedom as I watched the clock for when my parents would get home. For the time being, I relaxed, watched TV, and enjoyed being alone in my own company. I felt wonderfully free. Then, I went to bed and pretended to be asleep. With the exception of throwing up, it was a glorious experience.

Beyond that kind of small escapade, though, I did not drink on my own for several years. Later on, toward the end of high school, I would drink with a buddy at the drive-in movies on occasion. In contrast, I am quite sure that Carolyn did not drink outside of home until she went to college.

So, those early memories of alcohol were mostly social, and mostly good. In particular, I remember Huntley Drinkley as a pleasant time when we all would share about our day and comment on the news. Carolyn and I would often share about our friends and school. Carolyn was a straight-A student but tended to be concrete in her thinking, and there were times we would have to explain the point of a news story or the meaning of a joke. This was always done in a loving and gentle way. Once in a while, my mother, Maxine, would get a little high and my father would notice. This was not hard to tell as her voice would get louder incrementally.

"Now Maxie, I think you have had enough," Fred would say.

She would finish her drink and then set the glass on the table next to her. I always wondered how she felt about this as I would not have liked being told to stop, especially in front of other people. My parents never disagreed in front of us but presented a united front and she did not say anything.

I didn't want to lose my privileges and was careful not to show I had a buzz. I did not want my father to notice I was a little high and tell me I had enough. I never knew if my sister got a buzz or not but suspect that she did.

Mother would usually talk about how my sister and I were doing with our piano lessons. She was a musician, and our music education was important to her. We were often in recitals together and Fred was expected to attend so he would get notice when one was approaching.

"Remember that there is a recital coming up," she would say. "Carolyn is doing well with her pieces, though Janny still has a way to go."

To be fair, this was usually true. Carolyn practiced more than I did, as she wanted to please Maxine. I liked my lessons, but there were also other things important to me and I had limits to how much I was willing to practice. I needed to see my friends, to draw and paint and to do homework without a time limit that practicing would create.

Also, during Huntley Drinkley, my father would share about things that happened with friends, about coming events and the business. He had a great sense of humor and would often make fun of things in the news.

On occasion this would be when he would tell us, "The business is a little slow and we need to be careful about what we spend."

He owned an automobile dealership, and things would be slow in the winter months. We always paid attention to his requests but never got too worried as we were used to the change of business seasons and we knew it would get better soon. Besides, we knew our father was a good businessman.

For years after that, we did "Huntley Drinkley" whenever we could, which meant that Carolyn and I, from an early age, became daily drinkers, just like our parents.

* * *

PLEASE NOTE: In the following text there will be certain sections that will be in italics. These contain information that is important about bipolar disorder.

THE BEGINNING

I WAS BORN INTO A HOUSEHOLD CONSISTING OF my father Fred, the owner of an automobile agency in Walla Walla, Washington, my mother, Maxine, a musician and my sister, who was four years older than me. My Uncle Kip, my father's brother had moved to Walla Walla to work for my father as a salesman. He was single and lived with us, helped around the house and became an important part of our family, especially for me.

FRED

MY PATERNAL GRANDFATHER WAS GONE PERIODICALLY, as he was not interested in raising children. He would return sporadically and on five occasions my grandmother would have another child. I know the last absence was long. My father was born ten years after his next sibling. Though little was said about my grandfather, when we were older my sister and I realized that he was Jewish. I can only guess why this was never discussed. It has also occurred to me that this grandfather may have had another family.

My grandmother Dora ran a hotel in Portland, Oregon. Because she died before I was born, I know very little about her. I did understand that she was a competent businesswoman, though she was not often available for mothering duties. My Uncle Kip was the one who took care of her in her later years, and when she died Kip came to Walla Walla and lived with us. It was my father's siblings who essentially took on the task of raising Fred. When he was fairly young, for instance, he had polio and required a lot of care. The experience left him with a limp, and I know that he was teased by other kids, though he overcame the limp through sheer determination. By the time he was in high school, that limp of his was barely noticeable; and once he was an adult, it was gone. One leg did remain with lesser muscle tone, but you could only tell if he showed you.

During adolescence, Fred lived with his oldest sister, Eve, and her husband Sid, who was a lawyer. They lived in La Grande, Oregon. Sid became a judge. Actually, he had the reputation of being a "Drunken Judge," as he did drink a good deal. My father was very grateful to his siblings for helping him when he was growing up. As an adult, he was very generous with them and employed not only Uncle Kip but also his sister Frieda's husband, Reed.

Fred wanted to be a lawyer, partly because he admired Sid. So, he went to the University of Oregon to study. Years later, I remember that he did have a set of law books, which he never threw out, even though he'd never gotten that law degree. It was, after all, the middle of the Depression, and after the second year, he could not afford school anymore, so he'd gone to Enterprise, Oregon and worked as the accountant for the Ford dealer there. This was in about 1933. Fred and his best friend, Kelly had a little side business. Prohibition was still in effect, so Fred and Kelly had built a still in the hills outside Enterprise. They made moonshine and sold it to the fraternity boys at the University of Oregon.

A rebel and an entrepreneur: that was my father. And that became, I think, no small part of myself. When I did rebellious things, he often said little and I always thought he was reminded of his own wildness when he was younger. Years later, when he died before I opened my own agency, I was sorry that he hadn't been there to witness it.

MAXINE

UNLIKE MY FATHER, MY MOTHER, MAXINE, WAS AN ONLY CHILD. When my grandmother became pregnant, her husband said that he would stay if it was a boy, but not if it was a girl. He left when mother was born and my great grandmother Belle came to live with her daughter and help with the new baby who was named Maxine.

My great grandmother Belle was a character I wish I had known. A suffragette, she had strong political views and enjoyed intellectual discussion. Clearly, she was an independent and capable woman, and she believed that women were oppressed. Even physically, she demanded attention, striking as she was with snow-white hair by the time she was twenty-one years old. Back then, she'd married an older man who had been a soldier in the Civil War. When he was wounded in the war, he was given alcohol for the pain, and Belle believed this was the cause of his alcoholism later in life. His name was James Case. They had two children, a boy whom I know nothing about, and a daughter, my grandmother Nelle.

James died when Belle was still young. So, she packed up the kids, got on a train, and left Iowa for Oregon to homestead a property on a mountain. There were hints about a miner who lived on the mountain who was of help in building their cabin. Belle lived there for a few years until she felt that it was time to move to a city where the children could get an education. Then, she settled in Eugene, Oregon, keeping the cabin, which, years later, would be where she took Nell for an extended stay when she had a "nervous breakdown." During this time, the isolation of the cabin was a blessing, as Belle had to tie her daughter to the bed for days when she was out of control. Fortunately, Nelle did recover, though it reportedly took about a year before they went back to town.

I do have a memory of Belle. When I was about four years old, she came to visit us in Walla Walla. At that time, my sister had been dealing with a bully in the neighborhood, and Belle decided to do something about it. One day the bully walked by the house on his way home from school. Either my mother or

Carolyn pointed him out to Belle. The next day when school let the kids out, Belle took me with her to the front yard. There was a small hill at the side walk and we stood on top of it. As the bully approached, Belle handed me her cane and said, "Hit him on the head when he comes by." So, I did. It created a big fuss in the neighborhood that included a visit to the bully's house from their doctor, and a visit to my parents' house by his parents.

Maxine and Fred figured out exactly what had happened, promising that it would not happen again and telling me not to repeat what we'd done, though they didn't punish me. And, the bully never bothered my sister again. My mother said that Belle was a little demented. Her visit, in fact, had really been arranged, so that Maxine could see her grandmother before it got worse.

Years after the fact, I would check in with my mother to see if I had remembered that incident correctly. She confirmed that I had. I think my great-grandmother and I shared things in common. To begin with, I like the way she met her challenges with action and determination, and the fact that she became a homesteader and a suffragette. Except for having me hit the bully on the head, an idea most likely derived from dementia, I like that she made a plan and saw it through. Besides, it had stopped the bully.

Indeed, there was plenty to admire in the women of my family. Industrious as her mother, my grandmother Nelle was successful as a business woman, and a musician who opened a music store with studios above it that she rented for music and dance lessons. The downside, though, was that Nelle seems to have been quite narcissistic and was not a mothering type. While she wasn't nurturing, Nelle did make sure that her child had opportunities. For instance, once Maxine was old enough, Nelle sent her for lessons in flute and piano in the studios above her store. This served two purposes, to begin her music education and to replace the need for a babysitter after school, which also gave Belle a break. Fortunately, Mother was talented and excelled at playing both the piano and the flute, and she played both the rest of her life.

So, in some ways, music saved my mother; and it taught me a bit about her, too. When I was young, she used to tell me about it, explaining how, when she first started playing the flute, she would sit on a high stool and get dizzy from breathing hard enough to produce a tone. She worried, she told me, that she might fall off the stool, but she never did. Later in life, when mother was tested by the doctor for her breathing, she would blow the meter high off the mark from years of playing the flute.

Although she didn't particularly relish spending time with her child, my grandmother Nelle was a woman who did not like to be without a man, and eventually was married four times. And, as though I needed a reminder of the brazen women from my past, when my mother died, I inherited the diamonds from Nelle's wedding rings. I have to admire her that in her era it was quite unusual to be married four times, and she did it anyway. Two of her husbands died while still married to her, but she found another man after each one. And, to commemorate her ingenuity, I designed a new ring using her diamonds and adding a sapphire centerpiece so that I can wear it and think of all that history. Indeed, someone I know who explores family histories exclaimed the unusualness of mine in that someone in my background had five last names.

I suppose such colorful histories can have their downfall, though, and my mother described Nelle as narcissistic, always making decisions that served herself over the needs of others. Nelle was not an affectionate mother. Maxine told me a story that when she was ten years old, Nelle promised her she would take her on a train ride. The day came, and they went to the train station. But when the train arrived, Nelle got on it with a strange man and sent my mother home, not caring how that would affect Maxine, who was bewildered and crushed.

Instead, Belle was the parent who looked out for my mother when she was young, who interacted with Maxine as a caregiver and showed interest in her development. Mother describes her childhood as an only child as having to learn to entertain herself and that this was one reason that she became an avid reader. I don't know if my mother had childhood friends, as she never mentioned any.

When mother was still quite young, Nelle married a man considerably older than her. Mother described him as a nice but very serious person. He was a railroad man. My grandmother preferred that Maxine use his last name rather than that of her first husband. Her real father's last name was Kirk.

Mother thought of making my middle name Kirk, but Nelle would have had a fit, so mother settled for "Kay" for my middle name. Nelle was not forgiving of Mr. Kirk's abandonment.

Maxine went to the University of Oregon and graduated in English literature. She was a Phi Beta Kappa, which she was not shy in letting people know. It seems likely she had an affair with her English professor, who was a poet. Mother intimated this on a number of occasions. He was the Poet Laureate of Australia. Her friends were artists, writers and musicians who were all going to go to New York City together after graduation.

These were young, intellectual, talented free spirits, and people of the arts. When Belle and Nelle got wind of the New York plan, they would not hear of it. Next, Mother applied to teach English to students in Korea, which was met with even more opposition. I believe at that time Korea was politically unstable. I can guess mother's plans were a little too wild for their liking.

So, my mother ended up taking a high school teaching job in Enterprise, Oregon where the father of a good friend was the Superintendent of Schools. This is where she and my father met. Belle accompanied Maxine to Enterprise. I suspect the plans to go to NYC and Korea had something to do with it, as well as there were not too many young women who lived alone then.

My father was the wild guy that the townspeople told my mother to avoid. It was a small town, and people were aware of most things that went on. My father and his best friend Kelly were two of the eligible bachelors in town, and they were particularly under scrutiny. Kelly, with my father along, rode his horse into the apartment house of a young woman he was courting. Indeed, with my father's help, he rode the horse all the way down the hall and up to her door. With stunts like those, of course they became the talk of the town. Moreover, perhaps the most significant thing they did was build the still and make that bootleg liquor. If they sold it to the fraternities at the University of Oregon in Eugene, it is a sure bet they sold to others in Enterprise.

Fred was outgoing, handsome and had a good sense of humor. People liked him. He was employed as the accountant to the Ford dealer so was well employed in the middle of the Depression. Of course, Maxine was drawn to him, particularly because he was the "wild one." It did not take long for Fred to win over Belle.

Perhaps I got my attraction to "wild guys" from Maxine, and unknowingly because of my fondness for my father. I would have a few in my life over the years. I also have a feeling when I did get in trouble due to my own "wildness," I always noticed that my father seldom got too upset, perhaps remembering his own wild days and identifying with me a bit.

My parents decided to marry but did it secretly because it was still the Depression and women who were married were not allowed to work. The school year would end in a few months, and mother did not want to leave without a teacher to replace her. So, Fred got an apartment across the hall from Belle and my mother. Belle would check to see that the coast was clear, and Mother would sneak over to join Fred each night. I have always loved this story and how it reflected on the character of all three of them.

When the school year ended, they no longer kept their marriage secret, and Belle went back to Eugene to live with Nelle who was now married to her third husband. After Belle left, the opportunity to buy into a dealership with a Dodge Plymouth dealer in Walla Walla came up, and they moved from Enterprise. The dealer in Walla Walla wanted to retire in a few years, heard of my father from the dealer in Enterprise and offered the opportunity to my father to learn and eventually take over the business.

MY PARENTS TOGETHER

BOTH MY PARENTS HAD FATHERS WHO DESERTED THEM and mothers who were not available to nurture them. Fortunately, both of them had others who took over and raised and nurtured them. My father had his siblings and my mother had her grandmother.

Maxine supported Fred in his business, and Fred supported Maxine in her music. They clearly had differences but did not deal with them in front of my sister or me and never spoke ill of each other in front of us. They were there for each other through medical difficulties and presented a united front in dealing with our crises and rebellions. I believe they loved each other very much.

My parents were happy in Walla Walla. My father was doing well with the dealership and Fred became friends with many of his customers and business associates. Mother became friends with some of their wives and with people in the music community. Maxine played the flute in the Walla Walla Symphony and taught piano. They also became good friends with many of our neighbors. The business was stable as Fred was a driven businessman and worked very hard. They also joined a Congregational Church. Maxine sang in the choir and Fred was a Deacon.

In their fourth year of marriage, my mother had gotten pregnant with my sister. I think my father was happy and ready to have children. Once, however, I overheard my mother tell several friends that she had never wanted to be a mother, but everyone was having children, so she did, too. So, I don't think Maxine was especially happy about the pregnancy. I doubt she talked about this with Fred. My mother had not exactly had good role modeling for motherhood. She was also succumbing to social pressure, something that would continue. To make matters worse, Carolyn was born with life-threatening asthma. The doctor said she was wheezing with her first breath. So, Mother was on call for whenever Carolyn might go into an asthma attack, which was frequently.

When he was twenty-seven, my father was diagnosed with ulcerative colitis, which was quite serious. The doctors recommended surgery, but he refused, as it meant he would have a colostomy. He managed it with medication and diet. He had a good nurse in Maxine, who made sure doctor's orders were followed which included a special diet. It was also recommended that he should be under as little stress as possible. This was the difficult part, as he was a driven businessman; and, after she was born, Carolyn's asthma was a constant stress. And for Maxine that meant that now there would be two special diets and doctors' orders to follow.

Fortunately, my mother had some support from a woman who managed the apartment house where they lived. Her name was Maudi, and she was a very nurturing older woman. Later, Maudi was also a trusted sitter for Carolyn which was important respite for both Maxine and Fred. My parents were very fond of Maudi and my father was always there for her when she needed a little help with something. After Fred and Maxine moved from the apartment, they remained friends and visited regularly. After I was born, Maudi was our most frequent babysitter, and Carolyn and I became fond of her, too.

MY SISTER CAROLYN

CAROLYN WAS BORN IN 1939. Her asthma had a serious impact on her childhood and early adult life. She was poked with needles to stop attacks and scratched to determine what she was allergic to. Moreover, she had an exquisite allergy to peanuts, and was allergic to dust, pollen, most animals with hair, and a number of other foods that were not as serious as the peanuts. She could not run much, as it would bring on the wheezes. When she had attacks, my parents would rock her for long periods of time, rubbing her back soothingly and trying to help her relax. Often, the doctor would be called to the house to administer an injection of a strong medication to stop the attack. There was some worry that those treatments, though, could impact her heart.

Throughout all of this, my mother was a vigilant first responder when Carolyn had attacks. Other mothers and teachers were alerted to contact Maxine immediately if they suspected she was in any distress and that quick action was essential as an attack could be life threatening. They were also told not to feed her anything that she might be allergic to. The kids she played with were also instructed to be on guard and what to do which was essentially bring her home or get mother. So, Carolyn was presented to the world as a living time bomb.

Carolyn was a very beautiful little girl with dark, loosely wavy hair, big sky-blue eyes, and lovely skin. She indeed resembled Elizabeth Taylor. She truly did most everything well. She was very compliant to my parents' requests as well as those of others she viewed as in authority, as she always carried the anxiety that she might not live up to the standards that were expected of her. Clearly, she was not a worry-free little girl.

In retrospect, it also seems likely that she did not feel very lovable. I think this was closely tied to the anxiety, fear, and weariness that my parents felt. Asthma causes the bronchi to spasm and makes it difficult to exhale; and if you can't exhale, you cannot inhale. In most cases, the doctor would be called to give her IV medication. Time and again, the atmosphere was intense until the doctor got there. When the doctor did get there, he would give her the IV medication that involved a large syringe put into her vein and the tube would fill with blood.

When she was younger, I always wondered what she thought about my parents subjecting her to all of that harsh intervention. And what did she think about the blood, the concerned atmosphere, and the immediate response it always brought? She had to know that she was in danger, as it would feel like she was suffocating, and there was always such a fuss. Eventually, this relative chaos must have seemed routine, but she had to have picked up—at least implicitly—on the anxiety that everyone had around her even when she was not in an attack. I was glad to be me and not her. I also felt helpless to help her, because I was.

There were not many children my age in the neighborhood, which Maxine used as an excuse for me to go with my sister and her friends to play. The real reason, though, was for me to watch out for my sister and if she wheezed, to run back and get mother. This was the beginning of defining my role with my sister, that of rescuing her when she was in trouble. It was not a positive part of our relationship for either of us and came to be the source of deep resentment toward me on the part of my sister.

JANNY (ME),
THE YOUNGER YEARS

I WAS BORN HEALTHY, WHICH WAS A BLESSING for my mother, as both Fred and Carolyn needed a lot of attention. Mother suffered from post-partum depression after giving birth to me. This went untreated until I was nearly ten years old. Mother became pregnant again when I was still under one year. That was more than she could deal with, and she went to the family doctor, who was also the doctor in town who kept the prostitutes clean and did abortions. He was aware of my mother's depression and the situation with Carolyn, Fred, and an infant. So, my mother got an abortion. I never knew what my father thought about it, or if he was consulted. I can only guess he did not approve of the abortion and this would, perhaps, have a serious effect on a turning point in my life some years later.

When I was in my late forties, I was having some difficulty neurologically and went to a neurologist who had me get a brain scan. It indicated that my brain was smaller than was normal for someone my age. The doctor told me that I probably had meningitis as an infant that had gone untreated. She asked me if I knew how attentive my mother had been when I was very young and suspected that my mother missed the fact that I needed more medical attention than I was given. I could believe it.

I told her, "My mother was overwhelmed when I was first born."

I asked if a small brain might affect my intelligence, and she assured me that it would not. My problem for going to this doctor was due to a medication I was on and when I got off of it, I was fine. I did not find it good, though, that I have a small brain.

Lucky for me, Uncle Kip was a very kind and gentle man who adored me. He was a part of my care when I was a baby and when I was old enough, I followed him like a shadow. I watched and "helped" in the garden with my little garden tools he had gotten for me. I watched, fascinated, when he tied flies for fishing. He pushed me in the swing on the maple tree and guided me up the ladder of our big wooden slide and caught me at the bottom. He greeted me as I came downstairs each morning and rocked me and read to me as mother prepared breakfast. He clearly provided the nurturing my mother was unable to give, and I was able to flourish.

Uncle Kip helped out with a lot at the house and was a talented gardener. I was with him most of the time when he was home. One of my earliest memories was being with him in the back yard when the two Irving brothers, who lived across the alley, came to the back gate. We stood looking at each other through the chain link fence.

They asked, "How old are you?"

I turned to Uncle Kip and asked, "How old am I, Uncle Kip?

He said, "You are three."

"What's your name?" I asked the older brother.

He said, "My name is Jimmy and I am three and a half. This is Jacky, my brother. He is younger and I don't know how old he is."

I remember the chain length fence and the Irving boys standing on the other side of the fence looking into our yard, their little fingers gripping the chain link. At this point in my life, Uncle Kip always seemed to be there when I needed him.

I was an active child, easily entertained myself, always finding things to do. I was quite artistic, which mother encouraged. I was given the nickname of "Mighty Mouse" because I was always busy and darting around, *perhaps a sign of what was to come.* I also was nick named "Sparkle Plenty," after a little girl in the Dick Tracy comic strip. Both of us had long blond curly hair. I thought she was kind of ugly, but my parents and Uncle Kip said she was cute. I didn't buy it. My sister looked like Elizabeth Taylor and I looked like Sparkle Plenty. Mighty Mouse was much better.

THE NOT SO EXTENDED FAMILY

MY MOTHER WAS AN ONLY CHILD, SO we had no aunts or uncles from her side of the family. My father made up for this with four siblings. My father's sister,

Frieda and her husband Reed lived in Walla Walla. Freida was a talented seamstress and did it professionally. Reed worked for my father as the Parts Man at the dealership. Frieda made lovely outfits for me and my sister. Mostly, I remember that they were very well made. One of them that stays in my mind was a dark green velvet coat with a matching hat with a front brim and a tie under the chin. The hat was important as when we were at Priest Lake one Fall day, mother had placed me on the two holer and because I was quite small, I began to fall in. The brim of the hat with the chin tie caught me along with my shoes before my mother could catch me. I remember her telling the other people we were with she was glad I did not fall in as she would have had to decide whether to clean me up or just leave me in there. I was pretty little but knew she was kidding, but it was not a nice thought.

We used to go visit Aunt Freida, but there were times she was not receiving visitors. Carolyn and I did not know why; it was just how it was. When we did visit, Frieda was very nice and treated us well. *Years later I would realize she was bipolar.* Freida did not have women friends, as she was obsessed that another woman might seduce Reed. He was far from handsome, and Maxine thought she was ridiculous about this. Mother tended to be somewhat judgmental and empathy was not her usual response to others. Freida did not want children, so much so that she was devastated once when she found a lump in her breast and thought that she might be pregnant. When it turned out to be cancer, she was much relieved. She did survive the cancer, and she never had children.

Family get togethers most often involved our aunts and uncles drinking too much and having fights that caused them to stop speaking to each other for months. Maxine did not like this and usually was not enthusiastic about the family gatherings. My sister and I did not witness the fights, though, as they occurred after we were in bed, and the adults had been drinking all day.

Aunt Eve and Uncle Sid still lived in La Grande, Oregon. They were the ones who Fred lived with when he was an adolescent. They had two daughters, both in their 20s, Doris and Sydney. The oldest daughter was quite beautiful and looked like Rosemary Clooney. The other daughter was cute. Both became alcoholic. The younger one died in her thirties and the older one struggled with it for years. It does run in families.

Aunt June was Fred's next older sibling by ten years. She and her husband owned a tavern in Bend Oregon. They had a son named Ben, whom I barely remember meeting. Some years later, June died in a car crash when she drove drunk and was smoking and the car burned up. I remember my father being very upset when this happened. I found it awful that someone would die that way. My sister and I never knew our cousins that well as they were quite a bit older than we were and seldom came to family gatherings.

I never felt that I missed much by not having a larger and more active extended family. It seems to me, the larger the family the more the problems.

THE HOUSE IN WALLA WALLA

WHEN MY SISTER WAS THREE, MY PARENTS built a house near the Whitman College campus at 728 University Street in Walla Walla in a neighborhood with a number of families with young children. My father knew what he wanted and worked with an architect to design a three-bedroom, Cape Code Colonial house: white with green shutters.

The kitchen was large and open. A large round table and benches were set back from the main section of the room in a bay window and left a big section of open floor where my sister and I would play. We would figure out how we could play inconspicuously in order to hear the conversations of my mother and her friends as they chatted over coffee. We would often draw and color pictures or do jigsaw puzzles or play checkers or board games on the floor near the table. The quieter the better. We did not want to draw attention to ourselves or disturb Mother and her guests.

But even if we tried not to disturb them, we did watch them. I remember when my mother and one of her friends sent away for a book about what were considered deviant sex acts. It was called "Psychopathia Sexualus" and was the kind of book you could only order if you were a doctor. The neighbor's husband was a doctor, so she had ordered it in his name and then intercepted it when it came in the mail. My mother and her friends were delighted; and, although they did not read it aloud when we were in the room, we did hear them laughing when we weren't there. Many years later, I found that book among my mother's belongings and took it to see what it was like. It was a little disappointing, though, after all that time, it was very antiquated compared to what is acceptable sexual behavior today.

Back then, when we were kids, there were still plenty of titillating secrets. Rumor had it, for instance, that our neighbor, Gracie, did not wear underwear, so my sister and I would play Jax on the floor near the table and try to look up her dress as she sat with Mother to see if it was true. Try as we did, though, we never confirmed the rumor.

There were other forms of entertainment, though. A large recreation room in the basement was where we could play when it was cold or stormy out. I remember it most as where my father would show movies every month. One of his customer's wife had MS and was bedridden. My father's friend had access to get movies from California for her entertainment. He would show them on one Saturday a month, and my father would pick them up on Sunday and show them in our recreation room or, in good weather, outside in our backyard. They came with a newsreel, a cartoon, a short Kit Carson serial and the main feature. When it was time, we'd put a sandwich board out in front of the house with the feature film on it so the neighbors were welcome to join us, which many did. I remember we had a big popcorn popper with a little handle that you turned to keep the popcorn from burning. I liked to be the one who got to turn the handle. We always made popcorn to go with the movie. On Monday, Fred would mail the movie to some town in Alaska and they, in turn, would mail it back to California after they showed it. I always thought that my father was very smart because of how he found things like those movies. He was very friendly with many of his customers and managed to get a number of things either by working something out like the movies or by taking in things in trade for cars over the years.

So, our lives went well, inside and out. In the back yard, there was a good-sized garden and a peach tree that was mother's pride and joy. She would can the peaches or bake delicious pies. To the side of the house were three very large old maple trees. There was ample room for the large wooden slide that Fred had gotten from a customer whose kids had grown up. There was also a great swing that Fred built that hung from one of the maple trees. There was plenty of room for running around. We had a sand box and at times pitched a tent for our playhouse.

When I was younger, I was especially fond of a great birch tree that produced hanging pods that squashed into flakes and became a paste when mixed with water. I fed these to the Irving boys. I heard my parents laughing about it. They were not laughing *at* me but because they thought I was funny. They were not fans of the Irving boys who were a bit mischievous. I was still told not to do that again.

In retrospect, we were very lucky kids to have the yard and a father who thought of us when designing the house. Indeed, Walla Walla was a great place for kids. It was safe for us to play in the neighborhood after dinner without supervision. We did have a curfew, but in the summer, we stayed out after dark, playing kick the can, hide and seek, and some games we made up. We would end the evening telling scary stories or "Shaggy Dog" jokes, rather long corny jokes with a twist at the end. I was not fond of the scary stories, but I did love the jokes.

Thinking back to those early days, I feel sad for kids who do not have the freedom and the kind of creativity at play that we did. Many have been robbed of much of this by technology. I see kids walking in my neighborhood with cell phones texting. Too often, I see them step into the street without looking for on-coming cars. And how can you appreciate the scenery if your eyes are on a cell phone? Sadly, the way we were able to be free and not worry about dangers in the neighborhood appears to have also become a thing of the past for most children today.

There was a group of us who hung out together. I had a special good friend during my early grade school days. Her name was Judy and I knew she was truly a good friend when she took me aside and informed me that I was a show-off and that the other kids did not like it. *Being a show off is not uncommon for people with bipolar tendencies.* We made a pact that if I began to show off, she would give me the high sign and I would stop.

A big change came when I was seven. Uncle Kip decided to marry a woman he had dated for many years who had been living in Portland. It meant he would move out. I was devastated at first, but everyone assured me that he and this woman would live in Walla Walla and visit a lot. My sister and I were prepared not to like her, and we thought she had a stupid name, Thone. Instead, though, she turned out to be a nice, kind, quiet woman. I did get to see Kip, as they would come for family gatherings and just to visit at times. I also got to see him when we went to the dealership with Fred. It just wasn't the same as when he lived at our house. I did get over missing him at home as I was growing up and getting busier with school and music and friends. He remained interested in me and how I was doing. I always loved him. I still give him credit for saving my early development.

He died when he was in his early 80's, while I was living in Seattle, my mother in Spokane. For many months after it had happened, my mother didn't tell me. I asked her why not, and she told me that she didn't think I would care. That is how far removed my mother was to how much time he spent with me and the emotional support and nurturing he gave me. By then, though, I was old enough that it was not a surprise to me that Mother would not be more in touch with how important he was for me.

FRED AND ME

FRED WAS CLEAR ABOUT HIS EXPECTATIONS OF MY SISTER AND ME. We were to behave ourselves in public, be respectful of adults and address them as Mr. or Mrs. or Dr. As we grew older, we were to be "straight A" students, and we were to respect our mother's demands regarding our music education. I am reminded of this frequently and I am forever grateful for the exposure I had to music from an early age. Although I no longer play often myself, I have been left with an appreciation for music of all kinds. I have always loved the symphony, jazz, as well as most forms of popular music over the years.

Fred often read stories to us at bedtime. Our favorites were "Billy Whiskers" about the adventures of a goat, and "Mrs. Piggle Wiggle," about a wise woman who gave advice to parents having trouble with their children. The best story was about a little girl who would not bathe, and Mrs. Piggle

Wiggle told her parents to put radish seeds on her one night when she was asleep. Because she was so dirty, the radish seeds sprouted and freaked her out, and she would bath after that with no fuss. Our most favorite, though, was "Winnie the Pooh," the best poem being the one about Wheezles and Sneezles because of Carolyn's asthma. My parents gave us each a stuffed bear that looked like Winnie the Pooh. My sister's remained pristine and I kissed the nose on mine so much he got a bald nose. I still have him on a shelf in my room. He is at least seventy years old.

Beyond reading us these bedtime stories my father Fred was also talented at making up stories that were clever and had great themes and characters. One of my favorite times with him was when we would go fishing alone and he told me stories of "Timothy Finny Tail" who was a young fish in Priest Lake who had many adventures. When a fish was caught I would ask, "Is that Timothy?"

"Oh, no," he said. "This is Timothy's mean cousin."

Timothy also had a mean uncle, a mean neighbor, a bully and so on.

Fred was always home in the evenings for family dinner. He also held Sundays sacred for being with us. He had a playful streak, a good sense of humor and clearly enjoyed being with us and we with him.

He was immaculate in his grooming, had good taste in how he dressed, and was particular in the care of his clothes and the care of other possessions. He had a special place on the workroom bench where he would polish his shoes, and I would often watch. He also was insistent that the cars the family used were in top condition, partly because they were often demonstrators for the business and partly because property was to be treated with respect. I always felt this was good role modeling though I have not always lived up to his example.

Until recently I drove a 14-year-old Toyota Avalon with at least six dents or scrapes. My garage is narrow. I would decide to get them fixed and then get another one. I told people it is a great car, which it was, but that it runs into things. I had a dream fairly recently in which my father came to visit, saw my car and took the keys away from me.

AN EARLY LESSON LEARNED

WHEN I WAS AROUND THREE YEARS OLD, ONE DAY I wanted to go out the back door, but it tended to stick and was particularly stuck that day. I called for mother who came and gave the door a big tug and it came open with force right on Maxine's nose and knocked her out cold. I did not know what to do so just stood looking down at her. I thought she was dead. She came to shortly and got up with a bloody nose and what was to become a slightly blackened eye.

I remember my mother telling some people that when she came to, there was a very puzzled little three-year-old standing over her with wide eyes. The long-term effect of this was a slight increase of a not too noticeable hump on her nose. For some reason, I had a thing about this.

Most likely due to my sense of mother's depression and some failure in our bonding, there was a time when I was about four that I got the idea that my mother might be a witch. One clue was that she had that slight hump on her nose. Another was that sometimes she seemed not to respond when I thought I needed attention and I was not sure that she liked me very much. In fact, it crossed my mind that she might prefer not to have me around. I just did not feel that she cared that much. It wasn't so much what she said as what she did not say.

At first her lack of response frightened me, and I would lay awake in the dark with my sister sleeping across the room from me. For a period of time, when I was convinced that my mother was a witch, I worried that she kept a big black bear in the attic above the closet in our room. I would have deep fear that it would come down and get me in the night. After some time, though, I became tired of being afraid and decided to muster my courage and look in the attic. I carefully retrieved a fairly substantial step stool that was kept in the kitchen and a flash light from the tool drawer and went into the closet, setting up the step stool and climbing up to reach the attic door, which was not on the ceiling, but rather down a way on the wall. I was able to see in pretty well with the help of the flash light. And there it was, an empty, dusty attic. This was the beginning of my knowing it is best to investigate things feared before making life miserable being afraid. The notion that mother was perhaps a witch did not end, it just meant she did not keep a big black bear in the attic. Over time, the witch thing did fade away.

THE SANTA LIST

When I was about four, my parents, as usual, asked us for a Santa list for Christmas. My parents always tried to make things equal between us. I hated this because Carolyn would make her list, and I would make my list, and we both got what was on her list. So, this time I asked for a dresser drawer. My parents had no idea what I meant, but my sister did, as we had one of those early sibling communication things. So, they asked her if she knew what I wanted, and she explained that I wanted a suitcase. I really did feel hurt when they ignored my list and this time, I was going to do something about it. I was sure that my sister did not have a dresser drawer on her list, and they were sure to notice my unusual request.

We always opened presents early on Christmas Eve. This time, for once I got one thing on my list that was different from Carolyn. It was a small black suitcase. As soon as presents were all opened, I took my suitcase upstairs to my room and packed my most precious things. I put on my coat and boots and walked out of the house unseen and down the street to my babysitter's house. I told her I was running away from home and asked if I could stay with her. She called my father and said she would give me dinner and he could come get me after that. So, my father came, and I have a very clear memory of walking hand in hand back to our house with him carrying my little suitcase in his other hand. I was really glad that he came to get me, as I was worried that he and mother did not really care about me, but this proved that they did. At least he did.

It is clear to me I was picking up the fact that mother was not really there for me; and I was correct. It would be revealed to me some years later that she did not really want children but did have us, due to social pressures, something that was to become somewhat of a driving force in her life. Also, it was obvious that her mother did not want to be a mother, either, and turned Maxine's care over to Great-Grandmother Belle. The role model for motherhood was not there. In addition, her post-partum depression combined with the demands in my sister's and father's health problems placed on her were serious. But at age four, I did not put this all together. I was so lucky to have Uncle Kip and my father who were there for me.

THE GRADE SCHOOL YEARS

CAROLYN AND I WERE FOUR YEARS APART, and most of my teachers had Carolyn in their classes before me. I did not have perfect performance like she did, but close enough. I did not worry about being perfect but did want to do well.

I made friends in school easily and would go to their houses and they to mine after school to play. My sister's time to practice piano was after school, so I was free to be with friends. I had one friend whose mother was from Canada. When we went to her house we had "Tea" with real tea and milk and sugar and usually a cookie. Since then, I have always liked my tea with milk.

I had another friend who had a tree house, and one boy who had a train set. I really wanted a train like his, but my parents would not get one for me. We got dolls instead, always ones that were very popular at the time. It was no doubt part of that era when girls didn't have train sets.

There was no television in Walla Walla yet, so we really did play. We were creative, and I loved to make up new things. Our yard had three large maple trees with big roots that twisted and sprawled at their bases. My sister and I would make little villages and landscapes among the roots and make up stories about the people who lived in them. We liked making designer clothes for paper dolls, coloring in color books, and drawing original masterpieces.

We had fish, and I had a turtle that I forgot to feed, who died of starvation. I felt terrible about it, as did my mother. She felt she should have watched out for it more than she did. So, the rule thereafter was that there would be no more turtles or anything I was supposed to feed until I was older.

We tried to have a puppy, but Carolyn wheezed. Then we tried to have a kitten that I named Mittens. She made me sneeze and gave me itchy eyes. My mother made toys that were on a string or a stick so that I could play with her without touching her. It did not work out so well, as it was hard not to touch her. So, Maxine took Mittens "to someone's nice farm" to live, as she worried I might develop asthma.

My sister and her friends liked to play school. They were the teachers, and I was the student. I liked the game too, and learned early on the basics of reading, writing, and arithmetic. When I did go to first grade, I was very disappointed and bored that it was mostly the things I already knew. So, at recess I would go out with all the kids to the playground and just keep walking the two blocks to our house. I did this for a number of days, and Mother finally asked why I was coming home before school was out, so I told her. In response, she went to visit the teacher, and after that something changed, and I was no longer bored and no longer needed to leave at recess, though I do not really remember what changed.

I liked to learn and did well in school, I did have to follow my sister and her extra excellence. However, I did not come to class with a life-threatening condition. I got along well with the other kids, could run and play, and clearly enjoyed myself. I was polite and respectful of my teachers. Once in a while, I was anxious that I did not do things correctly, like bring a hanky each day, which we were supposed to do. One day I forgot mine and was afraid that I would be in big trouble. When I had to say that I did not have a hanky, the teacher just gave me a Kleenex. After that if I sometimes didn't do things perfectly it was not a huge deal. My teachers liked me, and school was good.

I still like to do well but have learned there are some things I will never do well, so I don't do them. I am just not naturally athletic and whenever I have tried, I have not done well. When I was younger the only exception was water skiing. But I always felt awkward and a bit disconnected regarding where my arms and legs were in relation to the rest of me in other sports. The thing is I have learned that if there is something I want to do well I need to learn about it and then practice. I did well in school because I liked to learn, and I did put in the time to study. I did well enough playing the piano and was able to compete because I practiced. I only won one competition and that was when I played a Chopin piece that I liked and won because I played with feeling. I like writing and try to practice that by writing something every day, even if it is not always worth saving or needs editing, but it does give me practice.

MAXINE AND ME

THERE WERE SOME TIMES WITH MAXINE that were important to me. When I was young, we would sneak into her room and shut the door, and she would get the peanut brittle that she kept in her top drawer. This was a secret from Carolyn because of her peanut allergies. Mother and I would sit on the edge of the bed and eat it together relishing every little bit. Peanut brittle remains a special treat for me. Since the special times with my mother were not frequent, this meant a great deal to me. What was perhaps more important was that it was unusual that it excluded my sister and I got mother to myself.

Other times that I loved included those when we would collect wildflowers in the woods at Priest Lake or the woods near our house in Spokane, name them, and press them for keeping. When I was a little older, a particularly lovely memory I have is when my mother and I would play Bach together, me on the piano and Mother on the flute.

This interest in the arts spread out in other ways, as well. For instance, Mother had been a serious student of English Literature, and when we were old enough, she would read Shakespeare with us. When we did not understand it, she would explain it to us. When we were even older, I think Carolyn was in college and I was in high school, we read Chaucer together. Maxine could read it in Gaelic and did for a few paragraphs, which we thought was cool. Then we would read it in English. But the thing that was best was that she knew the literature and was willing to introduce us to Chaucer's bawdy tales.

It was clear that Mother enjoyed our company much better as we got older. I once overheard her tell two friends she was more comfortable and much more interested in us when we were old enough to carry on intelligent conversations. This knowledge helped me to understand mother's behavior when I was younger. It was not me; it was Maxine.

If Fred did not have time to help mother with the upkeep of the house, he made sure that someone was hired to do it. For a time in Walla Walla, we had live-in students from a Seventh Day Adventist College who paid part of their rent by helping mother with the house. Mother's depression was quite debilitating and that was the reason for the live-in help. The college students stayed in a room off the recreation room in the basement. They did not eat with us because they were strict vegetarians. My grandmother Nelle had a walnut orchard and would send bushels of them to us. One of the students had finished her stay with us and mother went to the storeroom for something and found bushels of empty walnut shells. My parents took it with good humor.

The fact that Mother had a significant depression explains also why when we were still living in Walla Walla, Carolyn and I would find Mother in bed with her clothes on when we got home from school. She really tried to push through it, and she had, after all, gotten up and sent us off to school. Then she would try to do something else and not be able to resist going back to bed and sleeping. It happened a number of times that my sister and I would pull on mother to get her out of bed to lead the Blue Bird group or some other similar activity.

She realized that her depression was interfering with her mothering responsibilities and told Fred that, "I am not doing so well with this depression. I would like to go to a psychiatrist."

"Oh Maxie, I kind of like you a little bit nuts," he answered.

I think he loved her very much, and it was meant to be funny, but that comment was not too helpful, and it was indicative that he really did not understand how painful it was for her. She got some help from Reverend Claypool at our church, and the family doctor, but it wasn't until she was diagnosed with hypothyroidism that she got some medical help. The depression lasted ten years and by the time we moved to Spokane it was probably lifting on its own as most depressions finally do. There were no anti-depressants then, but treating the thyroid condition helped.

In 1950, when I was about seven, my maternal grandmother Nelle came to stay with us. She had cervical cancer and her husband was not able to care for her for a short period of time, so mother brought her to Walla Walla to stay with us. I remember her on the couch in the living room during the day, and the blinds were drawn so it was not very light in the room. We had never known her very well; in fact, I had no memory of her when I was younger. Mother was attentive to her needs and when her pain got severe, she would get a nurse who lived across the alley to come give her a shot. She did not talk much, and I just remember this as a dark and weird time. I think she was with us only a few weeks and then returned to her home. This is the only memory I have of Nelle. Maxine was not close to her mother and it was good of Maxine to do this. She was still her mother.

Nelle died some months later, and I remember mother and Fred going to Eugene where she lived to help settle her estate. Mother did not like Nelle's husband and there was some problem with settling things after Nelle died. I know that mother came home with the rings from Nelle's four marriages and Fred had a new ring made from the diamonds. When Maxine died, I got the ring.

PRIEST LAKE IDAHO

FRED BECAME A HIGGINS BOAT DEALER when I was still young. Higgins was the boat builder that made the troop landing boats in WWII. The boats my father sold were sturdy wood boats with Chrysler Marine engines and that was the connection to the Dodge Plymouth agency. We had a 17-foot speed boat that was kept in a marina on Priest Lake in Idaho. This was where we took vacations in the summer. It was a long drive from Walla Walla but worth it, at least for my father and sister and me. Mother was not so fond of going to the lake. It meant extra laundry, cooking in an inadequate kitchen, having to watch both Carolyn for her asthma and me as a young active little girl.

We stayed at a resort in comfortable but rustic cabins. The lake was pristine and not yet developed that much. The Forest Service owned the shoreline and did not allow obtrusive buildings on the water. There was also a little lake with a Thorofare that connected it to the big lake. You had to go slowly so it was quiet, and it was breathtakingly beautiful, like floating through the forest.

On the fourth of July, a wealthy man paid for a fireworks show each year that were shot off the swimming dock at the resort where we stayed. One year when I was six years old, someone forgot to cover the box that held all the fireworks not yet set off. One of the rockets misfired and fell into the giant box. Rockets and other explosive things took off and went uncontrolled toward the spectators on the beach. People were panicked and went running in all directions. One man fell into a hole someone had dug on the beach and broke his leg. Another man came close to smothering his young daughter by burying her in the sand. Mother gathered us up and went away from the beach to safety on the pathway along the beach behind some trees. I thought it was beautiful though scary. I often remember it on the Fourth of July as people shoot off a lot of unruly fireworks in my neighborhood.

When I was nine and my sister thirteen, we hung out on the dock where a bunch of teenage boys hung out. Our parents knew their parents and they were good kids. Fred liked to pull water skiers behind our boat. The boys started to have me ride on their shoulders. I was small and light weight and it was really fun. I wanted to learn to ski, and the guys taught me. My father was great about it, drove the boat with patience and cheered me on. I became good at it and would go out whenever I could. Other people with boats would take me too. My new nick name was "the cork" because I was often out there bobbing on the water. It turned out to be my best sport.

In the beginning the boys built their own skis, as they were not available commercially. Fairly soon they were, though, and things were changing as the sport became more popular. When Maxine and Fred were not around, I would go over the wooden ski jump. I did it easily and loved it. But when my parents saw me do it, they were very concerned, and I had to be more careful they were nowhere near by when I did it. When I was a teenager, my father let me get a "banana ski," which was a single ski, wider than the double skis, and with a metal fin on the bottom in back. It was great for cutting in and out and jumping the wake of our boat.

By then, Fred had a 23-foot Higgins Day Cruiser with a huge Chrysler marine engine. The boat was wide and threw an incredible wake and the engine was strong enough we could pull up to six skiers without a problem. My father loved that boat as did I. He named it the RNT which stood for "Release from Nervous Tension." We would load up with good food and beer and go to the upper end of the lake that had no houses on shore. Maxine and Carolyn and I would go ashore and pick huckleberries. Fred would stay in the boat and fly fish. Our parents let us have beer but did limit how much. My father named these outings "Becker Floatnics."

When I was fourteen, my father taught me to drive the boat. I was good at driving it and when I was a Senior in High School, my father gave his permission for me to take it out alone. I went with my Gonzaga boyfriend to Priest Lake and we took the boat out for the day. I enjoyed it a great deal and was particularly pleased my father thought I was responsible enough to do that. As my sister and I grew older, we went to the lake less often.

When I was a Sophomore in College, someone offered to buy the boat, and my father sold it to him. I was upset but had little ground to stand on as we so seldom got to the Lake anymore. We heard later that the man who bought it, along with a friend, were drunk and crashed the boat into a log boom and were killed. I did not know them but felt sad, I have to admit mostly because the boat was destroyed. It had been an important part of my life and my father loved it so. I guess it is possible to mourn a boat.

Today I do think about the Lake once in a while. It was an important part of my growing up. Becker Floatnics were great family times. Water skiing was the only sport I excelled at and I am content to realize those days are behind me. Some months ago, I mentioned my water-skiing skills to someone as we stood beside his new boat that was parked in a lot at work.

He said, "I could take you skiing if you would like."

I answered, "That is a nice offer, but I am seventy-five, out of shape, and now have balance problems. I think I need to pass on that."

SPOKANE

IN 1953 WE MOVED FROM WALLA WALLA TO SPOKANE. Fred was approached to buy a partnership in a Dodge Plymouth dealership in Spokane when I was just finishing third grade and Carolyn was in the seventh grade. There were a number of things that were attractive about moving to a bigger city. Carolyn and I were excited as they had television in Spokane. My father was seeing the move as an opportunity in expanding his business.

Maxine was coming out of her depression by this time and had a positive view of the move. There were good doctors for Carolyn and Fred in Spokane. There was also a large and sophisticated music community for mother with good piano teachers for Carolyn and me. I thought it would be an exciting adventure and it would be fun to meet new friends. We would also be closer to Priest Lake in Idaho. So, it was decided that we would move. My father sold his business to someone who was willing to keep Uncle Kip and Uncle Reed as employees at the Walla Walla dealership.

When we got to Spokane one of the most important things we got was a TV. It was a piece of furniture on its own. The screen was fairly large, and the cabinet looked like mahogany and perhaps it was. We had it in the room we used as a den. When Fred got home from work, we would watch "Time for Beanie" in which "Cecil the Seasick Sea Serpent" was our favorite character. Mother would be in the kitchen fixing dinner and Carolyn would be practicing piano in the living room. Time alone with Fred remained precious to me.

Carolyn took piano lessons from a very special woman who was a graduate of Julliard and played concerts professionally. Her name was Margi Mae Ott and she was a wonderful teacher. Carolyn adored her and worked hard to do well. My teacher, Mary Virginia Miller, was associated with Margi Mae and was also a professional musician who played classical organ in churches and concerts as well as piano. She was another important person for me. She was the first political liberal that I knew and was married to a well-known artist in Spokane. They went to the Unitarian Church. She was a role model of what I wanted to become. She expected me to practice and to attend Saturday sessions at Margi Mae's house once a month where both their students played for the teachers and each other and were critiqued in order to improve. I believe this was excellent training for me to learn that being critiqued was an ok thing and to learn from it.

Mary Virginia was always very kind and showed an interest in me. I loved to go see her for my lessons. She never put pressure on me to perform, though was proud when I did well. She did not expect me to keep up with my sister. She accepted me for myself and knew that music was important to me but that I had other interests that were important too. She wanted me to compete as it set up goals for working on certain pieces and getting to understand different composers. I was fine with it and believe that it helped me to overcome stage fright which has been helpful for being comfortable speaking to large groups both professionally and in the Program.

Early on I felt that Carolyn got the more well-known teacher who I knew was also more expensive, so there were more competitive feelings between us. Later, though, I realized that was not what was going on. I think Mother and the teachers knew that I was talented but not cut out for serious competition. I now believe that my mother selected the best teachers for each of us and that she was very wise to give me a different teacher from my sister.

Fred did think we should have chores around the house, but my mother argued successfully that we would learn how to keep house on our own and that practicing the piano and doing our homework was much more important. My father, though, was right when it came to me. I have never been that good at keeping house. Even so, Fred would come to our recitals, though he admitted that he often would count the ceiling tiles when others were playing, but he swore that he did listen when we played.

Fred had a good reputation as a businessman and was active in the community. He was six feet tall and always kept himself at a healthy, slim weight. He was somewhat of a clothes horse and was always appropriately well dressed in suits for work and had nice casual clothes, too. He was well liked by others and was a good friend in return. It was not long for there to be more people driving Dodges and Plymouths in Spokane.

Mother became active in the music community and became a member and later president of "Friday Musical," a long-standing group of musicians in Spokane who gathered for a performance by members once a month. This organization was Nationwide, and the Spokane group was the first one West of the Mississippi. Maxine was proud of this. She was in a trio in which my piano teacher, Mary Virginia, played piano, a woman from Holland played cello, and Mother played flute. Maxine did play well and had exceptional tone. I painted a picture of her trio which is now in my living room near the piano.

So, our move overall was a good one. In Spokane back in 1953, we lived in a rented house at first, and it was a fairly big two-story house with four bedrooms. It was not a particularly attractive or comfortable house, though, and it was drafty, but we knew it was temporary until my parents found a house to buy. In the rented house, my parents had a master bedroom with their own bathroom. Carolyn and I had our own rooms that were for our personal things, but we did not sleep in them. My sister and I shared one bedroom at night which was the "Allergy Room." It had venetian blinds, no rugs or carpet, the mattresses were covered in durable plastic and there was an air filter that sat on the floor to purify the air in the room. The room was thoroughly cleaned once weekly by my mother's cleaning person.

I did not like it that I had to sleep in there when I did not have asthma like my sister. I made the case to sleep in the fourth bedroom by myself and finally won. I think that room was an addition to the house, as it was a step down from the hallway and was colder than the other rooms. Mother made a special bedspread for me, and curtains to match, which I appreciated. But I had a cot rather than a real bed, which I did notice. I had never slept in a room without my sister, and I remember well the first night I was afraid to be alone. However, I survived and learned that it was a silly worry, and I did fine after that.

Soon, my parents began looking for a house to buy and would take us to see the ones that became a possibility. They looked for quite a while and saw houses of many different types and in various parts of town. There was one that Carolyn and I liked that was very big and old and was like a castle. My parents decided that it was too big and probably needed work as it was so old.

There was another that was in an upscale neighborhood that was lovely but expensive. It was that house that made them decide to build one that could be designed to meet our needs specifically. So, they bought a smaller house in the same school district where we had been. We knew it was just for the time it would take to build the new house. We were there about sixteen months while my parents looked for a place to build and the new house got built. Fred designed the house along with an architect. They chose a lot that was on the edge of an undeveloped area with a woods on it. Ours was the last house before the woods. Of course, the area became built up fairly soon after we moved in.

In the smaller house Carolyn and I shared a bedroom on the top floor. Her asthma got worse during this time, and I woke up too frequently with the doctor and mother standing over Carolyn as the doctor injected medicine into her vein with the large syringe that had blood in it. I got used to it, though, as it was nothing new. Mostly, I would just turn over and go back to sleep. I felt bad for my sister but did not know what I could do to help.

The doctor and Mother, though, would talk softly, and I could hear what they were saying.

One night, mother asked, "Is there something we are not doing that we need to do? She has been so much worse lately and things just are not getting better."

The doctor replied, "You might consider sending her to a dry climate like Arizona. They have live-in schools there for kids like Carolyn. They know what to do when they get sick and she would not be missing school like she is here."

I thought this was a great idea. Carolyn and I were in competition about a number of things. We were not as close as we had been when we were younger. She was in high school now, and I was in fifth grade. We had different interests that conflicted at times. We would have verbal battles. It was getting to be frustrating because it was disruptive when she had an attack. I felt guilty for resenting her. Also, there was a victim thing coming out in her and it was not attractive. There became secondary gains with people feeling sorry for her and also she would get out of things she did not want to do. At the same time, I wanted her to get better. I felt conflicted about my relationship with her and had for a while.

CAROLYN GOES TO ARIZONA

MY PARENTS HAD ALWAYS FOLLOWED DOCTORS' SUGGESTIONS, so they looked into a school for Carolyn in Arizona. My father did the research and had arranged for her to go to a specific school in Tucson. We would drive her down and I got excused from school. I would have to give a report on the trip when I returned. My father had a brief conference in Las Vegas so we planned the trip around that, and we would stop for it on the way back to Spokane.

So, we drove Carolyn down to Tucson. The roads there were interesting because there were "dips" in the highway with warning signs to go slower as we heard there were accidents because of them. The scenery was also very interesting with the barren desert and big cactus—all very different from the pine trees and green vegetation in Washington. I have heard recently from a friend who has a home in Arizona that the highways are now flat and straight. I am glad I experienced them with dips.

When we arrived in Tucson, the school she was to go to had just been closed because the owners had been arrested for fraud. My father responded by grabbing a phone book and we went off to find another school. The one he picked seemed reasonable and was on a ranch and had many activities as well as school on the premises.

So, we left her at the Fenster Ranch School. It was well kept, and the people who owned and ran it were very nice, as was to be expected since my parents were paying a good deal to have her there. As we pulled away, I looked back and saw Carolyn standing alone watching us drive away. It was a bit sad as I knew she did not want to be there. I knew she felt dumped.

"I hope this is helpful, but I have to admit it is a relief to have her away for a while," my father said.

I suspected some of what he wanted to be away from was Carolyn and me bickering, and I realized that he had also picked up on the victim thing, which was getting old.

Mother commented, "It seemed like a fine school and the cottages were nice. It will be a relief not having the crises so often."

"I hope she likes it there. " I said, though really I was thinking, "What a relief!"

On the way back home, we stopped in Las Vegas for Fred's conference. He went to his meeting the next day. Maxine and I went shopping and out to lunch. There were a lot of expensive clothes for sale and a lot of women with amazing make-up and fancy hair.

Mother told me that, "If you look closely you can tell which women have had face lifts. They are the ones who have stiff smiles."

I had never seen that before, but I could tell what she meant. I found it exciting and wondered who these people were.

Mother and I went to our room, changed for dinner and went to the dining room where Fred was to meet us. When he entered the room, people turned to look at him as he walked to our table. He was six feet tall, a handsome well-dressed man with distinguished silver hair and a tan from golf that summer. People thought he was a celebrity, and I felt proud.

So, we left Carolyn to hopefully get relief from her asthma, but it turned out that she hated that school. It was owned by a Jewish couple, and she was the only non-Jewish person there. They were very nice to her and included her in their holiday celebrations. Apparently, she even got drunk from the wine at one of them, and they told her to go easy the next time. Wine or not, her asthma did improve, but she was very unhappy.

Having Carolyn gone gave me and my parents some needed relief. By now, our competition thing had increased. I perceived her as a better student and musician. She saw me as having more friends and being more social. She thought I was closer to Fred and that he responded to her coldly. I had artistic talent. I was basically optimistic, and she was depressed.

Carolyn came home for Christmas and convinced my parents not to send her back to Arizona. I have no doubt that Carolyn was somewhat traumatized by being left in Arizona, so she went to Lewis and Clark High School in Spokane. Her Asthma was better, and she became involved in a social club (High School Sorority), went back to working with Margi Mae for piano lessons, and came home with straight A's. She was also invited to join a music club that mother viewed as prestigious. Maxine liked prestigious.

Carolyn related to the friends she had before she left and developed some new ones, as well. There was also a small group of boys and girls who hung out together and would come to see Carolyn at our house. I thought they were wonderful and sometimes hung around to be a part of their visit.

Her relationship with Mother had begun to be rather symbiotic. When she got home from school, they would sit at the dining room table and go over her day in detail including what she thought and what she did. I took a dim view of this as thought it was asking for trouble. I didn't want Mother to know what I thought and only part of what I did.

Carolyn had trouble making decisions. She would ask advice and then have numerous reasons not to take the advice offered. Once she asked mother how you decide to do the right thing and mother told her to see herself on the piano bench with Jesus on one side and Margi Mae, her piano teacher, on the other. I thought this didn't really answer her question and left her with, once again, the idea she had to be perfect.

Maxine would pick Carolyn up after school so that she could practice the piano and also to try to avoid asthma due to cold weather. This meant that she was not able to go with friends after school to the main department store for cokes and gossip. Later Carolyn would blame mother for interfering with her learning how to have friends. I suspected this came from her therapy sessions as I did not think she would have come up with that on her own. It always seemed too hard for Carolyn to be directly angry with our mother. I look back and realize, though, from this point on that I saw Mother and Carolyn as joined at the hip and I was happy to stay out of it. They were like a bag of old yarn all tangled around each other and very difficult to untangle.

GRADE SCHOOL IN SPOKANE

WHEN I WAS IN 6TH GRADE, I WENT STEADY with my first boyfriend, Freddy. He was the son of a major grocery store owner on the South Hill where we lived. We exchanged name bracelets, a custom my father thought was odd.

"If something happens to you, they will think you are Freddy," he said teasingly. I supposed he had a point, though mainly, I always loved my father's sense of humor.

I wasn't in love but was "in like" and he was a popular guy, cute and fun. The other girls thought he was cute too, so that made it better. Our parents were friends and were fine with it. I can't remember how long it lasted but probably only around six months. I was looking forward to seeing Freddy at our 50th high school reunion but when I got there, I learned that he'd died a few years earlier of a brain tumor. It's hard to have that happen when you are traveling back in time to being a teenager and think everyone will survive like you.

Back in those days, though, when we did all still feel immortal, we knew how to have fun, often holding parties at kid's homes, mine being a popular one. After my first boyfriend, there was another boy in particular that I thought was special, and I had that crush for many years. It was rumored that his father ran the bookie joint in town.

But, there were always more boys. I remember another who was very handsome but shy. Once, his mother invited me to dinner at their house, and I guessed that she was concerned that her son didn't have a girlfriend like most of the other boys. I wasn't sure that I wanted to go, but Maxine thought it would be nice of me to do it, so I went. He was actually a sweet person, but his mother blew it by asking him in front of me if he needed to go to the bathroom before dinner. I felt sorry for him that he had a mother like that, and I think he felt the same way too. He never asked me out. Over fifty years later, I saw him at our high school reunion, and he was with a very beautiful woman who was his wife.

Wilson Grade School, where we went, was a good school. Teachers were good, and the school was pleasant and interesting. It was in 8th grade that I had one of the best teachers I ever had, Mr. Harmon. He was a wonderful man that was an inspiration. He was well organized in his teaching approach and made things interesting. He was serious about our learning but also had a good sense of humor about it, too. He knew what we would need to be able to do well in high school and even in college. He taught us good basic math and most importantly how to write term papers with research and footnotes. I was very grateful in later years in school.

Also, when I was in 8th grade, I felt like some kids my age did not like me, I think now it was mostly that adolescent negative self-image thing that most have at this age. I came home from school and told Fred that some kids did not like me.

"If you are liked by everyone, you are most likely doing something wrong," he told me.

I have remembered that on many occasions. I especially remembered it later when I was a boss and had to make unpopular decisions for the good of the agency or when mentoring someone in sobriety I needed to confront them about their behavior. I never had trouble confronting my clients about their behavior as felt that was part of my job but I tried to do it gently.

My best friend in seventh and eighth grade was Suzie. We tended to dress alike, and both had ponytails. We were cheerleaders for our team, and I met other girls from one of our competing grade schools, Roosevelt. We became good friends and remained so throughout high school. There were four of them, Betsy, Ellen, Judy and Andrea. They were serious students and active in school activities.

Judy's mother was a much-loved teacher at our high school and Andrea's mother was a graduate of Wellesley and Andrea was headed that way. Betsy and Andrea's fathers were doctors. Ellen's mother was a character and quite different from our mothers. She seemed to act young for her age. When Andrea went to Helen Bush School in Seattle, I wanted to go there too. My parents felt that I would get a good education at Lewis and Clark, and my father made a joke that private schools in Seattle were for potential juvenile delinquents from wealthy families. When we all got together for Christmas, Andrea did seem to be ahead of us in dating, smoking and drinking. Well, not drinking for me because of Huntley Drinkley, and within a year I was smoking up the chimney in the recreation room. I did not need to go to Helen Bush School to accomplish this.

On the whole, my memories of grade school in Spokane are pleasant. I was fairly used to things at home, mostly things that were difficult around the health problems for Carolyn. By now I had pretty much stayed out of things between mother and Carolyn. There were only a few rocky things in eighth grade, mostly with the beginning of adolescence and the doubts some of that brings regarding some degree of self-esteem. I liked all my teachers and got along well with the other kids. My parents got along with each other and presented a united front for my sister and me. I was fortunate to feel essentially stable and well-loved in the family by now. The competition between Carolyn and me was still there, but it was beginning to feel less important to me.

THE HOUSE FRED BUILT

My parents found a lot on which to build on the edge of a wooded area on the South Hill. The wooded area would be developed within a few years of our moving there. It was in the same school district as our school so again we did not have to change schools. It was fun to watch the house be built. Before the walls were up, it looked small to Carolyn and me and we referred to as "the room." Fred did not appreciate this as he was paying for a fairly large house. In 1956 it was completed, and we moved in.

It was a mid-century modern, 3600-square-foot house. A "living kitchen" which today would be called a "great room," was a main feature. There was a fireplace and built in grill and rotisserie, and an area for a dining table. The TV set was away from this area as was a couch near the fireplace.

There were two chairs beside a table. These were Maxine and Fred's chairs. The kitchen itself was off in back of the TV area with a long hall like space with the laundry at the end out of site from the main room. There was a large window with a table and chairs near the back door where mother spent time working cross word puzzles and where Carolyn and I would sometimes chat with her. She could keep an eye on the kitchen from there when she was cooking. The "living kitchen" area was painted a light yellow. Most of our family time was spent in this part of the house. We would gather around the TV to watch the news which would later become Huntley Drinkley time.

The formal dining room was just off the "living kitchen." It was open to the living room which had a large flagstone fireplace and cathedral ceilings. The grand piano was in the living room. The ceiling was finished with a special material that was supposed to provide good acoustics for the piano and my mother's trio when they practiced and when Friday Musical met at our house. The walls and ceiling in this area were painted a dusty pink. On the fireplace wall was a brass Griffon on his hind legs and with a penis that all the boys who came to the house noticed. At first Carolyn and I were embarrassed, but soon it became something to laugh about, and it was interesting to see how different people reacted.

The Grand Piano was special to me and still is. When my mother moved into senior living, she gave it to me. That was because my sister had a piano but had not played it in a number of years. I was delighted to have it. It was especially important to me, as my father had special ordered it from the Baldwin Company for my mother when we moved to the house he built. I have it today in my living room. Since I have had it, there was a period of time I took lessons to get back to playing. I was pretty rusty and did not practice enough to make a big difference. Currently it needs tuning, but I will get around to that soon. I only play it when Brent, my roommate, is not home as I am terribly rusty and would not wish it on anyone to hear me play.

The bedroom wing had a square hallway with three bedrooms and a bath off it. Fred did not like long hallways as felt they were a waste of space. The master bedroom was on the front of the house and had three large closets, a shower and toilet in its own closed space and two sinks on an L-shaped counter. There were built in drawers plus a large dresser, a drum table and two chairs at a large window looking out on a small garden with two large and beautiful Douglas Fir trees.

My sister and I each had our bedrooms on the back side of the house that were identical except that mine had two large windows and Carolyn had one as only had one exterior wall. Both of us had two twin beds, a desk for studying, two closets and built in drawers between. Our bathroom was between our rooms and had a large square tub, toilet and sink which were blue which was very 1950's.

The basement had a furnace room/workshop and a safe that fascinated me. Mother and Carolyn never learned the combination, but I remember it to this day. The main room in the basement was a very large recreation room with a large curved bar and a fireplace. It was typical of mid-century modern fireplaces to have a raised hearth that you could sit on. When I began smoking, I would sneak downstairs, make sure the draft was open and sit on the hearth so I could put my head inside the fireplace and light my cigarette where the smoke would go up the flu. Sitting on the raised hearth with my head in the fireplace must have been quite a sight. No one ever saw this as the chimney had an efficient draft and I never got caught smoking.

My friends liked having parties in the recreation room. It had a sitting area near the fireplace and a big open space where we could dance. My parents would make a lot of noise coming down the stairs to check on us so we knew they were coming, and we would all be behaving ourselves by the time they got into the room. They were loud on purpose.

Because our house was on the edge of a wooded area where kids would go to park and make out, we had young men coming to our house to use the phone. There were no cell phones then. They would be stuck in the mud or have a flat tire and needed to call for help. My father enjoyed answering the door when this happened and would let them know he knew what they had been up to in a teasing way. We liked to hear this and see how the boys responded. Most appeared to get pretty nervous.

MY PARENTS' COMMUNITY IN SPOKANE

AFTER WE MOVED TO THE HOUSE MY PARENTS BECAME good friends with a number of couples in the neighborhood. Also, by then Fred had developed friendships with many people in Spokane through both business and through community activities. Fred was active in several organizations. He was on several boards over the years. There was one organization that was for automobile dealers where they would get together and share business ideas and tell tall stories about how well they were doing, and he had some position with AAA since it was related to automobiles.

Every year, Maxine and Fred had quite a few large dinner parties that were catered both for business and for friends. They belonged to bridge clubs in the neighborhood. There were also cocktail parties attended by a fair number of people, sometimes attached to special projects, business and social events. The piano was in the living room and mother fed the cat on top of the piano so the dog would not be able to eat the cat food. She also would often serve smacks from the top of the piano during cocktail parties. One evening she forgot to remove the cat food dish before the party. During the party, she was talking with one of the guests by the piano. The man reached over and scooped up some of the dry cat food and popped it in his mouth. My mother was about to say something to him then thought better of it. He did not seem to find anything wrong with the cat food.

When they weren't entertaining at home, my parents played golf and belonged to the local country club. They also belonged to the City Club which was originally a Gentleman's Club in the early days of Spokane. I remember that there were little windows with curtains that covered up pictures of naked women. The curtains were closed when women were present, and my sister and I would always peek in when we could.

So, my parents had found a hobby they could share. They played golf and often went on vacation to play on high-end courses. Moreover, golf was sometimes included in business conferences for Automobile Dealers and is common as a business tool in developing customers. Carolyn and I took golf lessons, too, as our parents felt that it was a good skill to have in adulthood. I was not a good golfer, though, as I did not always know where my arms and legs were in relationship to the rest of me.

Fred was a bird hunter and joined a hunting club called the Kalispell Duck Club. It was an old organization that owned land outside of Spokane that had duck blinds on a lake, cabins for each member and a main farmhouse where the groundskeeper and his wife lived. She was the cook for the club. Membership was by invitation. There were doctors, lawyers and businessmen, including automobile dealers as members. It was men only. We called it "The Boy Scout Camp for Fathers."

It would have seemed that my parents had it all, though we still couldn't have pets, so there was something missing from the image of our perfect home. To make up for things, some years later, my sister's husband gave my father his dog since Carolyn could not live with a dog. The dog's official name was "Gun Thunder of District 10" but was known in our house as "Mr. Ringo." He was a beautiful Black Lab with a loving disposition, and he made a very good hunting dog because he bonded so well with Fred. The dog, though, was not without its down sides, too. For instance, one evening my parents were playing cards in the living room while doing Huntley Drinkley and cooking a beef roast on the rotisserie in the living kitchen, Fred went to check on the roast only to find a small part of it on the ground. Mr. Ringo had gotten it off the rotisserie and eaten most of it. Fred went back to the living room and told my mother, "Mr. Ringo was a bad dog and ate our roast. He will have to go to bed with no supper! I guess we will too."

This reminds me of that house with the built-in rotisserie, the fireplace with the raised hearth and the area around the TV where we did Huntley Drinkley. It had all been good at the time and reminds me once again about my father and how I admired him for designing such a great house that truly did meet the needs of our family. I got my "thing" about houses from him, there is no doubt. After we sold it, we heard that the people who bought it grew marijuana in the basement and were found out and arrested.

It was sold again and when I was in Spokane some years later when my mother died, I asked my friend Rita, who was with me, if she would like to see the house where I grew up. She said she would, so I drove over to it. There was construction going on with the door open and workers coming in and out. I stopped and explained that my father had built the house and that it was where I had grown up, and I asked if I could look inside, and they said yes. So, my friend Rita and I both went in and saw where they were building a huge island in the kitchen, though it really looked out of place to me. I also saw that they had taken up some ugly shag carpet my mother had put over beautiful wide plank oak floors with wood pegs, which was a very good thing. I remember thinking mother did not appreciate just how beautiful they were. I loved that house and though I did not agree with the kitchen island thing, I was glad that whoever now owned it had realized it was a good house and worth a remodel. It was built like Fort Knox.

MY SISTER'S TEENAGE YEARS

WHEN CAROLYN WAS IN HIGH SCHOOL THERE WERE THINGS about my sister I admired. She made some nice friends who seemed to all have fun together. She excelled in school and of course in music. She chose nice clothes and was pretty. I did begin to think she was too willing to please mother. Though I did not purposely displease her, I was not always willing to compromise with Maxine and did not feel badly about it. One issue was how much I practiced the piano. I agreed to one and a half hours per day instead of the three hours plus that my sister practiced.

.When Carolyn turned sixteen, Fred got her a car to drive so that my mother didn't have to always pick her up after school. It was a 1949 Dodge, big and clunky, an uninteresting green color with a running board because it was high off the ground. It also had a visor on the outside in front that ran across the top edge of the windshield and it had a semi-automatic transmission. When my father drove up with it, mother, Carolyn and I went out to the driveway to look it over, Carolyn was speechless. She hated it. I, though, thought it was really cool. We named it "Rodan the Roadrunner." One of my sister's best friends was the daughter of the Ford dealer and she got a brand new 1955, first year model, of a baby blue Thunderbird convertible.

Around that time, my sister began to go with the boy next door, literally. He was the son of our neighbor who was my orthodontist. He was headed to become a doctor. He was also Catholic which was a concern for his parents since we were protestant. His father and mine were close friends. Carolyn and this boyfriend went together for three years and I wondered if I would ever have a lasting boyfriend like that. He was handsome, too, and a good student, polite, and just really a nice person all around. He went to Gonzaga High School, and he was clearly fond of Carolyn, just as she was pretty much in love with him. When they went off to different colleges, though, they stopped dating. I was never quite sure why. Some years later, Carolyn told me that she had been very much in love with him, and it was hard for her when they broke up. At the time, I hadn't known that she was upset, as it had seemed to me that we were beginning to grow further apart. Still, back then, Carolyn continued to have asthma attacks, but they began to usually come on when big events were supposed to happen, things like a big dance or some big event at school. There began to be more of the victim role in it with people feeling sorry for her. I felt bad for her but by now just went about my own business. I don't think I was ever hostile to Carolyn. I just got tired.

HIGH SCHOOL

IT WAS FINALLY TIME FOR ME TO BE OFF TO HIGH SCHOOL, during which time I remained friends with the girls from Roosevelt Grade School. I was the only one of these friends who joined a social club. My mother was quite insistent, and I began to notice her preoccupation with what she perceived as social status. Most of her friends' daughters joined, as had my sister, though I was a little ambivalent. On the one hand, because my sister had belonged, I knew that I would probably get in, too, if I applied. The main thing that I found worthwhile, though, was that the clubs, including the boy's clubs, put on dances. I thought some of the girls in the clubs were kind of shallow, overly interested in boys, competitive about it and did not have things like music or many intellectual pursuits. I suppose I was a little judgmental, though I was quite serious by then about my music in that I enjoyed it and liked my teacher, Mary Virginia. I also preferred the company of the Roosevelt girls and felt that they made good friends. And we were not competitive about boys. We started to play Bridge together and had more interesting discussions than just about boys. I will mention I did not really like to play Bridge but did so because I liked my Roosevelt friends. Part of it was that I wasn't very good at it. I have never really liked playing games of any kind unless it is a solitaire type. I do play Mah Jongg on my tablet.

I thought that a number of the girls in the club were sort of rude when they would pay more attention to putting on their make-up in the meeting than in the meeting itself, of course in preparation for seeing their boyfriends afterward. It was an era of heavy eye make-up that my mother insisted Carolyn and I do in moderation. Maxine claimed that the other girls looked like panda bears.

In high school I began to date but would only go with any one for no more than a few months or even weeks.

Once, I asked Fred, "Does it bother you when I go steady?

His response was, "Not really. You only go with them for about three weeks and then it's over."

So, without anything to hold me back, I did the typical teenage things of going through a stage of dating boys that my folks might not approve of just to make them nervous, the beginning of a much bigger rebellion. They did not react much, though, so I didn't do that for long. Besides, I had other ways of standing out at that time. For instance, when I was in high school, Fred and I would watch football or some other sports together and smoke cigars. I was not to inhale which happened only a little at times. I always loved this with Fred which usually happened when mother was cooking and Carolyn was practicing the piano or when they were away from the house. I doubt mother knew he was allowing me to smoke cigars. To this day, I still love the smell of cigars.

The boys from grade school were still around, so I chose one, beginning to date the son of the football coach. He was the leader of the pack, so I was attracted to him. The problem was that he liked to French kiss, and I hated that. Instead of telling him, I finally broke up with him and infuriated all the other guys who all suddenly disappeared from my social life. So, I began to date the Catholic boys from Gonzaga High. The boy I missed the most was the one I always had the crush on.

Fortunately, there were other things beside either boys or my family to win my attention. When I was a junior, I became interested in conservative politics of the time. This was due to a neighbor lady who was for the John Birch Society. I was not for that but did begin to read some books she gave me, including, I remember, "None Dare Call It Treason," which was about conspiracy theories. I did think it a bit much but decided that I was a Republican. After that, I wanted to have discussions with other kids who might be interested, so I started a Teen Age Republican Club. There were only a few members, mostly more right-wing than I was; but I did start to spout off Republican doctrine and began to bore and even offend some friends. So, I cooled it.

Once you start to talk, though, people tend to listen; and one day I got a call from a man in Spokane who invited me to a study group at his home North of Spokane. He somehow found out about the Republican Club I started. So, I went only to discover he was John Cantwell, the man who had been the chair of the Washington State House Un-American Activities Committee. He had made life miserable for many professors at the U of W for some time accusing them of being communists. This had fallen out of favor by the time I knew him.

The other members of the study group were all his kids and nieces and nephews, except for the boy who lived across the road. They had a compound in the country out North of Spokane. I thought they were very radical Right. I did find it kind of interesting and went to three sessions until the fourth session was to include target practice to be ready for the communists if they should invade. That was too much, though, and I never returned. Moreover, I found out that the boy from across the road didn't return either. This little chapter of my life has rarely been shared with others as it does not fit with my later political life. I was never sorry I attended these classes as it was a great learning experience and helped me to develop my political beliefs at the time. They differed from Cantwell.

And so, things change. By the time I was a junior, I was going for longer periods of time with one boyfriend. The most memorable one that I really did care about was from Gonzaga. There was something sweet about him. He was from a large Catholic family with five boys. He was smart and had a good chance for a productive future; eventually, he became a lawyer. I probably would have had sex with him, but he was a good Catholic boy and never would have done that.

When I went into high school, Carolyn went off to College. My parents insisted she go to the University of Arizona because of her asthma. She hated it, though, and when my parents went down to pick her up for Christmas break, she was all packed up, and they had to bring her home. What she'd really wanted was to go to the University of Washington, but by then she had to wait until the following Fall to get in. So, she'd spend the next semester going to Whitworth College in Spokane. Fred got her a car to drive there. It was a demonstrator from the business and much more acceptable to Carolyn than the Roadrunner.

Throughout all of this time together, Maxine, Fred, Carolyn and I continued to do Huntley Drinkley. That was a part of our family life, and it was still a pleasant time. Carolyn was still a straight-A student. I began to realize I did not have to compete with this though I did fairly well. I wanted to get into college and therefore did my homework and actually liked to learn. One day I came home with my report card with several A+s and one A. My father looked at it, paused, and handed it back to me.

He said, "Why wasn't the A an A+?"

I knew he was kidding me and was pleased with my grades.

Also, during that time, I had a good friend named Spencer who liked to hang out at our house, especially at dinner time. My mother got a kick out of how he managed to be invited to dinner a lot. He liked mother's cooking. He was a good buddy kind of friend and was the only one I would drink with a few years later. We would go to drive in movies with a bottle of liquor and drink while watching the movie. We were not sweethearts, just good friends and drinking buddies.

Soon after I turned sixteen, one of my sister's friends had a big wedding with the reception at the City Club. My sister was a bridesmaid and my parents were good friends of her parents. My friend Spencer went with us. There was a champaign fountain and it was easy to fill my glass. I got very drunk, and Spencer took me outside the reception room and sat me on a bench at the entrance of the club while he went to get my parents. I threw up on the bench just before my parents came to get me. Until then, I had thought my drinking was sophisticated and glamorous. Throwing up at the entrance to the City Club, though, was neither.

On the way home, I went into my first black out, regaining consciousness only once I was in my own bed at home with mother at my side. During the blackout, I had been talking with little inhibition, and, as it always happens in blackouts, I was not aware of what I was saying and did not remember it afterward. Apparently, at that time, I'd confessed to smoking cigarettes, and my mother grounded me from driving for two weeks. I did not get grounded for getting drunk and making a scene.

There were other more positive distractions, though, especially as I had started skiing when I was a freshman. It was more difficult for me than water skiing, but I stuck with it. I felt awkward and tired easily from getting up after falling. I took group lessons at first and then when I was a sophomore, I found a private instructor.

My mother met him when he came to pick me up as he was giving me a ride to the mountain. She noticed that he did not use deodorant. He was Austrian, an avid skier, and I don't think they did use deodorant to go skiing or perhaps ever. He and his brother rented a little ski area with a rope tow where we went for lessens. I think my mother was suspicious that he may have had ideas beyond skiing, but she was wrong. He was a perfect gentleman and really loved the sport and teaching it.

There were a few others who went too but it was more individualized than the group lessons. I did improve and was able to go on the intermediate runs, including a ski trip to the Big Mountain in Montana with a group from my high school. Life is never without its lively moments, though, and, on the way to Montana, I'd sat next to the boyfriend of the president of my social club, and we began flirting, without much thinking about the consequences. It was fun but when we got to the mountain we went in different directions as he was a better skier than I was. In the middle of that first day, though, I fell and injured my knee and ended up spending my time in the lodge with the chaperone for our group. She was a smoker, so I smoked along with her. My injury was not minor and would require surgery when I got back to Spokane, which ended my skiing career. Both the surgery and that loss were painful, and somehow smoking helped; and, because the chaperone was smoking, I thought it was alright for me to smoke with her. After all, she was the chaperone.

On the trip back to Spokane, the flirting guy sat with me again and we did a little more than flirt. Upon my return to the social club, I was put on probation for smoking in public, though I knew it was really due to my behavior with the president's boyfriend. I was not too upset as it meant I could not attend meetings for the several months of the probation period. It was not exactly punishment for me. I did have an attitude back then.

Soon after I got back from the ski trip, my parents went on a vacation. I stayed with some older kids whose parents were on the trip with my parents. Our parents had hired someone to "sit" with us. We thought she was a weird woman. It seemed she had little personality and was intimidated by us. I was seventeen, the other three were in their 20's, and there was a twelve-year-old boy. The woman found some venison in the freezer and fixed it for dinner. It had apparently been in there for quite a while and we refused to eat it. We decided that we could do better without her and fired her. Fending for ourselves, we did fine, and we looked out for the boy, too, who also did just fine.

The whole situation was quite different from what I was used to, and I did not have a lot of support. I did not know the others well and they did not know me. They did not know about the trouble I had created for myself on the ski trip. I was not doing well between the injured knee which was in a cast, staying in a strange place, the trouble I had created on the ski trip, and the fact that some people at school knew about it. The other fact was my parents knew about it and were not happy with me. *I was a little overwhelmed and experienced my first depression.*

I was able to be just ok enough to go to school. I did get a little help from my sister via long distant phone calls as she was in Seattle at the University. She was helpful as had experienced depression on several occasions, twice when she was in Arizona and a few others. I did not look forward to my parent's return, as I knew that they were not happy with me. When they did return, though, things were not as bad as I had expected. But by now I was feeling like a rebel, which I did not mind in and of itself. It was just not comfortable being a lonely rebel, and I had pretended I was tough and with an attitude, though I was really a mess inside.

This was the first really difficult time I can remember from adolescence. It was not really the social club thing as it was just that I was not sure who I really was or even who I wanted to be. I felt rebellious inside but was not really sure about what. It was a time of searching and discomfort.

So, still not really happy with the social club, I waited to get through the probation period and then resigned. Maxine was not pleased. She was even more unhappy when I tried out for the musical group my sister had belonged to and was not invited to join. It seems the mother of the girl whose boyfriend I had the little ski trip escapade with was the adviser for the club. Someone had told Maxine that I had played well in the try-out but was rejected because of my behavior on the ski trip.

So, I paid dearly in Maxine's opinion, I was sure. But in truth, I really didn't care too much because I was relieved to be out of the social club, and I'd only tried out for the musical group under pressure from Maxine. The incident did not affect my friendships that mattered. My father probably didn't like it much but said little, and I suspected he was reminded of his own escapades when he was young. I did realize that what I had done on the ski trip was not only stupid but not a nice thing to do with someone else's boyfriend. At the same time, I had begun to develop more disdain for my mother's thing about social standing.

Despite all of this, my senior year of high school went well. I spent time with my Roosevelt friends. I dated enough including some boys from Lewis and Clark but no one special. I remained focused on doing well in school and was looking forward to College. My grades remained solid, and I had participated in various extracurricular activities and there was no question that I would get in.

And so it went, my parents continuing to do Huntley Drinkley each evening, and allowing me to join them whenever I was home. If I was going out for some reason, I wouldn't drink, even if I was with other kids. For whatever reason, I just happened not to have friends who drank. But at home, I did—with Fred and Maxine, I always did.

At this time, I was preparing for my Senior Recital and I was working hard with Mary Virginia. My father was always trading things with customers toward the price of cars. Somehow, he had traded something for a large organ that Mary Virginia played very well. So, we had my senior recital in our living room, and she played the symphony equivalent on the organ and I played the piano of a Shostakovich concerto. I also played some Mozart and Bach and Chopin. A decent amount of people attended, and I played well. I felt good about it and my teacher and mother were proud of me.

Also, around that time, I went to work for Fred at the dealership for the summer as the receptionist on the desk in the showroom. Several years before he had moved to a partnership in a Buick agency. Carolyn and I had both worked for him before and I knew the phone and intercom systems and the other jobs it entailed, so it wasn't too stressful, and I actually rather enjoyed it. I got to see Fred in action, and of course was treated well by the other employees.

This was a good transition time for me because I was interested in how my father's business all worked, and my position was right in the middle of it all. Fred expected the best from me, and that was ok. The other employees knew it and were quite supportive and at times we would joke a little about Fred being somewhat demanding. I suppose they thought I had to deal with that at home too, but I did not feel I did. I usually found he was quite reasonable and was wise about most things.

During those last few months before college, I dated but don't remember exactly who, and spent time mostly with my Roosevelt friends. Andrea's parents had a cabin on a nearby lake and they let us use it sometimes. We would play bridge on the dock and swim and talk about upcoming college. Andrea was headed for Wellesley, and the rest of us were headed for the University of Washington. They were also going through rush. We knew that we probably would not end up in the same sororities, and I actually was a little worried that I might not get in any because of the incident that might have tarnished my reputation. Even so, my own worry had started to surprise me. Since when did I worry that much about what other people thought?

By then, I was always allowed real drinks for Huntley Drinkley hour. It was absolutely consistent that we all gathered around the TV before dinner.

Scotch on the rocks and not much water was my drink. I always had at least two. My family was pretty compatible. Sometimes mother would still get a little high and Fred would notice. It wasn't hard as her voice would get louder. I remember looking forward to Huntley Drinkley and enjoyed these times. We did drink together at other times, to ease the stress of situations and to celebrate good things, in other words we drank to about everything.

As I left high school and prepared for college, Carolyn graduated from the University of Washington with honors. She'd majored in political science and Russian language and was headed for Washington, D.C. to try to find work there where it could relate to her degree. Fortunately, her asthma seemed under better control as she got older, and she did get her first job at the Bureau of Standards and was able to use her Russian, so it seemed like a good plan. It was not what she wanted permanently, but it worked for the time being, and she kept looking. Some years later, she told me that what she'd really wanted was to be a spy. Before long, though, she'd found a job as an administrative assistant to a Representative from Ohio. He was the minority whip while Kennedy was President. It sounded pretty glamorous to me.

MY COLLEGE YEARS

MUCH AS I HAD EXPECTED, I FOUND THAT I was not that fond of Rush. It was awkward, and I didn't like being in the position of being judged, nor did I enjoy the idea of being a legacy to be chosen because my sister had been a Delta Gamma.

Despite all of that, what if they rejected me? For one thing, after the fiasco with the social club back home, I knew that my mother would really be upset. So, I tried—if not for myself, then for her—and apparently I did alright because, in the end, I was invited to join Delta Gamma; and I accepted.

Despite having that community—and all of the stress of getting in behind me—I still had a hard time during my first quarter at the UW. For the first time, my grades were coming in with "B" averages, and I realized that I was having trouble.. What was worse, I was flunking my bowling class due to that old problem of not being in touch with where my arms and legs were with the rest of me. Of course, I felt inept, but there was nothing to do but keep trying.

And that's just what I told my teacher: "I am really trying."

"You certainly are," she answered.

But perhaps the biggest problem was, in my Spanish class, especially because the professor seemed to pay unusual attention to me in class. Once he began popping up randomly on campus, I became pretty sure he was following me. That possible stalking frightened me and put me in a difficult position, and my sorority sisters encouraged me to report him. Once I did, though, I regretted it a little. Of course, he found out about it and was unhappy with me. But he did leave me alone after that, and he did give me a decent grade. But the whole thing was upsetting and did influence how I was functioning.

Over the years, I have found it amazing men are still doing things like this, especially now that there is no question that it is abusive to women. At least other women are reporting these things more these days. At the time, it was not that often reported, but I was glad that I reported him because when he had been lurking around me, it felt awful and creepy.

Even if I'd escaped harm from my instructor, though, gender dynamics were still complicated, especially because there was a significant emphasis on dating at the DG house, and I suspect at all the sororities. I did not seem to be a superstar at it, at least I did not feel I attracted the kind of person I would have a long-term relationship with. I thought perhaps there was something wrong with me. I knew I was attractive enough. I think I put up a wall about dating as it seemed to me it was a lot of work, and besides, I did not find the fraternity guys that interesting.

Just to make life more exciting, one of my friends and I were friendly with the Housemother. The three of us decided to play a few pranks on the other girls. We thought they were a little full of themselves. We named ourselves "The Purple Pansies." My friend and I did all the dirty work as the housemother did not want to put her job in jeopardy. Probably the worst thing we did was put powdered sugar in the beds on the sleeping porch. It was a bit cold at night and everyone had electric blankets. They did not feel the powdered sugar when they first got into bed but as their beds warmed up and they sweat, the powder sugar would get sticky and be uncomfortable. Of course, they would have to wash their sheets which was not fun. Another thing we would do is smoke cigars in the basement so the smoke would go up the stairs. We had fire doors leading to the hall area of the stairs and men were not allowed to go behind them except for things like repair men. When the cigar smoke drifted up, we could hear the girls calling "Man behind the fire doors." My friend and I would post signs in the halls and stair wells stating, "The Purple Pansies will strike tonight." We were very careful and never got caught.

Two of the brothers of the Gonzaga boyfriend lived in an apartment a block away from the DG house. Their apartment was nice enough, typical of what two college guys would have. The furnishings were probably what came with a furnished apartment. Most importantly it was functional. They kept it relatively clean for students. I felt welcome and appreciated their hospitality.

To soothe my unhappiness, I would go visit them and ended up attracted to the older brother, who was in his first year of law school. He was apparently attracted to me, too, and we began a mini-affair that never became sexual, partly because he was a good Catholic and partly because it turned out he was engaged to someone from Spokane. But he and the other brother were good to me and provided a respite from the DG house. Our attraction dwindled with time, which was ok by then. Some of the attraction for me came from that rebellious part of me. The friendship had served me well, let me know I was attractive to someone and helped me through a difficult quarter. And by that time, I was doing better in my studies and adjusting more to my living situation. Ironically, many years later, the older brother would work at the Bank where my father had his Will and would be the Trust Officer after my mother died. When I realized this, I thought things were in good hands, though I would be proven wrong.

It was the City Club that put on the White Cotillion that presented the young women to society. This was, keep in mind, in Spokane, Washington. It was a real mini-version to those in cities of size and cultural importance. But it was a part of my sister's and my life, along with many of our friends, we were little princesses. The Cotillion took place at Christmas time the first year of College. My friend Betsy from Roosevelt and I were not cracked up about it, but we did it as did our sisters before us. I would add that it was 1961 and the time of the "Twist" and the era of the "merry widow" corset like undergarment with stays from hip to mid-back. I have a vivid memory that it was very painful when I "twisted." My escort for the presentation was my father. Afterward there was a dance, and my date was a friend named Ripley who was handsome and gracious about it all.

WASHINGTON, DC

THAT SPRING OF MY FRESHMAN YEAR, it became apparent that Carolyn was very unhappy and depressed in DC. So, I was sent to DC to the rescue for the summer to try to help her. She had a roommate who was rather strange, also unhappy and working in some high security job, which meant that I had to have a security clearance. This was good timing as some years later I got involved in political activities that might have made passing a security check difficult.

Carolyn did have a good friend from Spokane who was married to an administrator for a Senator, and they had been very good to Carolyn and welcomed me. She was an Occupational Therapist who worked at The National Institute for Mental Health, And I was fascinated talking to her about it. She proved to be a good adviser, too, in dealing with Carolyn.

What was even better was the fact that Carolyn's boss had found me an internship with Senator Tower of Texas. I felt very lucky. Every day when I went to work and walked over a mat that said, "UNITED STATES SENATE," I felt a little thrill. There were only two of us in Tower's Office who were not Texans and it was clear we were viewed as outsiders. The other person was a young man from Maine. We became good friends and drinking buddies. At the time, the legal drinking age in Washington DC was nineteen, which meant that we could go out to a lot of bars and drank a lot of Rob Roys (Sweet Vermouth and Scotch). It was during this summer that I had fleeting thoughts I was probably alcoholic. It was indeed troubling. I did not discuss this with anyone. I was, after all, just nineteen years old.

My job for the senator was not rocket science. It was obviously a gesture to please the Congressman from Ohio who was the Minority Whip. I helped open the mail and one thing I did was pull out the letters that went into the "nut file." A few of them wrote repeatedly and often. I even had my favorites and looked forward to their next letter, as their delusions were fascinating. Moreover, they mattered, because this was the beginning of my serious interest in major mental illness.

*   *   *

At the time, I also ran the signature machine and signed many letters from Senator Tower. The senator saw only a select few of letters sent to him. The staff dealt with most of them, often responding with form letters. A few years ago, when Obama was President, I wrote a letter to him regarding the mentally ill and certain basic needs that were not being met for them. I knew I would probably get a form letter back, and that is what I got. It was a letter about how he supported help to the mentally ill but was not relevant to what I had written. It was signed, I am sure by a signature machine. I framed it anyway, and it is still in my office displayed on a shelf. I can't say that I was disappointed, as I knew how these things worked in 1962 and doubted that things had changed all that much.

Back then, in the summer of 1962, Senator Jackson from Washington State had an office next to ours. At times co-workers would hold drinking glasses up to the wall and try to listen into conversations. I began to be aware of the shenanigans of Senators and Congressman. An 84-year-old Senator from Arizona pinched my butt in a crowded elevator once. If I had reported it, I doubt that he would have been asked to resign. At least there has been a little, tiny bit of progress around harassment in fifty-six years. A tiny bit. There was a joke that the women in Tower's office could be identified as they wore tenny runners in order to make fast get-away from unwanted advances. I suspected you needed to be from Texas to be a part of that. I wasn't.

One Saturday, Carolyn came out of the bathroom shaking an aspirin bottle, and asked me, in all seriousness, "How many aspirins does it take one to kill oneself?"

I answered, "60."

Then she went back into the bathroom and put the bottle back in the cabinet. I remember her roommate sitting across the room and looking up from her book and back into it again with no comment. The two of them were quite indifferent to each other, but this was definitely weird. Living with them was weird generally. Between my depressed sister and her depressed roommate, it wasn't much fun at all being in that apartment.

Carolyn never tried that again with me, though. The business of contemplating suicide and involving others is perhaps the epitome of manipulation, and I did not appreciate being put in that position. Years later, I now know that this kind of thing is known as "para suicidal behavior," wherein people leave clues that they are suicidal and just hope that someone will stop them. Sometimes they are not rescued in time, so it is hard not to respond. Apparently, though, I'd called her bluff by answering that question. Indeed, I knew my sister well enough to know that I was pretty sure she would go no farther with it. I did keep an eye on her for several weeks. In truth, I had no idea how many aspirins it takes to kill oneself.

In retrospect I have to add "Borderline" as a potential explanation for her behavior. When I consider her relationship with our mother, that diagnosis is pretty much on the mark. People with Borderline Personality Disorder most often have a parent who is rejecting or does not show affection or caring. Some have been molested and not protected or believed. In Carolyn's case, I think mother's rejection qualified. I was saved by Uncle Kip and did not need mother's nurturing. I have always been thankful I was not in Carolyn's position with Maxine. No matter what Carolyn would do in relationship to mother, it was never enough or became a nuisance.

Despite the discomfort of living in close quarters with my sister that summer, I am, today, still very grateful for my experience working in the U.S. Senate. It was a great opportunity, and I feel it was a privilege that only a few people get. The experience of working in the Senate had a down side, though, too. Not all, but some of our great leaders at close range were not especially admirable. There were a lot of rumors, probably true, of affairs, alcoholism, deals being made in back rooms, extravagant gifts. It was on both sides of the isle. Along with my fascination with the mentally ill, my experience in the Senate was the beginning of my political radicalization.

BACK TO THE U

AT THE END OF THE SUMMER, I LEFT DC and went to Spokane to get ready to go back to the University of Washington. By then, I was to enter a three-year undergraduate pre-law program in political science. Had I finished it, I would have gone into law school after my junior year. I mentioned this to Fred, whom I had told more than once about it, though he said he didn't remember.

His response, instead, was rather disappointing: "I would never hire a woman lawyer and will not pay for that."

"That means I need to change my major?" I asked. "Is that what you mean?"

"I guess so," he answered.

Even all of these years later, I have never been quite sure what that response was about. If it was the woman thing, I have to say it was something I would not excuse him for. I realized he was from a different generation, and so were a lot of chauvinist men. He did not understand this kind of oppression of women. It is only because he was so special to me that I even considered letting him off the hook. I would not have let it pass but I knew I would not be able to change his mind.

Though I was disappointed in his response, both because it disrupted my plans and fantasies of sometime standing, I was still surprised and disappointed in my father's chauvinist attitude. So, I looked into going to Medical School at the University of Washington. When I got in touch with them, their answer was quick and clear. They had a small quota for women applicants that had already been filled for some years to come. Besides, since I was applying to study Occupational Therapy, I already had identified studying in a Medical related field. I felt like it was a repeat of my father's attitude.

It did not take long for me to return to the decision to change my major to Occupational Therapy with the intent to work in mental health. That transition was a little bit miraculous, and it was one of those things that I did not understand at the time but is now clear it was what was supposed to happen as it did. Working with the mentally ill fit me more than to become a lawyer though I would have been fine with becoming a doctor. It just wasn't so bad coming from a prejudiced school program as it was coming from Fred. As it turned out, my career in OT is one of the things in my life that I treasure, and I am forever grateful for that.

Occupational therapy was developed to treat the shell-shocked veterans of WWI. The "occupational" word of the title refers to purposeful activity and is not related to vocational therapy. It refers to using purposeful activity and manipulating the environment to promote healing, both emotional and physical. Because OTs also work in medical fields, there was a variety of subjects we studied from medical sciences, including those related to anatomy, biology, kinesiology, (the study of human movement). Then there were classes for learning various crafts and art and how to adapt them for therapeutic purposes. For me it was a nice balance of serious science and creativity put to new use. Soon I was happy that I had changed my major.

What's more, back at the Delta Gamma house, I abandoned some of my negative attitudes and solidified several friendships, some which would pop up in later life. I actually enjoyed some of the other women in the sorority. By then, I was getting less judgmental and more accepting of others.

But my path still had its bumps along the way. By my second year at the UW, when I returned from DC, I began to think more seriously that I might be an alcoholic, though I honestly tried not to think about it. At the time, I was dating a man that I thought was terrific. He was a very handsome, first year law student, athletic, intelligent and coach of the Rugby team. I thought he was lovely. At Christmas, he offered to give me a ride to the train I was taking to Spokane to visit my family. As he put me on the train, though, he told me we would not be dating anymore because I drank too much. I was only stunned momentarily. I was traveling overnight and had a berth. I got on the train, pulled my scotch bottle out of my purse and drank all the way to Spokane because that is what alcoholics do.

As I recall, Carolyn flew home for Christmas. There was the usual holiday socializing, which involved a good deal of drinking at parties and at home with Huntley Drinkley. After the holiday, Carolyn returned to DC, and I returned to the UW. By now, the idea that I might be alcoholic surfaced periodically, and I worked hard at ignoring it. Sometimes, I would be absolutely determined not to get drunk, but always did. Instead, I began to think that I would be ok as long as I did ok in school. I thought I would probably have a glamorous but tragic ending at a fairly young age like Elizabeth Taylor in "Butterfield 8," a movie in which she played a glamorous and alcoholic woman who dies in a tragic car crash driving drunk.

Toward the middle of the second quarter, I decided that I had a crush on one of the houseboys, and he responded. Any fraternizing with house boys was forbidden, which made it more fun. He was attractive and a little on the bad boy side. We would meet away from the house. At the house we acted casually toward each other. We would have been in trouble if anyone found out. During Easter break, my friend from Wellesley was getting married and he borrowed a car from a friend, and we drove to Spokane. It was a fairly long trip as I-90 was not a freeway yet.

My parents were nice enough about it. I think he slept in my room and I slept in Carolyn's. The first night we were there we stayed up after my parents went to bed and I lost my virginity on my parent's couch in the living room. At the time, I thought that was funny, though it was really disrespectful of my parents. In spite of that I felt lucky that the houseboy was a good lover, and it was a good experience.

On the way back to Seattle when we were on the Vantage Bridge, the wind caught the hood of the car and pushed it open. My friend did not lose control of the car and we were able to get it back down and go on to Seattle, but it was very frightening. In the end we got back to Seattle and I got back to the Delta Gamma House without being found out. Over a fairly short period of time, we grew out of our little fling without any big problem and life at the DG House went on. It occurred to me that I seemed attracted to men who were not truly available for one reason or another. At the time, though, I wasn't overly worried about it; I just noticed.

My sophomore year basically went fine. There were no major crises. I liked studying OT though felt that mental health was not as targeted as I would have liked. My grades were good, and life was fine at the DG house. There was no question I was struggling with alcohol, but it remained private to me after the Rugby Coach stopped dating me. That is, no one else confronted me.

DC AGAIN:
ANOTHER RESCUE…ATTEMPT

MEANWHILE, CAROLYN HAD GOTTEN HER OWN APARTMENT in a nice area of D.C. and was living alone. She was still working for the Congressman from Ohio. As summer approached my parents began to be concerned about her. She was clearly depressed, and my parents wanted her in therapy. So, though I was not excited, I was willing, and it was decided I would go to DC again and live with my sister and see to it that she saw a psychiatrist.

So, I was once again off to the rescue, this time without a specific job other than to get a psychiatrist for Carolyn. Her apartment was on Tunlaw Road in a very nice part of DC. There were a lot of embassy people and other professionals related to government living there. It was an attractive building with nice apartments and a pool.

When I got there, though, it was clear that Carolyn was not in good shape, and I contacted our friend, the occupational therapist. She referred me to a psychiatrist who was well known for his work with depression. I got Carolyn an appointment and went with her the first time. The office was in a residential area and had a lovely garden entrance. The psychiatrist was an older man, very quiet and gentle. Carolyn was not impressed and apparently not too subtle about her opinion of him. She found it strange that toward the end of the session, the phone would ring once, he would pick up the phone, say nothing and hang it back up. I suspected they were letting him know the next patient had arrived. She referred to him as "Mouse."

Around six weeks into the time she went to him, he called me one day. "Do you know why your sister does not like me?" he asked.

I said, "I really don't know but I don't think she likes anybody right now. You really need to ask her."

I thought that was strange and inappropriate to call me about this. Apparently, the therapy was not going well.

I made friends with the life guard at the swimming pool who was a good supportive person. My friend Andrea and her husband had moved to DC and I spent time with her. I enjoyed her company and got to know her husband.

At the pool, I met an Austrian man, quite handsome but a bit stuffy. He was the Legal Attaché at the Austrian Embassy. He wore a tight speedo bikini suit at the pool which my sister made fun of when we went to the pool together. I dated him about three weeks during which he took me to the July 4th celebration at the U.S. Embassy. I met Dean Rusk, who was the Secretary of State, and tasted Buffalo meat. It was a beautiful party and it was exciting to be there. I did not like the Buffalo meat.

The Legal Attaché was a little hard to relate to, so I broke it off with him. He was furious and when he got into a crowded elevator with me (we lived in the same building) he actually spit on me. This was rather embarrassing and certainly not diplomatic.

I found a little work typing a manuscript for a professor that was interesting and gave me something productive to do. He was an eccentric and intelligent man. I enjoyed being in his home where he had an office. His assistant had been working with him for many years and was devoted and protective of him. She was nice to work with and I found their relationship interesting. I never knew for sure, but it appeared he was well known. There was evidence that he wrote a lot as there were papers strewn about, books piled up and in general an organized mess.

He was pleased with my work, which made me feel good. He was writing about a man who was some type of philosopher or psychologist. I don't remember the specifics of his writing as it was a long time ago and not my major concern at the time. It was about someone with the last name of White. Later I wondered if it had been William Alanson White as there was a famous Institute named after him in NYC where my own psychologist trained.

Most afternoons when I returned to our apartment from visiting Andrea or from the professor's house, I would go to the pool for a while until Carolyn was due home. I would put together a dinner as best I could. I have never been much of a cook. Then I would prepare for Carolyn's arrival. She was taking an antidepressant and I knew it would potentiate alcohol, that is, make it stronger. I would have a stiff drink ready for her, and one for me, of course. We would do Huntley Drinkley, and I would hear about her terrible day and the devious and unkind people at work. We had dinner and Carolyn would fall asleep on the couch. I would cover her with a light blanket and go back to the pool. In essence, I would "Mickey Finn" or drug her, so I did not have to deal with her as much. It was not a nice thing to do but was survival on my part.

Visits with Carolyn's friends were always a pleasure and often enough to help keep me going. By now, we could talk about OT and mental illness. At the end of summer, I happily returned to Spokane to get ready to go back to the UW.

Within two weeks of my return, Carolyn quit her job and came back to Spokane. No one was terribly surprised, nor were they happy, but my parents did not oppose it. So, she moved back in. Fortunately, she was willing to see a psychiatrist and began therapy shortly after her return. This, of course, was very important and would be helpful to all of us. She liked this doctor and remained in treatment with him for the next few years. She got a job with the Federal Home Loan Bank but continued to live with Maxine and Fred.

It was around this time Carolyn started dating a man from a prominent Catholic family. She was in love and apparently, he was too. They got engaged and began planning and announced the wedding. The recreation room was converted to display the wedding presents. It looked like a showroom for Tiffany's.

Then Carolyn had a serious asthma attack a few days prior to the wedding. I remember looking in on her and she looked tiny in her bed; she looked quite ill. Her skin was sallow and her usually pretty eyes were dull. The Bridegroom came to visit, took a different look at the situation and broke the engagement. Carolyn was of course devastated, and I did feel sorry for her. She stayed in bed for several days beyond the normal recovery from the asthma attack. It didn't seem fair. I think mother was devastated too as it would be the talk at the Bridge tables. My father felt bad for Carolyn, but he understood why the groom jumped ship. It was good Carolyn had her psychiatrist which was very helpful to her and everyone else around her though it would be rough sailing.

What to do with all the fancy presents? I was assigned to take the major part of them to the door of the people who had given them, hand over the present and state "The wedding is off. Thank you very much." This was my role as part of the rescue.

OUR WINTER OF DISCONTENT

I HAPPILY RETURNED TO THE UW for the first quarter of my junior year. By now I had enough seniority to have my own room in the DG House, which was good. Moreover, I liked my courses. Things were going well for me, and I was glad not to be in Spokane dealing with my sister.

At the time, I was dating some, and the person from grade school and high school whom I'd I had the crush on back then showed up, and I went out with him. That was when I'd learned about the pact that the Spokane boys had made to not to date me because I broke up with their hero. I was still attracted to my old heart throb. As I recall, he was leaving Seattle and I would not run into him again for many years.

Part way into the quarter, I got mononucleosis. I was put in the infirmary at the U for a few days, and my father was called to come get me. I felt very sick and the ride home was difficult. Fred was very kind to me, though, and I was glad to be going home to recuperate. When we got to Spokane, I was hospitalized with the complication of strep throat. I was close to delirious with a high fever. I remember being packed in ice and most people wore masks when they came into my room. I was allowed to go home in about four days.

So, there we were: Maxine, Fred, Carolyn, and me. I managed to finish the quarter by taking exams and writing papers from home. I soon got much better, though did not get my energy back right away.

The rest of that winter, though, was a little tough. We were a little bored, and Carolyn and I decided that we needed a kitten. Fred was about to leave for the Duck Club and a long week end of hunting and said "No." So, Carolyn and I found a Siamese kitten advertised in the paper. Mother did not forbid it, which meant she approved so we were off to get it while Fred was away. We knew once we had it Fred would let us keep it.

On the second day that Fred was at the Duck Club, he came out of his cabin and slipped on the step and tore out his knee. The Hunters were close friends and among them were several doctors. They assessed the situation, and splinted Fred's leg with kindling and duct tape. They all wanted to go Hunting so they put him on his bed with a bottle of Wild Turkey and left him for the day. They brought Fred home that evening. It was the first and only time I saw my father drunk. His doctor friends included an orthopedic surgeon who had booked him in for surgery the following Monday.

His return introduced Fred to a little kitten. He was not enthusiastic about it, but he was in pain and pretty drunk. We were a little worried. He had surgery and was home to heal in a few days. Fred would wear this kind of overalls with many pockets when he was home relaxing. We called them his zoot suits apparently after similar attire from the 20's. The legs were wide enough to accommodate his cast after surgery. We had an intercom throughout the house and when he was resting in his bedroom, we could hear him talking to the kitten who was snuggled up with him.

"You are such a cute little kitty," we heard him say.

It might have been the "Winter of Discontent," but it wasn't all bad. The kitten, now named Koshka (or "cat" in Russian), had won our hearts and was very entertaining. There were four of us, so we played bridge. Mother was still involved playing in her Trio and both Maxine and Fred continued seeing friends, going to dinner parties and Bridge clubs. And of course, there was Huntley Drinkley every evening. There were also those special times of drinking either to better deal with bad things or to celebrate the good. We drank to everything.

Carolyn was not quiet about her unhappiness, and it began to look like the major thing was that most of her friends were married and she wasn't. Her asthma was not a big issue during this time, except of course it had broken her engagement. She was also working through a good deal in therapy that apparently had quite a bit to do with her relationship with Maxine. Maxine would try to talk to Carolyn's psychiatrist, who in turn would not reveal much, which annoyed her.

There was one incident when Carolyn threw things at Mother when they were talking in her bedroom. I didn't know what it was about and really didn't care. I was kind to my sister and loved her as you love a sibling and felt sorry for her, as it did not seem fair she was having such a hard time, but I had grown tired of her victim role. There seemed an unusual degree of neediness, especially when I consider her relationship with a mother who just would not accept her. When I was able to return to school the next quarter, I was ready.

Today when I look back, it was admittedly a little hard to love my sister. I had been through too much with her. I felt bad for her but was getting very tired of her misfortunes that did affect the whole family. I was sad for her unhappiness but was not going to be victimized myself in its wake.

BACK FOR JUNIOR YEAR AT THE U

AFTER WE'D SURVIVED THAT COLD BUT KITTEN-FILLED WINTER, I went back to the DG House and OT classes. Happy to be back, I dove into school and dating right away. Meeting a first-year medical student, I knew that I might have sex with him, so I went to see a doctor about birth control. This medical student was a big man on campus, so I knew I should be prepared. I was nervous about the appointment and thought about how I would ask for help. Deciding just to be honest and clear about it, I sat in the waiting room for what felt like a long time. It was expensively furnished, and I thought the receptionist was snooty. Eventually, a nurse came out and took me to an office. Then I waited again.

Finally, the doctor came in wearing his white coat. It all seemed so formal. I told the doctor I was dating a man and thought I should be on birth control pills.

"Come back when you are married," he said. And left the room.

It was 1964.

I was mostly in love with the relationship than I was with the medical student. This is something that would happen again years later. I am hopeful I will recognize it early if it starts to happen in the future as the outcome is rarely good.

Although I was smitten with him, the man could be insensitive at times, and I had misgivings about him. We drank a lot. By that time if I drank at all, I drank a lot, which led to other things. One night, we were careless, though I quickly dismissed it as unlikely I would get pregnant. It was now Spring Quarter. But as the days began lengthening again, I began to wake up nauseated and thought it was a weird form of flu. I also noticed that drinking alcohol made me feel strange and was really uncomfortable.

Finally, though, I had to face up to the fact that I might be pregnant, and I called my old neighbor, who had been Carolyn's boyfriend through high school. He was a resident at University Hospital. He came by and picked me up and we went for coffee and talked about my options. I had no idea where to get an abortion and certainly was not going to ask anyone in the Delta Gamma House. It was dangerous and illegal.

He got me an appointment with a good doctor to find out if I was indeed pregnant. I was. Without many other options, I decided that I should go home and ask for my parents' support. I knew that women found abortions, but I had no idea how to or whom to ask.

My mother's first response was to go to Sweden where abortion was legal. I think one of her friends had taken a daughter there for that purpose. My father's first response was to go get his shot gun, not to demand a shot gun wedding but to shoot the father. Of course, this was wishful thinking. He was quite clear that he would not pay for an abortion in Sweden. And, although I couldn't cross him on that decision, I had always wondered if he opposed my mother's abortion, and this made me suspect he did.

All the same, I had already decided that I did not want to marry the father. Still, I wanted him to come to Spokane so we could talk about what to do. He did come, and we talked. My father and mother met him and said little. I could tell that they were not impressed, and neither was I. So, I decided to deal with it without him. Since the day when we met in Spokane, I have never had contact with him.

THE OREGON COAST

AFTER THE INITIAL SHOCK, MY PARENTS were not only supportive; they were actively helpful. Together, we came up with the "Secret Plan," which was to rent me a house on the Oregon Coast where I could spend the duration of the pregnancy. Fred did the research and found a house on the ocean that was available through January, which was around when I was due. He also gave me a car to use, and we found a great doctor in Salem, Oregon through our family doctor back home in Spokane.

During the time of my secret life along the coast, I found myself in a house that was good and solid and attractive enough. It was on a bluff over the ocean and had a fabulous view, especially from the dining room table. That was a good thing, as I would spend many hours at that table working on tests and papers, because I had arranged to finish the quarter at the UW that way. So, I was lucky as it was not the worst place to be. Things were in good shape. The kitchen was open to the dining area and the living area was a good size, and the upstairs had a big master bedroom and a guest room. The house was comfortable and pleasant, and I felt very lucky to have the parents I had to do this for me.

Moreover, I had company, as it was decided that I should take Koshka, the cat, with me. She graced me with gifts from the basement, a garter snake once and several mice. Mother had trained her to walk on a leash with a harness. Weather permitting, Koshka and I would walk a vacant lot that was behind my house that was not developed. It was quite pleasant most days. She was good company, and one day when I was discouraged and lonely, I sat on the stairs crying and she came over and licked my tears.

In terms of other company during those somewhat strange and solitary days, the house also happened to be located in a small artist community. I knew that I would need more to occupy me until January, so I began studying with an art teacher who was a real character, jovial and with a good sense of humor and a good teacher. She and her friends took me under their wing. I said nothing about the father, and I had a fake name myself, Mrs. James Case (my maternal great grandfather) and my mother's original wedding rings. My new friends decided that my husband was either killed in Vietnam or had died of a brain tumor.

There was a very nice, somewhat socially inept young man who stuttered and with whom they tried to fix me up, though that was the last thing on my mind. They did, though, include me in some of their social events, which I appreciated, and my art lessons and painting at home became important to me.

Maxine came to visit about every month to six weeks. She went with me to my art classes and was pleased when my teacher said that I was talented and a fast learner. The ideas about what happened to my supposed husband may have come from my mother. Mother and I explored the small shops, went out to dinner a few times but stayed around the house and talked often about her college days, her friends who went to NYC after graduation, how she ended up with Fred in Enterprise. I asked about my great grandmother and about my grandmother, and about what she knew of Fred's family. My ancestors were perhaps not the best of parents, but they were interesting and strong people.

On several occasions, my mother went with me into Salem to see my doctor. He was very good to her, and she liked him. My doctor was a good man who told me not to feel badly about getting pregnant. He assured me the only thing I did wrong was ovulate at the wrong time. By then I had pretty much accepted the fact of the pregnancy and did not think beating myself up about it would help anything. Nevertheless, I appreciated his comment.

By now I had a certain calm feeling about being pregnant that was very pleasant. It occurred to me that I could sit doing nothing but that my body was doing something very special. Interesting enough, alcohol made me feel very uncomfortable, and I did not drink throughout the pregnancy. I did not know much about fetal alcohol syndrome, which I now know can be devastating, so some Higher Power was looking after that baby.

Mother was pleased when the doctor told us that he had a wonderful family to adopt my baby. It was a prominent lawyer and his wife who very much wanted to adopt her. She was "good stock" from a college girl and a medical student. So, I agreed but did not sign anything. They would pay my medical bills. This did put me at ease, as it meant my father was off the hook. I was not at all sure yet if I would give the baby up, but there seemed to be a good prospect for her if I did.

Still, it was quite a decision. I spent a good deal of time going over in my head the different scenarios that might be available to me, if I did want to keep her. Early on, I eliminated going to my parent's house. They had enough on their hands with my sister. Moreover, it had been my being drunk and careless that had led to my situation. I already felt very much appreciative of their response to my situation and I did not want this option. This was clear and definite.

At twenty-one, I also knew that I needed to finish my education, even if I felt responsible for the baby first. So, I decided that I would take my time to figure it all out before the baby was born, and I would not obsess about it. There were months, after all, to figure it out. I would just have some options to choose from by the time I needed to decide.

During this time of wondering, Fred also came to see me once, and it was evident that it was hard for him to see me pregnant. Because I loved my father, this was one thing that did make me feel very sad. I had really let him down. My mother was with him, and we did have a good visit, despite both our discomfort. I think I understood my father well and accepted the fact that it was too hard to visit. I knew he was doing what he could to support me both emotionally and financially, and I was very grateful. He did not need the pain of seeing me pregnant. We apparently both knew this, and it was fine this was the only time he came to visit.

My sister, though, came to see me a number of times, which was not easy, either, as she was quite preoccupied with her own situation and not terribly good company. She meant well, I am sure, but it was a little draining. She wasn't working currently, and it was easier for her to get away than it was for my parents. I did appreciate her efforts and dismissed her self-centered problem as best as I could.

Beyond that, I really did not mind being alone, as I got a good deal done by myself. Painting was wonderful, as was my art teacher. I also worked my way through those tests and papers to finish the quarter, which gave me a good deal of satisfaction. Moreover, I decided that I did not want to go back to the U, as occupational therapy students there took the medical science classes at the Medical School, and I just did not want to run into the baby's father. It became increasingly clear; I needed a new start somewhere else.

So, I began to research a number of OT schools and began applying to start in the fall. Most significantly, I was interested in Columbia in NYC, as they had a special focus on psychiatric OT that was headed up by the author of the main text for mental health practice. I did apply elsewhere too, U of Pennsylvania, Scripts in San Francisco, Tufts in New Jersey and several others, just in case; but once I was accepted into all of them, I chose Columbia right away. Fortunately, my father agreed to support me financially, and my mother thought it very good that I had been accepted at all those "good schools." Beyond that, I was sure that the Bridge Club in Spokane would hear about it with some story about where I was currently, but I didn't much care. After a summer working for Fred, I would be off to NYC the following fall In the meantime, though, life was not without its dramas. Carolyn was in Oregon with me when there was a huge storm on the Pacific Coast. The pass between me and the hospital in Salem was closed, and I was not too far from my delivery date. I called my doctor, and he told me not to worry, as he was in the Air Force Reserve and could come get me by helicopter if need be. That was a good thing, I suppose, though my mind still flashed headlines, "Janice Becker, Pregnant Unwed Mother Rescued from Beach Front Home." Fortunately, none of that was necessary, though the storm was pretty amazing.

The damage, too, was equally impacting. All along the coast, cattle washed up on the beaches. My little house was up on a bluff above the beach, and the front hedge along with about four feet of the lawn disappeared in the night. Carolyn's company was appreciated, and we got through it with some good humor and a little bravery together, before my sister, for all of her trials and tribulations, went back home for a while.

When it was time, though, both Maxine and Carolyn came down for the delivery. I remember thinking there was only one way out of the situation and though I was anxious I don't think I was afraid. We drove to the hospital which was in Salem and by the time we got there I was having more and significant cramping. But it was to be a 32-hour ordeal before I delivered a healthy baby girl. After delivering, I had a very special euphoric feeling—something that I would recapture in a different way some years later.

Despite all of those months meditating on what to do, I still had not signed papers for the adoption, as I was not totally sure that I would give her up. But, when the moment came, my better sense told me that I was probably not going to do well with an infant at Columbia in New York, where I had no support system; and no baby should be brought into a situation where mother and child do not have that. Because of the prominence of the potential adoptive parents, I had a lovely private hospital room that had just been vacated by the Governor's wife. Indeed, the prospective adoptive parents had a connection with the Governor.

Not surprisingly, the social worker was persistent, coming to see me two to three times a day for the next two days with the adoption papers. I'd told her that I wanted to see my baby before I signed anything, which put her in a panic mode that she did not hide well. It became apparent that they did not want me to see her, so I stuck more firmly to my guns, even offering for Mother and Carolyn to go with me, though they declined. Mother was obviously worried that she might return to Spokane with an illegitimate grandchild, but that was not one of my concerns. I was just trying to make sure that my decision was mine and that it was the best for the baby, rather than being based on what would look best for Maxine's social standing.

So, the social worker and I went to see her. She was, of course, a beautiful baby with a sweet face, not like Mr. Magoo like so many Caucasian babies I have seen. She had exceptionally long legs. I was satisfied, and I signed the papers. She was most likely headed for a privileged life, so I wished her well and hoped that she would be healthy and happy. As I write this now, knowing what was to come for me, I have no regrets regarding that decision.

Sometime later, I would think about contacting her so that she would know that I'm an ok person and wanted the best for her. At one point, I hired a private investigator to look for her. I told them what I knew of her parents, which was not rocket science. When they came back saying that they'd found nothing, I knew they were a scam. I thought again about my finding her and realized that it was her place to decide if she wanted to find me. There was a registry in Oregon for finding original parents, and I put my name on it and let it go.

I am comfortable with this final decision to let her find me. It is now fifty-four years later, and I have never heard from her. I hope she is having a good life and is well.

BACK TO SPOKANE

AFTER ALL OF THAT, IT WAS GOOD, FOR A TIME, to be home again doing Huntley Drinkley with Fred and Maxine. It was still a pleasant time, and I knew that they were relieved that the Oregon Coast period was behind us. Mother was no doubt most grateful she did not have an illegitimate grandchild to explain at the Bridge Table. Fred was grateful that the drama was over. My baby was never mentioned again by either of them. Most of the time, this felt ok. I did want to give them that room.

At the same time, the Buick GM dealership was doing well. I had agreed to work for Fred until leaving for New York City. By now, there was a prevalence of Buicks in the driveways of our neighborhood. At this time, the son of Fred's partner was working with Fred to learn the business. He was my sister's age and we got along well. He was a flirt and had a great sense of humor. He was married, and I was Fred's daughter, so the flirting was all in fun.

There was one incident when I put through a mailing that was to be 5 cents apiece at 50 cents. I knew Fred would see it and there would be a disaster. So, I contacted the Post Office and somehow got them to intercept it and Fred never knew. Everyone working there heard about it and held their breath until I rectified the mistake. Other than that incident all went well.

When I worked for Fred, a part of what went on with me was I had a fascination with the fact my father owned his own business, that he knew how to run it and was good at it. I also had a fantasy that I might learn how to run it and be able to do so one day. But I also knew that my father did have an old chauvinist thing about women and the kind of work that was appropriate for them to do. The biggest clue had been the thing about me going to law school. The closest I knew I would come was to work for him which I did on several occasions. Without question, I know that this had an influence on me in developing my own agency. My agency, though there have been some rough times, has survived for the last thirty years. It is still not always easy, but it remains helping a number of people with very difficult disabilities. It provides employment for a number of people who do good work. It has been worth all the worries and troubles along the way.

DICK

I HAD ONLY BEEN HOME FOR A FEW WEEKS when I ran into an old high school acquaintance named Dick. He was the only adopted son of a wealthy couple who lived out by the Country Club in a beautiful house and a fair amount of land where they kept horses. He'd been popular in high school and had gone to a number of "party" colleges including the University of Arizona, University of Hawaii, University of Colorado and a few others. By then, though, it was 1965, the time of Vietnam and the draft, and Dick and his father had run out of deferments, so he was waiting to go into Warrant Officer Training in the Fall. We started dating.

His father had been the manager of a major mine in Mexico during WWII and made a great deal of money. He was an alcoholic and quite a wild one. Not too long before I met Dick his father had ridden his horse into the men's grille at the Country Club and had been banned from there for several months. He was very nice to me and I liked him.

My new friend was essentially a golf bum, so we played golf, not my best sport. We spent a lot of time together. As usual, Fred had some questions for him in relationship to me. The most outstanding was could he keep me safe when we were out. He responded that he could do that as he kept a loaded gun in his glove box, which freaked Fred out a little bit, but he let it pass.

By this time, I knew that we were both alcoholic. Our drinking was a major focus of our relationship. I just accepted it as a fact and thought there was not much to do about it except try not to get into trouble. Our golf game was focused on a case of beer in the golf cart for Dick and a large gin and tonic for me at tee off and a refill at the bar at the end of the 9th hole. I never liked beer as I got full before I got high. We would play the rest of the course then shower and change and meet for dinner in the clubhouse. There were the usual drinks before dinner, wine with dinner and then dancing. We were the youngest couple there and everyone thought we were so cute. I have no idea how many knew how drunk we were, but I think we did pretty well not to be too obvious. I think my tolerance for alcohol was increasing and I did not pass out or go into black out.

We did a lot of other things together on dates. I told Dick about the baby, and he swore to secrecy but wanted to get her back. I told him we could not do that. He settled down. He was basically a good person, and worried about his immediate future in the service. His parents loved and spoiled him. I saw a nice part of him, and I was in love. He made my time in Spokane special, treated me very well and by the end of the summer we were engaged. My parents were ok with it and had come to like him. So, we were both off in the Fall. He went to Warrant Officer Training and I went to NYC and Columbia. Then, the plan was that Dick was to come for Christmas in New York, when we would announce our engagement.

NEW YORK CITY

FINALLY, THE TIME HAD COME TO START OVER, and I was excited. I was going to Columbia and was experiencing New York City. My friend Betsy had married a PhD candidate headed for a career as a professor, and they were also living in NYC near the Columbia Campus. They picked me up at the airport which I very much appreciated, especially as I must admit that I was a little afraid of being on my own in a totally big, strange place. So, it was wonderful to have a friend there. They showed me around NYC, and I was immediately aware I was in a very foreign place. But, there were still a few days before I was to move into the dorm, so I stayed with them. They did not have children yet but had a huge St. Bernard dog that was wonderful. Of course, I think most dogs are wonderful. We all got along just fine.

That time was a first for a number of things. To begin with, I had never witnessed people sleeping in doorways or begging for money or food. The signs of wealth and poverty were side by side. It was astounding. Everyone seemed so busy. People even walked fast. There were not too many greetings to others, and everyone pretty much stayed to themselves.

I had never been so small in such a big world. The Princess from Spokane was about to get right sized, perhaps one of the best things living in NYC did for me. I had never seen street venders or people performing music with a hat on the sidewalk for donations. There were good musicians playing on the street. People were so diverse in New York, and I liked that. I had never been among so many kinds of people before, and it was certainly helpful to be with Betsy and her husband for my first exposure. By then, it was 1965, and things were politically alive. I was certainly excited that I was on my way to a very new adventure. I had no idea how much my life would change. I just knew it would.

A few days later I moved into Johnson Hall on the main campus, which was located on a bluff separating it from Harlem. It was an old but well kept up building. I had been assigned to a top floor suite of two bedrooms separated by a shared bath. The rooms were quite large, and my roommate was an OT student a year ahead of me, and two dental hygienist students shared the other bedroom. We each had our own desk and the good thing about mine was that one of the drawers accommodated a fifth of Ballantine Scotch perfectly. There was no ice machine in the dorm, so I drank scotch without the rocks. And yes, I drank regularly in the evening and often while I studied. In retrospect, my three roommates must have been appalled, but I did not notice or care. By this time, I needed to drink.

Most of our classes were in the College of Physicians and Surgeons about a 20-minute subway ride north from main campus. A large group of us commuted on the subway together. Both OT and PT students had a number of classes together. Specifically, OT had its offices and special classes like those related to mental health at the Medical School. Soon after we began to study diagnoses, we would diagnose people on the subway in pig Latin. Of course, we weren't very good at it, but it was just a silly game to make the subway ride a little better. Schizophrenic was schabitzaphrobanobic, for instance.

The OT program also had some classes in the Art and Psychology Departments on the main campus. I really liked these as I was very good at the art-based classes and liked the way we used them therapeutically. The psychiatric based classes were excellent and extremely interesting. I enjoyed studying and, in spite of the drinking, was a good student. The first year was focused on psychiatry and was taught by Gail Fidler, the co-author of the main text used for psychiatric OT at the time. She wrote it with her husband who was an analyst. The text was referred to as "Fidler and Fidler" and described clearly the relationship between mental health, the environment and productive activity.

Gail was very knowledgeable about psychiatric issues and an inspiration for me. I admired her intellect and creativity. She was a skilled teacher and held our interest. She understood that I was very serious about working in psychiatry, and I felt she challenged me at times.

Gail was also clear about therapists developing insight into their own issues, defining appropriate boundaries with clients and what therapeutic relationships with them were necessary for establishing trust and motivation for treatment. She believed it appropriate and even necessary to engage in our own therapy to be clear about our own issues and therefore not contaminate the professional relationship with the client. I was up for therapy, as I felt I needed it to sort out my family, for one thing. I waited for about a year before I began that journey. It would last a long time.

We spent a good deal of time in group discussions sharing about our practicum experiences. A good deal of this was talking about relating to patients, taking things personally when not appropriate, understanding patient behavior, how to make helpful choices in therapeutic activities and how to interpret behaviors for treatment purposes. It was all fascinating to me.

We also got to know each other from these experiences together. For instance, we sat in a circle for these sessions, a technique that I would later learn was quite purposeful. With nothing to separate or protect us like tables or desks, it would draw us closer and perhaps open discussions up more. Our experiences were not all alike, as we were individuals with different views about what was going on.

But there were certain things that held true in psychiatric terms. It was not appropriate to take things personally nor to be too quick to judge such things. As therapists, we meant different things to individual patients. Sorting through these dynamics was part of the puzzle. Because the approach we were training in drew some on symbols and cultural meanings for each individual patient, it was very interesting. Things could have interpretations depending on our own background and experiences. It needed to relate to that of the patient. I was and remain so grateful I chose working in mental health and that I got to study at Columbia with Gail Fidler.

A LITTLE SOCIAL GROWTH

As I had since the beginning, I continued spending some time with my friend Betsy and her husband, and I met some of their friends, becoming good friends in particular with one whose name was George Harrison, (not the Beetle). He was an intelligent and fun person who had been a classmate of my friend's husband. He was also the first black man that I knew personally. Throughout that time, I met many diverse people and became friends with quite a few from school contacts and through others I met socially. Arriving in New York City at twenty-two years old, I understood that there were going to be big changes now in how I saw the world, and some would be surprising.

Fairly soon, I began to become more liberal in my political beliefs, quickly realizing that I'd been sheltered and spoiled, the Princess from Spokane. Now, I was witnessing things I had never seen before. I got to know people who were African American and successful, and people who were students and immigrants from many different countries. It turned out that I was a very small duck in a very big puddle, and that realization was very good for me. At the same time, I also saw wealth beyond anything I had known before. The contrast was staggering, particularly as I lived in a neighborhood that was predominantly Black and Puerto Rican.

In no way did life slow down during this time. On Halloween during that first year, I was invited to two parties. One was at Betsy's and was a costume party and one was an invitation from a Columbia student I had dated for a short time. I decided that I could wear a costume to both parties because, after all, it was Halloween. So, I put together a pretty good devil's outfit. red with a forked tail and horns. I went first to Betsy's party and had a really good time. Then I went to meet the new friend at his party. Walking in the door, though, I saw that all the men were in suits, and every single woman had on a black cocktail dress with pearls. People stared at me, but I decided that I didn't care and would stay and talk to people. My new friend never asked me out again. The rebel in me, though, was awakened, and I did not care. That fellow was just a little too East Coast sophisticated and humorless for my taste.

Politics were raging in the country and were particularly acute in NYC. In retrospect, I was pretty naive and did not know I was. I just knew that we had no business in the Vietnam War, killing a lot of people, both our own and the Vietnamese. The homeless situation in the city was also raging. I believed these things were basically wrong, but I did have a lot to learn.

CHRISTMAS 1965

My fiancé was coming for Christmas from Warrant Officer training, and I was getting close to being an anti-war activist. I was uneasy. He arrived and it was not good. We had grown in different directions and we were worlds apart. He would pull out a wad of money on the street to buy a hot dog, which freaked me out. I think he was trying to impress people, but it was dangerous. He also talked about killing "Viet Cong Charlie," which was hard for me to hear. He was disdainful of people on the street. One saving grace was he had gotten tickets for "Funny Girl" for Streisand's last performance. I was not sure that I should go, but I did, and it was wonderful, though it was the last thing that I was going to do with him. After the play, when we stopped for a drink, I explained as tactfully as I could how I had changed, and it wasn't going to work out for us.

Dick left for Spokane the next day. His parents had gone to Hawaii for Christmas. My parents invited him to spend Christmas with them. So, naturally, I was the bad guy. I can only guess what their conversations were like. I'm sure they thought I'd become a wild thing in New York and had broken up with Dick recklessly. I'm sure they thought I had become a nasty protester; and what worse could I do to be rebellious against a family like mine? Not much.

But, I did get some sympathy. One of my friends at the dorm who was a PT student was sorry to hear that I'd ended my engagement and didn't want me to spend Christmas alone, so she invited me to go home with her, and I accepted. So off I went with my Italian-American friend to the Jersey Shore.

Her parents were very upset, as well, that my engagement was broken. I accepted their concern but offered few details. Sometimes, things are just better left unsaid.

It was pleasant being there, though. Their house was large with expensive furnishings, and they were extremely generous toward me. There were many visitors to see her father, who apparently was someone important. The visits were on going, somewhat brief and jovial and in a den off the living room. My friend, her sister and mother and I went to a lovely spa for manicures and pedicures. Meals were wonderful traditional Italian. On Christmas morning, I was given numerous very nice presents. I was appreciative of their hospitality and kindness. I also suspected that my friend's father did something special considering all the devoted visitors.

After our break-up, Dick became a navigator on a combat helicopter. Sadly, a few years later on a mission over Laos, his helicopter went down, and he was MIA. I was very sad and wished that things might have been different, but they weren't. I appreciated how he had been sweet and kind to me when I returned to Spokane after the Oregon Coast. Neither did I forget that I truly had been in love with him back then. For a while, I wore a bracelet for him—a custom during that time—and tried to remember the good things as best as I could.

PSYCHIATRY

AFTER MY VISIT TO THE JERSEY SHORE, I RETURNED to New York City and continued to love school. We started our first contact with patients on the psychiatric units of New York Psychiatric Institute, a part of Columbia Presbyterian Medical Center. There were two patients who were very interesting and quite famous. They were known as the "Finn Twins." They were diagnosed as being "Idiot Savant." They could calculate the day of specific dates in some phenomenal range of years. They were somewhat behavior problems and Gail Fidler was part of their treatment team.

She arranged to have them deliver newspapers to patients throughout the hospital as a job. They took their job very seriously, and their behavior was fine around that. She worked with them on their behavior generally, somehow attached it to their job and it improved. They were well known within the hospital, and people would ask them to do the date calculation. They were identical twins and would stand side by side, hold one index finger in front of their face and one would rock back and forth sideways, the other forward and back.

Along with my classmates, I was a bit anxious at first, but I got over it quickly. The patients were interesting and generally appreciated what we were doing with them. Soon, we also became privy to the charts, and I found them fascinating. I was beginning to understand major mental illness and to enjoy knowing the patients assigned and to understand and appreciate occupational therapy as a useful approach.

Particularly interesting to me was Fidler's diagnostic activity battery that tested organizational skills (mosaic piece), self-perception (drawing of self), and the ability to define oneself (a material such as clay that was inherently messy). When well interpreted the battery revealed reliable information toward diagnosis and provided a basis for what therapeutic activities would be appropriate.

Alongside the good energy of my work, I had begun dating again and was quite promiscuous. There was something connected to having had a baby, coupled with the fact this was the 60's. And frankly, I enjoyed sex. There was always an alcohol haze during my social activities. By now I accepted that I drank to get drunk and believed that as long as I functioned for school and moved closer to a career, it would be ok. I had a theory, typical alcoholic thinking, that when I was hung over, I exerted more energy and attention to what I was doing and actually did better than I would have if not hung over as overshot the mark. Drinking, by that point, was becoming a lot of work.

At the beginning of my second year, I began seeing an analytic psychiatrist. He was very serious, and I was not especially comfortable with him. Even so, I had not expected a warm nurturing person and thought I would adjust to his manner in time. He also was seeing another student whom I did not know well and actually had never thought she was someone I would be friends with. But I did wonder if the doctor acted the same with her as he did with me. I tried to just go with it but at times considered bringing up shocking and strange things to see how he would react, but I didn't do that consciously. The time never came when I adjusted to working with him. After just short of a year, I brought up my feeling that he did not like me, and I thought I would find another psychiatrist. He said, "That is a good idea."

It was likely he was conservative politically, and I was becoming more liberal, even radical in his view. I think the last straw for him was when I started my last internship, I met and began dating a black man who had been a Black Panther. I met him at the Bronx VA. Someone suggested the psychiatrist was even frightened of me. It felt pretty strange to have a psychiatrist who did not like me. I was glad that I had figured it out and had gotten out of there when I did.

A CLOSE CALL

IN LATE WINTER I WAS DATING A STUDENT a few years younger than me. He was from the East Coast, and his parents had a cabin in the woods a few miles outside of New Ipswich, New Hampshire. He invited me to go there with two other couples for a weekend. When we got there, we had to leave the car on a road about a half mile from the cabin. There was snow on the ground but the hike in was not too bad. We built a fire in the fireplace to warm up, had dinner, drank and partied for a number of hours. Snow became heavy and of blizzard magnitude. In the storm, we hunkered down, drank some more, stoked the fire, and went to bed. Several hours later we woke up with smoke in the cabin. My friend went outside with another fellow, looked under the cabin, yelled to us to get dressed and pack up. The timbers under the fireplace had caught on fire and were smoldering. They packed the area with snow and managed to put out the burning embers. We had to walk out to the car in the dark and in the blizzard. As we trudged outside, we realized how close we had come to a disaster potentially fatal to us all. Once again, looking back, something was looking out for us.

I had a neuro-anatomy final the next Tuesday. I was tired and distracted and needed to cram for the exam, something I seldom did. One of my friends suggested that I take some form of speed to help me with this and gave me several tablets of what she used. I was able to stay awake to study and felt that I would be ok with the exam. Then I laid down to try to sleep and do not remember if I did. When I got to the exam, though, I totally drew a blank. I had no choice but to hand my paper to the professor with an apology. What I learned was about "state specific memory" meaning, I had learned the material under the influence of a stimulant, but I'd tried to take the test in a different state and had no recall. Would I have had recall if I had gone to the exam on a stimulant? I don't know. I do know that I got a "C" in that course, which I suppose was lucky, even if difficult to swallow.

CHESTNUT LODGE, MY PSYHIATRIC INTERNSHIP

AT THE END OF THE FIRST YEAR IN THE OT PROGRAM we all had internships. We did our psychiatric placement first as it would be relevant to all areas of practice. Gail Fidler suggested strongly that I go to a private psychiatric inpatient hospital in Rockville, Maryland called Chestnut Lodge. It had been founded by Harry Stack Sullivan and Frieda Fromm-Reichmann, two Neo-Freudian psychiatrists. The hospital was set up with cottages that patients lived in with a few other patients. There were housekeeping staff and cooks who worked in and maintained each building. The cottages were pleasant, and the grounds were large and well kept. The administrative office and treatment offices were in separate buildings. As I remember the OT clinic had its own building. The clinic was well equipped and in an adequate space that was attractive. It was 1966, and the fee to enter treatment was $300,000. There were a number of famous people in treatment. Some patients had been there for many years.

I lived above one of the patient cottages in nurse's quarters and had my meals with the patients. I learned quickly to meet challenges, what we called "testing," by the patients with honesty and direction. My first day, when I went downstairs for breakfast, a patient was waiting for me at the bottom of the stairs. He was masturbating and was watching to see what I would do. I was a bit surprised but not scared. I knew a little about him and I pretty much knew he was a gentle soul. He was the son of a famous author.

"Put it away, George. It's time for breakfast," I told him.

So, he did, and we went in to eat. He would meet me every morning, without the challenge, and we had breakfast together for the next three months of my internship. He was essentially non-verbal, but we had a special relationship.

It was an unusual institution as practiced an analytic approach with major mental illness. This was controversial. Whether this was appropriate was not the issue, but how much I learned about psychiatry was the issue for me. In service trainings with the Psychiatrists were wonderful and challenging. I worked beside some incredibly skilled therapists, not only O.T.s but art and music therapists. There was a patient who did absolutely beautiful modern collages. The art therapist encouraged and supported her in this work. She had been at the hospital for eighteen years.

I had the great opportunity to work with Marion Chase, one of the founders of Psychodrama. She was seventy-four at the time, and she invited me to work on Saturdays with her to learn about Psychodrama and Movement Therapy. She was very special and very skilled at working with extremely difficult patients. I remember a specific patient who was mute whom she would meet every Saturday under a large tree. She would take her place beside the patient, make eye contact and then they would walk together for an hour. I would walk a number of steps behind them in silence. They did not speak. The patient was always there to meet her. They had done this for some years.

I also went to her psychodrama sessions for the rest of the three months that I was there and liked it very much. It was basically picking a relevant topic about issues and role-playing solutions to it. This is a very simplistic explanation but makes the point. I have found that many patients liked this method of working through problems. I learned that people with significant mental health issues are able to benefit from it. I also noticed that a number of them were talented at role playing and working through problems by acting it out somehow frees people up to go deeper toward the solution.

Perhaps more than anything from this time, though, I will always remember the music therapist who worked with a woman who had been a concert pianist. The therapist reported that she had assigned a Beethoven piece to her and when she played it in their session it was very strange. They had recorded it and after the patient left the session, the therapist listened to it several times because it did not make sense but there was clearly a structure to it. She finally realized the patient had played it note perfect backwards.

On another occasion, one of my patients taught me a huge lesson. He was a well-known person, and I had given him a choice in projects, and he chose weaving. One Friday, he went on a pass. While he was gone, I pulled the weaving back to the place of an error so it could be fixed. He returned on Sunday. I saw him the next day and told him what I had done and why, admitting that I hadn't thought he would object.

But he told me, "Don't you know that I am paranoid and would think someone did it to hurt me?" His gaze was long. "Just don't ever do that again."

I apologized and I have never done that again.

There was a pool on the grounds, which I used some evenings and on days off. The lifeguard was interesting company until he was caught renting out the pool shack to patients for extracurricular activities. The new lifeguard was not so industrious and was good enough company for the rest of my stay.

These experiences are all still with me, clearly, and I remember how they began to shape my work skills and knowledge. It was a privilege to be at Chestnut Lodge for my internship, particularly as I began to see that working with the severely mentally ill it was possible to help them find meaning and gratification and that they often had skills and talents that could be tapped. I learned that patience and careful observation often gave clues to what people with severe problems could do when given opportunity to explore this. So, I'm grateful to Gail Fidler for arranging my internship, encouraging me to experience different approaches, just as I'm grateful to the therapists there who took an interest in me and taught me skills I draw on today—skills that have never left me.

Even now, I attend staff meetings at my agency as a means of keeping a pulse on things. It does mean I go in twice a month, which interrupts my retirement, but I'm comfortable enough with it. And, just the other day, I had a reason to pull on my experience at Chestnut Lodge. One of our therapists has struggled with the fact that one of her clients is periodically elusive and she may go several weeks without connecting with her. Nevertheless, the client has stopped screaming at her and has even been pleasant on occasion. The therapist does take her a coffee and a treat each week and leaves it for her if she is not there. The other thing involved in this service is also that the family knows that someone is checking in on her and that she is ok. I shared the story of the woman who met Marion Chase under the tree once a week. They never spoke but did have a relationship. I think the same thing is true of this client and the therapist and that it is important to continue to be there for her. It is also a service to the family to give them some peace of mind that there is contact with their family member. All these years later, it occurs to me that I'm still drawing on things that I learned in that internship.

THE SECOND YEAR IN NYC

AT THE END OF THE FIRST SCHOOL YEAR AT COLUMBIA, I had agreed to share an apartment with a friend of mine who was in the PT program. It was a one-bedroom apartment in an old building on 115th street off Broadway. It was near Johnson Hall, so we knew the neighborhood. I looked forward to the freedom it would give me as she knew I drank, and it was a bit more comfortable than drinking in the dorm.

My friend George Harrison liked us both as friends and was around a bit. One evening he brought some pot with him, and I smoked it for the first time. It was a joint that he had brought and that I thought looked kind of small and poorly rolled; but, paying attention to his instructions, I smoked with him and got high. It was a bit of a combination of a mild out of body experience, a bit of euphoria and a bit of paranoia with hunger at the end. I liked it. Of course, I drank with it, too. Some years later when I was married and not drinking, I would smoke in place of Huntley Drinkley for about eighteen years. I'd applied sobriety only to alcohol. I was wrong.

Back at Columbia, most of my classes were focused on studies related to physical disabilities, general medicine and pediatrics. Human anatomy presented a problem for me, as we shared a cadaver with medical students, and anatomy lab was almost intolerable. I could barely deal with the smell of formaldehyde and found touching the corpse close to impossible. I went to see the professor and begged him to not have to touch it if I got A's on his exams. I explained that I was going to work in psychiatry and would probably not have to deal with anatomy in my career. He said we should go to the lab session and he would talk with me afterward. Then, of course, he called on me first and asked me to pull on a tendon in the wrist that raised the middle finger. I wasn't sure I could do it without fainting or throwing up, but I did, though he also saw how difficult it was for me to touch it. I was pretty freaked out, and it wasn't until sometime later that I realized what finger he had me move. After the lab session he agreed that if I got A's on the exams, I did not have to touch anything, but I did have to go to lab sessions and observe what others were doing. Well, that was good enough for me.

The rest of the second year of classes were medical oriented with therapeutic activities that related to medical patients. I found most of it interesting and though I was doubtful I would use it that much as was still determined to work in psychiatry. I would use it years later when I worked at Eastside Mental Health with clients who were mentally ill with physical and medical issues.

You never know. It was interesting and was part of the program and I would have two more internships in which I would need to have this training.

My second internship was in White Plains, outside of New York City at The Burke Foundation. I took a commuter train from New York with a number of men who lived in the city and worked in White Plains. There were frequent advances and flirtations from the men. I noticed they checked out my left hand. They were just too obvious not to be creepy. There was always some kind of catchy line to get my attention. I didn't like it, though, and I grew tired of it quickly so bought a nice silver wedding band and started to wear it. It worked pretty well, and I named it my "masher smasher." A few years ago, I was organizing a jewelry box and found it. Brent, my roommate, saw it and thought it was nice, so I gave it to him. It fits his little finger. He had it on recently with a nice silver bracelet.

"That's a nice ring you are wearing. It reminds me of one I had," I told·him.

"You gave it to me," he said. I had forgotten.

The internship with very young children worried me. I had never been around children this young and felt I just would not know how to relate to them. I was the youngest in my family and never baby sat. The closest I came was when I had taught music lessons to younger children when I was a teenager. But these children were much younger and were severely disabled. The majority of them were victims of their mothers having measles while pregnant which was devasting to them both physically and mentally. So, I did my best and passed the internship with good recommendations, which surprised me. Being kind and interested in the children while doing OT, it turned out, was not hard. I felt very sad for the mothers and for the children. All the same, I did not feel that competent and it just wasn't my favorite kind of practice. Because of this, I think I just plodded through the internship, found it very sad and just got through it. I did learn some things, one of them being I had trouble working with young children, especially those as severely disabled as these were.

THE LAST INTERNSHIP

MY THIRD INTERNSHIP WAS IN Physical Disabilities and General Medicine at the Bronx VA. It did not have a good reputation overall and was not an especially pleasant place. But the work was more interesting than at the last internship. I was assigned to the OT clinic that covered a number of different disabilities. One was working with Pulmonary patients. Most of these patients were older vets, a number of them with tuberculosis. Most were a little crusty, and some of them saw me clearly as a vulnerable young lady. Initially, they delighted in testing me by spitting on the table, telling dirty stories, and generally making fun of whatever we were doing. But I kept cool, dealing with it all through some measure of indifference or simply by declining to comment and by explaining the reason for what we were doing. After a few weeks, they let up on me and things went fine.

I also worked with paraplegics, quadriplegics, and stroke victims, noting excellent reasons for seat belts and safe driving and reasons not to participate in extreme sports. Whatever the issue, though, it was interesting in that there were a number of things that were clearly helpful to do with them as an OT. Still, it was clear to me that I would work in psychiatry.

In the lunch line one day a handsome and friendly black man, named Dick, began a conversation with me. We had lunch together, and I found him to be an interesting person. He was a physical therapist and worked mostly with spinal cord injuries, developing adaptive equipment and other ways that allowed them to function around their disability. He had been significantly involved in developing adaptive equipment for driving with hand controls for paraplegics. We began to eat together daily and then began to date.

Whenever we got together, he would meet me at our apartment, and we would go out in the city. Soon we would go to his apartment in the Bronx, at times for the week end. He was actively political and had recently left the Black Panther Party over an issue of tactics that he did not explain in detail. He didn't tell me for a long time, but apparently some of the Black Panthers were still in touch with him and gave him detailed descriptions of where I went and when. That was creepy. He made it clear that I should not worry about it, as they would not hurt me but were letting him know they were keeping track of him and knew he was dating a white woman.

But there was no question that he was politically active. He had grown up with Stockley Carmichael and had worked with him in the Student Non-Violent Coordinating Committee, and I deduced that his differences with the Black Panther Party were around non-violence. His political activism was very interesting to me, as I was becoming more drawn to more leftist positions. He was, in turn, interested in my fascination with psychiatry.

When we went out it was most often with my friends or alone. Only once after we had dated for a number of months did Dick take me to a party with his friends which also included his brother. Not surprisingly the women were not too friendly. That evening, though, I did dance with his brother, who looked down at me and said, "I'm a racist, but I might accept you."

Despite the complexities of the politics and history around us, I found my friend to be a good and caring person; and he was handsome. His political beliefs were close to mine, and I enjoyed talking about that with him. I was sure that he cared about me, and I for him. There were times when there were political activities that I was not privy to, only to know he could not do something we had planned. There was one time he called me to say he had to do something that might not turn out well, to know it was for an important reason. He just wanted to tell me in case it hit the papers and I added in my head, in case he was arrested or worse. Then when I saw him, he explained his good judgment had prevailed and things turned out well.

But was I truly genuine in the relationship? This is a question that I still ponder. Certainly, I did care for him and thought he was a very special person. Still, it was confusing for me, and I wanted to be fair, but knew there was some racism deep within me that would probably surface if I were challenged enough. I doubted that our time together would lead to anything permanent, so I just began to enjoy being with him. After I finished this internship, we continued to see each other but we did gradually see each other less often as I began to work my first job out of school, which was in the city, and he remained at the VA in the Bronx.

Still, to this day, there are times when I wonder what life would have been like if I could have overcome my own racism at that time and stayed in that relationship? Would we have been able to sustain things? Did Dick have the same reservations as I did? We never really discussed a future. He may have figured me out back then. I do think I loved him, though, and wish I could know how he is and what his life has been like since then.

GRADUATION FROM COLUMBIA

IN APRIL OF 1968, I GRADUATED FROM COLUMBIA. In spite of my drinking daily, I graduated with a 3.75 grade point. It was an accomplishment, and I was proud to have done well and to have found a career I was sure I loved. I had gotten a grant for tuition from United Cerebral Palsy Foundation for one semester with the stipulation that I work at least five years as an occupational therapist. There were no strings attached about working with cerebral palsy patients. I was glad for the grant, in that it meant a little financial relief for my father. I have fulfilled that stipulation ten times over.

Still, I was a little upset that my parents did not come to my graduation. There had been a big fuss when Carolyn graduated from the UW, and I was hurt that they had not made more of an effort than they did for me. So, my mind had gone back to that old competition thing that was fairly ingrained between my sister and me by then. Perhaps flying to New York was just too long a trip for my parents. Whatever the reason, I never asked why they did not come; and I'm sad to say that I held some resentment because of it.

BELLEVUE PSYCHIATRIC HOSPITAL

As I ended my internship, I got hired at Bellevue Psychiatric Hospital. This brought the opportunity to get a very nice apartment in the Village that was owned by NYU who ran Bellevue and was available for faculty and employees. I started work on the first work day of January 1968 and applied to get into the apartment complex.

Fairly soon, after I quit seeing the analyst who did not like me, I began seeing a psychologist. He had trained at the William Allanson White Institute and was married to one of my OT professors. His name was Jerome Fine. He was a wonderful change, and I soon became very comfortable with him. We worked on family issues, on my current relationships and activities.

For a period of time, I was also dating a Puerto Rican named Julio. This was a stretch of time when my parents did come to visit New York, not that the timing was good or very helpful to me. Still, I introduced them to the man I was dating, and I know that my parents were very uncomfortable. It was not a very serious relationship nor long lasting, but I was rebelling and again, what more could I have done to get at my parents than to date casually a man whom they would be uneasy about. It wasn't necessary, I know, to have made them see that. But I wanted to show them my life, so I also took my mother to the hospital to see where I worked. When we were in the elevator with a few patients in hospital robes, I looked at my mother and there was a tear running down her face. It was a good part fear but also sorrow for the patients, and I felt sorry I had taken her there with me. Equally bad was the fact that I'd upset my father, introducing him to Julio. So, we shifted gears, and instead, I took them to the Village Gate where mother enjoyed the jazz and then to other tourist areas.

As I was becoming more political, I was also beginning to see my mother differently. Her concern about her social standing was becoming increasingly unattractive to me. There were many more important things to be concerned about in those days, and I saw her priorities as quite shallow. Sometimes people would ask me what my mother did, and I would answer: "She is a social climber."

Similarly, my sister was someone I was happy to be away from. Although I felt sorry that things frequently went wrong for her, I didn't tend to think that she had tried much to change her end of things. It seemed to me that she remained in that same victim role that she'd inhabited for most of her life. In particular, she was victimized by Maxine, and it seemed to me Carolyn could not come to terms with it. She kept trying for mother's approval, which just annoyed Maxine. Although he disagreed with much that I believed in now, I still saw my father as a good person who did good things for other people. He remained very special to me. I was pretty sure our relationship would survive this period and it did.

For all of these reasons and more, I preferred living in NYC, being involved with issues I felt were important and meaningful. This was the 1960's, and most of my friends were in the same position with their families. I did think my parents thought my work was a good thing but did not think they understood it. I no longer cared much about that. It felt good to be away from them. It was not that I did not care about them, I was just in a different world and was growing and liked that. I began to better trust my own insight and to change my behavior. I was no longer a Princess from Spokane.

I still didn't share with my therapist how much I drank. On my own, I continued to do Huntley Drinkley, drinking every evening, often drinking at home before going out to drink more. Clearly, I was beginning to have blackouts. On one occasion, I woke up with a strange man in my bed and a gun beside him on the table. I did remember early in the evening having gone out with girlfriends to some bars looking for men but had no idea where that guy had come from. He was either a gangster or a cop of some kind, though he was actually quite nice in the morning as we had coffee. Still, things were getting worse, and my hangovers were increasing in intensity but were still tolerable. Fortunately for me, I was functioning well at school, and later at work, as I was feeling more competent and was liking myself more, despite the progression of negative effects from drinking. By then, I'd decided that "Looking for Mr. Goodbar" was not going to happen again. (It was a popular movie of the time in which young women hung out at bars with pretty bad results.) And for the remainder of my time in NYC, I did not go to bars looking for a man.

CAROLYN GETS MARRIED

IN 1968 CAROLYN MET A MAN WHO WAS IN SPOKANE for a friend's wedding. Carolyn was a bride's maid, and he was a friend of the groom and also in the wedding. He was an attractive banker from San Francisco, and he and Carolyn began to date and fairly soon became engaged. This time, the presents would not go back.

Flying home for the wedding, I was happy for Carolyn. Most of the males in the wedding party were independently wealthy, though by then I was on my way to being a revolutionary and was not particularly impressed. Carolyn's fiancé, in fact, was not actually all that wealthy, but he ran with that kind of crowd. They were a particular breed of men, and I didn't think they were aware of the Feminist Movement. Clearly, they were mostly interested in how attractive women were and were not interested in *who* they were. I didn't express my opinion to any of them but did mention to my parents that I did not like them and basically found them shallow, full of themselves, and obnoxious. Mother said nothing, and my father subtly acknowledged my opinion. I had a slight suspicion Maxine had a slim hope I might be interested in one of them. A wealthy son-in-law would have been nice.

Carolyn and her husband went to Lake Louise and Banff for their honeymoon, though, unfortunately Carolyn returned with a horrible rash. Even worse, the doctor determined that she was allergic to her husband's dander. It seemed to me this could only happen to Carolyn, a victim again. To make matters worse, she was put on a steroid which caused a fast and significant weight gain. The rash cleared up, and her new husband cooperated with the allergy clinic and combed his hair into a petri dish that they used to immunize Carolyn against him. Still, this was not a good way to begin a marriage.

To make matters even worse, the weight gain began a fixation for Carolyn to never gain weight again. She was diligent to lose the weight as soon as she was off the steroids. From then on, she watched her weight closely. I was not concerned about this, and we did not discuss it with each other. Actually, we did not discuss much anymore. She became pregnant two years later and lost two pounds during the pregnancy. I found this concerning for her baby. In later years her obsession with her weight would become a major health issue.

THE COLUMBIA SIT IN

After the wedding, I returned to New York and work. It was good to get back. I began to date a fellow from Columbia named Walter. He turned out to be involved with SDS (Students for a Democratic Society). It was the spring of 1968, and Columbia was alive with activities leading up to occupying campus. The precipitating issue was that Columbia wanted to build on land that was a playground and park for kids in Harlem. Of course, the issue of the Vietnam War came into it and things were off and running. Walter had talked about going in to occupy Fairweather Hall the second day of the sit in and I talked to my supervisor at Bellevue about taking a leave to join him. She supported it. I had worked with her for a number of months and pretty much knew I was safe to ask.

As I was getting ready to go to campus, Dick who was still living in the Bronx, showed up at my door. I hadn't seen him in a while. It was good to see him. When I told him what I was about to do he wanted to walk me to campus. I packed my back pack and as I slung it over my shoulder the phone rang. It was my mother.

"I certainly hope you are not with those nasty kids at Columbia," she said, and I lied.

"No," I told her. "I'm not there." Well, I wasn't there yet.

Then I picked up my backpack and walked with Dick to campus. At the gate, he said he wouldn't walk me all the way onto campus, as the building across from Fairweather Hall where I was going was occupied by the Black Students, and they were armed, and it would not be smart. That was the last time I saw him. I remember looking back as I walked away. He was smiling, and I realized how much I had been missing him. As I write this, I think of him fondly and do have some regrets.

But instead, I put my energies elsewhere, joining Walter inside Fairweather Hall as we began to join others in putting out news releases, printing leaflets, and hanging out while discussing politics and the tactics we should use. Walter was a sweet man, and we stuck together. One of the leaders of SDS was the head honcho at Fairweather Hall. He was well known in the press. Some of the women inside Fairweather, including myself, were not too impressed as, at least at that time, he had not been too successful in stifling his chauvinism. He was not alone among men in the movement at that time. They just didn't get it. It seemed that women were better able to run the mimeograph than to participate in political discussions.

Led by my supervisor, my colleagues from Bellevue Psychiatric Hospital came to our building with baskets of food and other supplies, which we hoisted up from the street on a rope to a window on the main floor. There were students from Julliard who came with their string instruments through a ground floor window and played for us one evening.

For a while, then, things were not all serious, until, in the afternoon, we heard the police were on their way to arrest us. People divided into groups of those who were going to resist arrest and those who were not. I was in the not resisting group, mostly because I was scared. It was not based on any political principle. Walter was going to resist. A few of us went to the roof to smoke up the pot that was in the building. From the roof we had a good view of the police approaching, some marching toward the building and many on horses. Buses were lining up on the streets.

At that point, my Fairweather roof-top friends and I left the roof to be arrested and put in the buses, stoned. It proved to be not such a good thing for me as everything was happening in slow motion. It was scarier than if I had been straight. I was worried about Walter and the others who were resisting, and I did not know what was coming for me. I knew my judgment was impaired when I asked a female arresting officer if her name was "Lovely Rita," and she put her hand on her holstered gun.

The women and the men were separated, and we were booked into the city jail. We spent the rest of the night crammed into a large cell now full of women. There were no incidents among us though it was clear the black women did not view us as their comrades.

In the morning, there were lawyers to represent us before the judge. Mine was from The Lawyers' Guild and had liquor on his breath. It reminded me that I had not had a drink in over a week. I had not thought about it which was surprising. Most people were let go after being charged with Criminal Trespass and did not have return court dates. I, however, did have a court date. It seemed I was being considered an "Outside Agitator," as I had graduated officially in April and was not considered a part of the students.

BACK TO WORK AND THE VILLAGE APARTMENT

I RETURNED TO WORK TO FIND THAT THE STAFF had taken up a "Defense Fund" collection for me. It was a given that I would eventually have to pay a fine. I did return to court multiple times in the coming months to find that my lawyer always had liquor on his breath and that my arresting officer asked me out every time I went. Understandably, I felt harassed; and eventually, my lawyer asked him not to do that. In the end, I had to pay $50 for a fine. The Bellevue Defense Fund more than covered that, and I gave back the rest. This was a time when there was solidarity among people who had different views politically but did support others in the big picture. We used to say in the end you support those who are on the same side of the barricade with you.

So, there was plenty to feel good about. The community was close-knit, and my work as an Activity Therapist for the Adolescent Unit at Bellevue was great. Bellevue was run by NYU, and the students and doctors were from their medical school. There was quite a lot of research going on. Staff were to attend in-service trainings. I was informed that the unit I worked on was the first program specializing in adolescents in the Country. It was well run and with skilled professional staff who took me under their wing and were great about teaching me things when I needed them to. They also were very accepting of the fact I had some great experience from my work at Chestnut Lodge and in my training at Columbia. Specifically, I was encouraged to use it and began Psychodrama and Movement Therapy. I did diagnostic activity batteries, which were met with acceptance, and I began to develop friendships with some of the staff, both in my department and some on the Ward.

To round out my experience of that time, I got an apartment in the buildings owned by NYU in a group of four buildings called Washington Square Village. Mine was on the corner of La Guardia and Bleeker Street. It was a large studio with a nice open kitchen, dressing room with a big closet, a good bathroom, and air conditioning. The floors were parquet oak, very 1960's, and my windows looked out over the grounds in the center of the four buildings. In order to furnish it properly, I bought a convertible couch, one that made into a bed, and a matching chair, both deep blue and lovely. A second chair that I got looked nice, as well, complementing the other furniture. Then, I got a wool rug that picked up the colors and delineated the living room space and bought a really beautiful Rosewood table that doubled as a desk and a dining table and two chairs that looked good with it. There was a plant shop in the complex, so I got a large rubber tree, and found, too, some prints and framed them. It was all very comfortable and attractive. Finally, between my work and my apartment, I felt like an adult, and I liked it. I liked it so much, in fact, that I would come home each evening and "feel" my apartment—how nice it was—and would do Huntley Drinkley.

In part, this ritual helped me appreciate what I had. I was very lucky to have a nice place to live, and I knew it. Many of my friends lived in tiny apartments, one with a bath tub in the living room, and often they paid a lot more rent than I did.

Not that things were perfect. Like all New York City tenants, I also had roaches, though the maintenance people came through regularly and sprayed. I could have pets, too, and decided that I was fairly permanent in my housing, so began to watch for a cat. Soon I found out one of my co-workers raised Persian cats, and one of the females was pregnant, so I put down a deposit.

It was 1968, and my rent was $350 per month which was incredible for NYC at the time. There were some retail shops on the ground level including, first and foremost, a liquor store. There was a large grocery store on the corner. I had a little cart for carrying groceries. Best of all The Village Gate was just across the street on the other corner. I could walk across the street after Huntley Drinkley, listen to Mose Allison or other great jazz musicians and drink some more. Then I would walk home. Mose Allison was my favorite.

Where I live has always been important to me. I have always fixed up the places I rented and still live in the first house I bought. My home has always been precious to me, and I have been fortunate to be able to make them comfortable and attractive. I am grateful every day for the house I have lived in for thirty-one years and also love the gardens that surround it and the neighborhood. I am always happy to share my home and do host a lot of both small and large events.

Finally, after an excited wait, my kitten was born. I named him Godot as in "waiting for." He was a "blue," meaning that he was gray. He had a lovely face and coat, a precious kitten, and beautiful when he grew up. As long as I had him, he was very loving and always good company.

Indeed, I had community all around me in that lovely studio apartment. One of my favorite co-workers, lived several floors up from mine. She was from Israel, an excellent OT, supervised me on the adolescent unit and became a good and trusted friend. She was really quite lovely; and, through her, I began to learn more about Judaism. With the last name of Becker, most people thought that I was Jewish. While it is true that I have a rather Jewish looking nose, no doubt a result of my genetics from my grandfather Becker, this issue never came up until I lived in New York. I began to wonder why my family's possible Jewish history was always so secreted? Today I just happen to live in a Jewish neighborhood with two Orthodox Synagogues around the corner from my house.

Always, always there were new ideas. At work, I continued to learn from the staff who shared their expertise. I was invited to join residents, interns and students in observing interviews with manic depressive patients through a one-way glass that was a very interesting part of an early on-going study of Lithium. The in-service training programs were excellent, and staff were welcome. I really liked this aspect of working at Bellevue. Lithium was fairly new and manic depression, now known as bipolar disorder, was a big topic.

Even the patients themselves educated me. One day, for instance, the Princess from Spokane went looking for a patient and happened upon a number of the girls doing lines of cocaine on the sink counter in the girl's bathroom. When I found them, it took a few seconds for me to realize what I was seeing, as I had never been around cocaine use. Honestly, I did not stop and stare. But I did not feel comfortable "busting" them and knew some other staff were closer to them as a group. This part of the staff was referred to as "the Mamas." They were older very caring Black women. The girls would do better changing their behavior if the Mamas confronted them rather than the Princess from Spokane and I also knew this activity would not escape the notice of the Mamas.

After a while, I was asked to run Psychodrama with the patients, most of whom liked it and appeared to be talented in role playing. The most common topics were families and things that happened in "the Hood." Out of this, we wrote a play and eventually presented it at Grand Rounds. It was about life for the adolescent on the streets and was based around the death of a young character. Because the Adolescent Unit was a long-term treatment program, we were able to do long term projects like the play. A number of the patients were good actors and carried the play, and we got very positive reviews. I was proud of how well they did.

In addition, I was also assigned to do group therapy. Generally, we did it with a co-therapist. I had excellent supervision both on the ward and from my department. A few times I felt over my head but had good support and soon felt reasonably competent.

Early on, I understood why I had been attracted to working with the severely mentally ill. As a population, they are usually without strong and consistent advocates. I still respond to this with action and have done a good deal of community service as an advocate for several disabled populations. The mentally ill are a population that are often talented, sensitive and generally intelligent. Their thinking process is often quite different due to their disorder and to understand their logic is fascinating. I was once told I spoke "Schizophrenize" because I was good at understanding what the more severe patients were saying.

Their suffering due to their disorders is significant. Their disorders are mostly genetic, biochemical and often exacerbated by environmental issues, in other words not something they are responsible for. They are aware of the stigma that is attached to their illness, at least in our culture. They are not often violent, in fact statistically less so than the general public.

MORE PERSONAL RELATIONSHIPS

After working on the Adolescent Service for a few months, I began dating one of the psychiatrists who was handsome and very intelligent. Together, we went to movies, a few plays, and out for nice dinners. He was in his own analytic training, which fascinated me. He and a friend owned a very old, well-kept house near Tanglewood in Connecticut, and we went there a number of times for the weekend. His friend brought another woman along. They had known each other for a long time. I thought it a little strange that I had my own room and that we did not have sex, but I enjoyed his company and enjoyed being out of the city.

One evening he called to tell me that we would not be going out anymore, that he enjoyed my company and hoped we would be friends. He said he had been working in analysis to determine if he was gay, and I was a test case. He'd decided that he was gay.

My immediate reaction was how dare he make a test case of me? I went on in a rage. In that moment, it was all about me; plus, I did not know much about homosexuality at that point. It was not that I was homophobic, it was all personal to me and my not getting what I wanted which was a relationship. Also, of note, is the fact that, I had just done Huntley Drinkley before he called.

In therapy, I had been telling my psychologist about our relationship, and he'd said he thought that that was what was going on. An additional and ongoing problem, though, was the fact that we had to work together. Somehow, we managed, though I remembered that, in psychodrama, the patients portrayed him as effeminate, and I was a little surprised. In fact, they made fun of a lot of the staff, and I just dismissed it, not wanting, back then, to really look at it all. Sometimes, I've realized since then, the patients can be more perceptive than we give them credit for; and for a while, I'd been in denial about that. Later on, when I learned more about the Gay Movement, I felt really bad about my response and the fact that my behavior made it difficult for that man to remain friends with me. Truly, he really was a very nice man.

Soon after this, I met another man who was studying for a PhD at the New School. His name was Charles. He had friends with whom we often spent time. Some of them were into drugs, which I was not really interested in, as I had my alcohol and knew reliably how it affected me. I had seen enough adverse reactions from drugs at work and something told me to pass on that.

Mostly, they were into Psychedelics. The people did not push it but did comment more than once that they knew of few people our age who still preferred alcohol. It was the drug of choice for parents.

One day, however, Charles asked me to join in on a special outing to the Cloisters, a museum that is a castle in a park in upper Manhattan. It is beautifully done with medieval artifacts, including knights in shining armor. They were going to drop mescaline. Charles went into some detail of what I might experience, which included throwing up. I hated throwing up but knew what to do about that part. So, I agreed to try it.

I knew that one of the psychiatrists at work was into drugs and had nitrous oxide parties at his country place. I asked him if he could get me some Compazine to help me not to get nauseated when I tried drugs for the first time; and he was happy to do so, thinking that it would be an interesting experience for me—though actually, his comment made me a little more nervous about it all.

So, the morning that Charles was to pick me up to go to the Cloisters, I took the Compazine. We met our friends, and I waited to hallucinate with everyone else. I felt a little high in a pleasant enough way, but everyone else was telling about what they were seeing, and it was not what I was experiencing. We wandered through the Cloisters, which was quite wonderful. I was preoccupied with the potential of hallucinating and should one day tour the Cloisters again straight.

Then we went walking in the adjacent park. My experience was very pleasant, but nothing spectacular. Eventually, we came to a tree that was decorated with draft cards, many of them. I thought that was cool enough; and then I finally remembered taking the Compazine, and it dawned on me that it is essentially an anti-psychotic. I had inadvertently taken an antidote to the effects of the mescaline. I thought about it and decided that I was just not supposed to artificially induce psychosis in this brain of mine. As I understood why I was having a different experience from the others, I was glad that I'd taken the Compazine, as something told me not to mess with my sanity. The main effect was that I was awake through that night and the next day with difficulty sleeping the following night. It was not pleasant, and I was no longer interested in trying psychedelics. It was not worth the risk for me.

Charles was Jewish, an only child, and his mother did not appreciate his dating a non-Jewish woman. To make things worse, soon after we started dating, his father died. When I went to the funeral, and his mother was distraught. I started to tear up, and the woman sitting next to me poked me.

She said, "If you are crying for her, don't waste your tears. She is always overly dramatic."

After his father's death, Charles began staying at his mother's place at night. Then he told me she insisted he sleep with her. I told him that was sick. Apparently, he heard me, and soon after that, he would stay with me most nights. He said he refused to sleep with her anymore. Not too long after this, he took me to dinner at his mother's. In front of me she referred to me in the third person.

She said, "Tell that Shiksa that dinner is ready."

That was essentially the extent of her interactions with me; and indeed, I found it uncomfortable and rude. I knew that a struggle was futile, and I seldom brought up his mother after that. We never visited her again.

One day, I came home from work to find my very special Persian Cat, Godot, dead. He had been ill for a time with a urinary tract problem that the vet had been unable to treat. It was not a surprise that he died, but I was nevertheless very upset and called Charles. He came right over, put my cat in a crate, and off we went in his car to Riverside Drive where there was a memorial, the name of which I cannot remember. He got out a shovel and went behind the memorial and buried Godot. Some years later, I saw the movie *Alice's Restaurant*, with Arlo Guthrie, and I saw the same memorial spot when he stops at one point in the film, so I guess we'd chosen a good place. Moreover, even though I was a dramatic mess, Charles was very good about it. Perhaps he'd had good practice with his mother. We continued to date, and I liked him very much. I appreciated his intelligence, even if he could get somewhat pedantic at times. A bit over a year into our relationship, though, he graduated from the New School and got a job on a Cruise ship teaching classes. So, he left. I wished that he'd gotten a job in New York City, but he hadn't. And, too, I couldn't help but wonder if it had to do with getting away from his mother? I have to admit also that our relationship did not make the cut.

RHUBARB

A FEW MONTHS LATER, A NEIGHBOR AND FRIEND OF MINE, Arthur, offered me a puppy. He had a male and female who were mutts and very cute. He had trained them, and they were in TV commercials. They were really great dogs, and the female was pregnant. I said yes and once again had to wait for the birth. When the mother was going into labor, Arthur called, and I went over and witnessed the arrival of my puppy. He turned out to be really cute, very smart and very special to me.

My building had kids and dogs, and the "in thing" was to be a dog walker. My seven-year-old neighbor girl, Pammy, had been having a hard time and was being bullied by some of the other kids. So, I asked her to be my doggie walker. Her parents and I thought this would be a great situation for both her and Rhubarb; and since Rhubarb was so cute the other kids were impressed that she was his walker. She learned fast, as did Rhubarb. There was a dog park across the street from my apartment building and it all worked out very well. I became quite fond of Pammy.

Rhubarb became an important part of my life and Arthur became a good friend. I met a number of interesting people at the dog park. There were others being developed throughout the city. Ours was named "The Houston Street Dog Run." People took it seriously and there were committees and officers involved. We followed the rules set by the city, as we were all dog people and we wanted this to succeed. There was a woman who ran for mayor who listed being president of a dog run as part of her political experience. She did not win.

Rhubarb was loving, funny, and good company. He enriched my life significantly, as have all the dogs I have had. He was my first of a long line of dogs that I feel fortunate to have had. Rhubarb was a reddish-brown color—hence the name Rhubarb—with some black throughout his coat. His coat was medium in length, and he was easy to groom. He was what I call a "fuzzy wumper," or shaggy dog. His tail was not docked and had long hair. His disposition was friendly and playful. He was great with kids and adults alike. And he was very smart. He went with me everywhere I could take him. He was much loved by friends.

MCHR AND THE UNION

THERE WAS AN ORGANIZING DRIVE at Bellevue Hospital by 1199, the Drug and Hospital Workers Union, focused on Social Workers, Nurses and among others, OTs. I got on it and became an active participant. I met a number of medical people involved and was introduced to an organization called the Medical Committee for Human Rights (MCHR).

They were very progressive people. Their projects, which included one of the first needle exchange programs, interested me very much. It was conducted from a van. They also offered medical care to low income people, often doing home visits. and gave support and medical care to people who were occupying abandoned buildings to protest the lack of low-income housing, which was a movement that was a focus in New York City at that time. Sadly, that's another issue that clearly has gotten worse rather than better over the years. They also supported universal health care. But they did other things, too, including organizing medical students and MCHR doctors to provide medical care to injured protesters at demonstrations, and medical care at rock concerts. Out of this work, they developed a way to substitute sutures to head wounds without shaving the hair, much prized by hippies who would refuse to have it shaved. They parted the hair down the wound and tied strands of hair over it with square knots. They found that there was no more infection than occurred with shaving around the wound. These treatments were all so interesting and innovative that I began going to their meetings, which required quite a sacrifice on my part, as I could or would not drink around them. Instead, I'd wait until I got home after the meetings and do a late-night Huntley Drinkley.

About this time, I was invited to attend a consciousness-raising group. I'd met several women at work who were forming one and I joined. We discussed the work of a number of feminist writers and talked about emerging new attitudes toward women and how that was affecting how we looked at ourselves. The group that I was in did not spend time "bashing men," as was the impression some people expressed about early consciousness raising groups. We were educating ourselves to better understand the often subtle and often not so subtle oppression of women. This was fifty years ago, and the struggle continues with far too much the same issues.

The first time I demonstrated, it was for abortion reform. I remember seeing one of the women psychiatrists from work among the counter-demonstrators and thinking that was an odd position for her to be taking. She had often recommended abortion for pregnant adolescent patients, and the method used was salting out. I thought this was not a kind method; it even seemed a little punitive. Eventually, I asked her about her opposing legal abortion, and it seemed to me to be a control issue for her and also in relationship to our patients there was racism clearly involved. The majority of our patients were black or Puerta Rican.

So, I began to be comfortable speaking out in discussions in MCHR meetings. I knew MCHR was made up of people with some political differences but did not know enough to identify which political parties they were from. At the time it did not matter to me. I knew I was naive regarding the differences they had, but I liked the work they were involved in, found them to be devoted to the work and that they got along on the whole within that context.

In the Fall of 1970, the Kent State killings happened, and things got very active. MCHR and 1199 were working together with others to organize a moratorium around Kent State and the War. Since I was involved with both organizations, they asked me to "seize," the mike at Bellevue Grand Rounds and call for the moratorium and I agreed to do it. I was a bit over my head, and I knew it and began to take valium. I was pretty well calm when the moment came. I got on the stage, walked to the microphone and called for the moratorium. The audience took a vote and agreed to support it. When the moratorium took place, I would be on a locked ward of one of NYC's finest psychiatric hospitals.

The next day was a big demonstration on Wall Street. There was a lot of construction where the demonstration was to take place. The workers were not going to like what we were protesting. We knew there would be big trouble and sent out many medical students and doctors to cover it for medical care. As it turned out, we were correct, and the workers attacked the demonstrators and were brutal.

I agreed to staff the phones to coordinate the medical people where they were needed and get the information to them. One of my motives was that I didn't want to be near the violence. We were working out of the Student Union at NYU; and, in late morning, my phones were cut off, so I went to the Dean's office nearby, telling him what had just happened and asking to use his phones. He agreed, and I returned to pick up my papers. At that moment, there was a bomb scare, and I was told not to enter the room. I pushed in and grabbed my papers anyway. My head was spinning. I went upstairs to a hallway where they had directed people to go. I sat down next to a stranger on the floor with our backs against the wall. I was panicked.

I remember turning to him and asking, "We're going to die, aren't we?" He said, calmly, "I don't think so."

THE FIRST EPISODE

DESPITE ALL OF MY WORK AND ACTIVISM, I'd been aware for some time, that something was building inside me, and that it wasn't going to be good. During the weeks before the demonstration, I felt very much over my head in the roles that I was playing; and, perhaps because of my background as a therapist, I knew exactly what was happening. *I felt my head spin out. I was in trouble. I had just crossed over into psychosis and literally felt it.*

I can't remember who it was, but one of my MCHR friends found me at the student center and took me to my apartment, which was within walking distance. Several other women came with us, and we all sat talking in my apartment for several hours. I was talking fast, and everything that came out of my mouth reminded me of another topic, so then I would turn and expound upon that. This dynamic kept on going. *Clearly, I was having "flight of ideas": a common symptom of mania. Things began to become very symbolic for me; and this was partly fun; clearly, there was a euphoric feeling about it. Underneath that, though, was a low simmering of fear.*

To this day, I can still remember sitting in that room with those women for several hours. They were kind and attentive, but because I was very involved in my own conversation, I do not remember what the other women said to me. Mostly, I guess, it was in response to whatever I was saying. Also, I remember getting an asthma attack for the first time, which I hated because of what my sister's asthma had meant to me. I did not want to be anything like her.

After a while, there were some phone calls, and I was told that I was being invited to stay at the commune, where a group of MCHR people lived.

I was clearly psychotic, and they did not want me to be alone. The couple who owned the house were the leaders of MCHR. He was a psychologist and she was a school teacher. They were very caring people who, I trusted, so I packed a back pack and called my boss to say I needed someone to take my dog for a few days. She came and picked Rhubarb up, and I went to the commune.

My memories of my episode are somewhat sketchy, especially as I got deeper and deeper into the psychosis. So, I share these details as best as I can, but I need to state that I have considered whether to share some things or not as *what I did while manic is humiliating in retrospect.* But I want to be open enough to present my experience realistically in my efforts to communicate what it was like. In being of service to those it might help, either those who are bipolar or those who treat them, and also others who might find it interesting, I will share it.

I was grateful those kind women had arranged for me to not be alone. I went to the commune and was watched over by a number of people. Some of them worked and were not available to be with me at all times. They were all members of MCHR, so I became a "communal effort." I will always be grateful for their efforts to keep me safe and of the care these people showed me.

By the time I had been at the commune a short time, it was apparently a concern that I was *hypersexual, typical of mania.* One of the doctors who knew I trusted him agreed to be the one to get me to put in my diaphragm. I do not know how I happened to have it with me, but I did. He asked me to get it out, and I did. I tossed it across the room like a frisbee. He sent it back. I took off my clothes, as assumed I needed to in order to put in the diaphragm and told him he had to also. He did. At that moment someone called through the door.

"Is everything ok in there?"

The doctor I was with inside the room laughed a little. "Yes, all is ok," he answered.

We threw the diaphragm back and forth a few times. Then he put on his clothes and brought the diaphragm back to me.

Finally, he told me, "This is serious, and I need you to put this on."

So, I did.

I was given valium, but it did not touch the mania. By then, I had decided that I was a witch and that it was important that I was a benevolent one. I remember telling someone that if I was not a benevolent one, that I would probably kill myself.

"You are a benevolent one," he told me, and walked away.

Although this comment confirmed to me that I was indeed a witch, at least I was benevolent. I remembered my thinking that my mother was a witch, and thought that's why I must be one, too.. *A lot of things were symbolic and related to each other*. So, I was satisfied I was a good witch and dropped the idea of killing myself.

Perhaps given my training, even while I was in that state, I was well aware that I was not accurately perceiving what was real and what was not real. It was not just uncomfortable; it was painful and was to become more painful as the mania continued. After a few days, I got bored and also felt that I was wearing out my welcome, which I no doubt was. So, I decided to go home. There were times people were busy and not immediately with me, and I just grabbed my back pack and walked out of the house.

My first task was to go to my boss's house and get Rhubarb. Off I went. She had taken Rhubarb when I went to the commune. She lived in the East Village, an area I was not too familiar with but remembered hearing that taxis would not always go there. So, I walked. Somehow, I found my way to her place, picked up Rhubarb, and headed for home in the West Village. I do not remember much about my visit with my boss. I just remember that I was getting very tired.

Then a biker on a very huge motorcycle came around the corner and parked near me. I had recently read a book called *Free Wheeling Frank* about Hell's Angels by Frank Reynolds. So, I said to him, "Hi. My name is Janny, and I read a book about Hells Angels that said you were not all that bad. Are you a Hells Angel?"

"Yes," he answered. "My name is Fuji. Would you like to go to a party?"

And of course, I answered, "Yes."

So, we walked across the street to a big apartment with a large party going on.

By this time, I was pretty crazy. At the party, I got a drink. It was a very hot, muggy day in New York City, and it occurred to me to take off my shirt. Another woman there saw me begin to do that and came over and told me not to. *My judgement was really impaired.* Then, Fuji invited me into a loft. I climbed up and laid down beside him. We had sex, and then he got down and I followed. Then Fuji started ordering me to bring him a towel, but I replied,

"Get it yourself, you Chauvinist pig."

Then, he pulled out a knife; and, before I knew what was happening, a man stepped between us.

"Leave her alone Fuji," he said. "You know she's crazy."

He turned to me and said, "Come on with me, I am taking you and your dog home." And we left in a cab.

This man told me that I needed to go to the hospital. He said he would wait in the cab while I went up to my apartment and to call my doctor right away. I did, and I told my psychologist what I had done and that I wanted to go to the hospital. He told me with little more discussion which hospital I should go to.

Next, I called my friend Arthur, who had given me Rhubarb. I told him that I needed to go to the hospital and needed him to take Rhubarb. He came and got Rhubarb within minutes. I changed my clothes and packed a bag. When I went down to the cab, the man was waiting, paid the driver to take me to the hospital and left. *I have no idea who he was, but he saved my life and I knew I was really crazy and was glad I was going to the hospital.*

I don't remember a lot about getting to the hospital or what happened for the next few days. They diagnosed me as having an acute psychotic episode related to trauma (i.e, the bomb scare at NYU) and put me on Thorazine. I got better.

I do remember some of my MCHR friends coming to visit me at the hospital. Among them was a doctor, Howard Levy, who was quite famous for being in Vietnam and refusing to serve when he saw what was going on. He had spent some time in Leavenworth before I met him. The staff knew who he was, and I think they were a little freaked out. When I was discharged, they told me to stay on the Thorazine and not to participate in politics.

That part was fine for a while, though I knew that I wasn't ready to work. I also knew the Thorazine made me feel like someone had poured lead down my arms and legs. *People who are bipolar do not like that. I was enough better, I thought, and stopped taking it. Again, my judgement was really off. This episode was not over.*

I decided I wanted to go home to my parents for a while. By then, my sister was married and living in California, so I wasn't really worried about that. It sounded like the calmest place to be. So, I arranged to sublet my apartment on a month-to-month basis, and I took a medical leave from work. Then I got plane tickets to Spokane. Rhubarb was too big to fly in the cabin and had to go in the luggage compartment. I was really worried about that. But we did ok and got safely to Spokane. *My mother said she knew I was crazy when she saw me get off the plane.* I remember that I had on a "Hippie like" dress from India with large sequins, and who knows how I was wearing my hair?

For a time, back in Spokane, I was getting worse and my father informed Maxine that he was going to stay in a hotel. She told him he was not going to do that and called my sister's psychiatrist who hospitalized me. This was 1970, and there were no psychiatric units in Spokane, so I was in a room on a general medicine unit. They tried everything but could not bring me down. I remember walking the halls and being fixated by a statue of the Virgin Mary who had a snake curled around one leg. *I could not figure out what that was about. My thinking was concrete.*

The doctor and my mother came to my room after a few days and told me that I could either go to Eastern State Hospital or agree to ECT, which is a form of shock treatment. They had tried everything to bring me down, including sodium pentothal, and nothing was working. Somehow, they got me to sign for the ECT. I had three treatments in the hospital, then went home and Mother took me in for three more treatments at the doctor's office. The one detail that I remember is that we went into the office by a regular door but came out the back way. Then, my mother would take me home. I do remember what the treatments were like for me. They gave me a light anesthetic, and I went out and woke up a little confused. It was not like *Coocoo's Nest*, not at all really bad. Still, I was glad when I was through with them and was glad that I was improving. Little by little, I was getting better, and I knew it. I have no question that those treatments saved me from the state hospital and allowed me a future. Each time, my memory would come back fairly soon after the treatment, even though I remember feeling vulnerable throughout that whole time. In other words, I was not functioning on all cylinders, but I did feel protected at my parents' house.

So, I stayed in Spokane with my parents for the next three months. The psychosis I experienced was hideously frightening, and it was actually the worst pain that I have ever experienced. *As I came out of the fog of psychosis I began to get depressed. I did not know this is very common after a serious manic episode.* It was hard to move physically, and I spent most of my time on my parent's couch in the family room. We did Huntley Drinkley every evening.

Somewhat surprisingly, my mother was quite patient with me, perhaps because she had experienced a deep and long depression herself. My father, on the other hand, finally lost his patience after about eight weeks and told me to get off the couch and find a job. He said he didn't care what it was, so long as it got me off the couch. This was apparently what I needed, as I somehow got a job doing inventory in a furniture factory. It was dirty and dark and boring; and about two weeks into it, I thought about the mental health work I loved. So, I quit, and within a few weeks I was on my way back to New York.

BACK TO NYC

Due to the union that I'd helped organize, I still had my job when I got back. To my surprise and disappointment, *they did not assign me to clinical work.* I did not object as needed to work. The compromise was that they created a position for me to do in-service training. *They were wrong that I would not be able to do clinical work again.* This did not help, and I became somewhat depressed, but I somehow mustered enough energy to work with developing some form of in-service course. I did not think I was doing a very good job of it.

I had Rhubarb with me, and my friend Arthur was around and helpful. I had taken back my apartment, too, and I was generally quite happy to be getting back into my life. Rhubarb was very important to me, and I think he was also happy to be home. I returned to my psychologist. I learned that he felt badly that he had not seen my episode coming on. He clearly became my rock during a very difficult time.

I continued to do Huntley Drinkley every night. It was clear that *people at work were polite but not friendly. I ran into someone from MCHR and though outwardly friendly I detected that was all. The lesson learned was that few of these people who were educated in major mental illness thought that I would not recover. This was not true as particularly with bipolar disorder, there can be full recovery if you follow treatment. Unfortunately for me, the common response among old friends was also "Once crazy, stay away."*

After six months of this, I also noticed that I had become what I called "hardened" to what was going on with people in my world. I would walk by people sleeping in doorways and not have a second thought. I was quite sure that I wasn't doing a great job at work, and I didn't like that, either.

So, I began to sell some of my things and gave notice to the landlord; and within six months of returning to New York, I decided to go to Seattle. It was a big enough city to have places to get a job in psychiatry. It also had good cultural events and was at least liberal overall.

I let my parents know of my plans and asked to stay with them until I got a job in Seattle. They were nice about it, so I gave notice at my job at Bellevue, polished up my resume, and was off to Spokane. Of course, Rhubarb came with me. I want to say that it was difficult and the short-lived return to New York City did teach me a few things. Once I was well enough to return, *people who knew me during the episode, or knew about it, were not ready to take me back,* even though I was still the person I had always been.

I was sure I would be able to work clinically and do a good job. I needed my old job back, and I needed my friends back. I needed these things to stay well and to get back into the life I had loved; but they were not fully available in New York anymore. Once again, I needed to make a new start just as I'd done after I left the Oregon Coast. I could do it again, but I needed a new territory. There was no question; *I needed to be elsewhere, and it had to be with people who had not seen me crazy.*

SEATTLE

IT WAS NOW LATE SUMMER OF 1971. I went for an interview at the University of Washington Medical Center. *They did not know of my episode, and apparently by now I presented well.* My background of Columbia and an internship at a famous hospital and working 4 years at Bellevue all served me well. I got the job on one of two in-patient psychiatric units and was told that I would be able to use my experience in psychodrama and group therapy. This was the first and only interview that I had.

While the news in Seattle was good, my quick trip home to Spokane to get ready for the move was horrifying. When I returned to my parents' house, my mother greeted me.

"I gave Rhubarb to my cleaning lady," she told me, "so that he can have a nice home with children who live in the country."

"What?!" I said, stunned. "You have no right to do that! You will have to get him back immediately! What made you think you could do that?" Truly, I could not believe it.

"I did it because it would be difficult for you to find an apartment that allowed dogs," She answered calmly.

"You don't know that," I insisted. "Why did you think you could do that? Don't you know what he means to me?"

Clearly, I was both furious and in shock. I was so shaken and so distraught that I just could not deal with her and went to my room.

A few days later, she changed her story, telling me Rhubarb had disappeared, and the family thought that he had been stolen. Still, I was crushed and did not believe her. "You'd better get him back," I warned her. "I will never forgive you for this!"

Soon after that, returning to Seattle, I was still heartbroken about losing Rhubarb. I could not believe that my mother had done that; but she had, and I had to go on, though I really did not think I could ever forgive her.

Fairly quickly I found a very nice apartment located near the hospital on Lake Union. It was one bedroom, large enough to be comfortable and in a newer building. It had a wonderful view of the city down the lake and it had a swimming pool, something not that common in Seattle at the time.

Going home to collect my things, though without Rhubarb, I could hardly stand to be around my mother, and I was just glad that I had a job and a place to live. I did have some conflicting feelings about my mother, as she had been good in helping me to recover from that awful episode. I just didn't understand how she rationalized other terrible aspects of her behavior. It was as though, briefly, she had cared about me and understood my episode then fairly quickly, she again lost the capacity to think about anyone but herself. So, I left just as soon as I could, moving into that beautiful apartment and starting back up in work that I loved.

In 1979, some eight years later, while I was visiting Maxine in Spokane I took her out to dinner.

As she sipped a martini she said, "That Rhubarb was such a cute dog."

I couldn't believe she said that.

"Don't you ever mention Rhubarb to me again," I warned. "I have not forgiven you for what you did."

She set down her martini, and we sat in silence for what seemed a long time, maybe a few minutes.

All these years later, I still find it hard to write about this. I still do not know how she thought she could do that. It is one of the most hostile things I have known, and it was my own mother.

UNIVERSITY OF
WASHINGTON MEDICAL CENTER

WORK WENT VERY WELL. I was so glad to be back into clinical work, and I also liked most of the staff. Before long, they respected me and accepted my clinical skills. Still, my heart was sore because I really missed Rhubarb. That residual sadness was not going to go away anytime soon.

The OT school at the U was glad to have me there, and they began to assign interns to the clinic. I learned that I had much to share and was a good teacher. Assigning one intern the project of picking a patient in the OT clinic, to diagnose them and write a treatment plan. I discovered when she'd turned in her paper, she had diagnosed one of the staff who did spend a good deal of time in the clinic. She got a good grade, as the staff member did have a diagnosis, which she had gotten correct. The staff person was on medication and functioned well enough to do her job. I did not have the intern initiate her treatment plan with the staff person, though I did assign a patient with the same diagnosis of schizophrenia. She had indeed developed a good treatment plan.

One of the psychiatrists from work lived in a house boat on the lake next door to my apartment building. He seemed interesting, and I would run into him from time to time in the neighborhood. He had a sailboat, and one day at work, he suggested that we might take a small group of patients sailing. So, we talked to our staff about it. I presented it as an OT project with specific tasks assigned to the patients. We would all work together to manage the boat and it would teach cooperation and responsibility. The psychiatrist would meet us at a dock near the hospital and we would go sailing. We took another staff person with us who would help and then take the patients back to the hospital after we landed when we were done.

Later on, as we pulled away from the dock after returning the staff and the patients to land after the sail, the psychiatrist and I would break out the bourbon as we sailed back to Lake Union, where he moored his boat. For a short time, I dated him, the main thing that we had in common being our drinking. After a time, though, I began to find him rather narcissistic, some-what immature, and not always kind. But the sailing was great and very pop-ular. By then, I was becoming aware that I seemed to be attracted to men with whom drinking was our major attraction.

Around the same time, I had started therapy with a woman analyst who was focusing primarily on my relationship with my mother. I had old difficul-ties with mother's narcissism and making what others thought of her the pri-ority. Moreover, I was still raw from what she did with Rhubarb. It seemed clear to me that she made all decisions according to her own needs rather than thinking of others. I have never understood what was behind giving Rhubarb away. I did some hard work and have always been glad for the experience with that therapist, though I didn't share with her that I was doing Huntley Drink-ley every evening. I just was not ready yet.

Then one day, I ran into my therapist at the grocery store, and I wasn't sure how to act, so I just said hello to her politely. At the next session she said, "You seemed to be uncomfortable running into me. Do you think I don't eat? Also, I don't wear a pill box hat and white gloves either."

I knew what she was saying. She was telling me that she was not my mother. After that, I relaxed a bit more in relating to her and began, too, to learn how I might relate to Maxine in a healthier way. I will always be grateful for the work she did with me, as she got me on track as to how I could grow to deal with Maxine.

Throughout all of this time, my father agreed to pay for the therapy, most likely hoping that there would be no more episodes. One time, he was late paying, so the doctor called him to ask about that. My father said that he had just overlooked it and would pay right away but he needed to let her know that he thought psychiatrists were shysters. She shared that with me, and we both laughed, since my father was an automobile dealer who many people think of as shysters.

The apartment was nice with the view and location close to the hospital, but the building turned out to be an active perpetual party. I was not in the mood and found it rather repulsive as there were public displays of outlandish behavior especially on the part of the men and women who were drunk. I don't know why it bothered me. I did have much in common with them. Quite often, I was drinking alone in my apartment while they were drinking at the pool. I was just not one of them pouring a pitcher of orange juice and vodka over someone's head.

Apart from the people in my apartment building, I did meet some nice people in my new city of Seattle. In particular, I became close friends with two of the nurses at the university. We even talked about the apartment situation when we would go out drinking together after work. I had signed a 6-month lease, and one of the nurses was looking for a housemate as the current one was leaving in a few months. So, I sat out the 6-month lease and moved to her house when it was up. We became known as the "hostesses with the mostesses" as had many parties often after work on Fridays.

That was a fun period of time, with just enough adult responsibility and just enough fun. We remained roommates for a year and a half, got along well and remained fairly close for a time. We had good parties with good liquor and a little pot now and then. A number of the resident psychiatrists and other staff from the U would come. Some of their friends would come along, too. My roommate had a dog, a black lab mix named Boris, who was smart and loving and helped me deal a bit with my need for a dog.

Around that time, I started dating a psychologist who was a consultant to the psychiatrists at U Hospital. In retrospect, our major thing in common was our drinking. Imagine that. I often had to drive us home to his house as he was too drunk, though I was never too far behind him with that. His two sons lived with him, and they would have to help me get him into the house and to bed, which I certainly didn't feel good about.

One of his sons was an excellent jazz saxophone musician whose band was in a national competition taking place in Chicago. That was exciting, so we all went, both boys, their dad, and me. The boys were going to visit with their mother for a few days before the competition.

Because the boys had traveled ahead of us, we were at liberty to enjoy ourselves during the flight; so, when we got on the plane, we started drinking martinis immediately. Of course, we flew 1st class, which I enjoyed. By the time we got to Chicago, we were both very drunk, and the crew was concerned enough about us that they put us directly into a cab to our hotel, where we sobered up enough to eat dinner at the hotel. The next day, though, life was back to business as usual. My friend took his boys to the Playboy Club, which I had no interest in, and also was not invited, so I set out on my own. I just happened to have a credit card from my life in New York, so I went shopping at the Bergdorf Goodman store that was conveniently located across the street from our hotel. I bought a full outfit there, including a purse and a pair of shoes; and that evening, we went out to dinner with the boys, their mother, and her latest boyfriend. That was an experience for which I pulled out my princess training and was quite sophisticated for the occasion. The next day, we went to the Jazz competition in which our guy did very well, in fact, his group won.

After all of that excitement, we got on the plane to go home the following day, only to realize that it was the same crew who had to take care of us on the trip to Chicago. They asked us to please watch our drinking, so I think we only had three martinis, or maybe I had scotch.

The next month my parents were coming to Seattle, and I thought it would be nice for them to meet the psychologist. Did I mention that he wore dashikis and beads with a full beard and shoulder-length hair? He was also twenty-some years older than I was.

When I introduced him to my father he said, "Hey man, what's happening?"

I saw the blood drain from my father's face. It turned white. It wouldn't have helped if my father knew this was a man who was highly respected in the psychiatric community, ran analytic group therapy for professionals that were difficult to get into, and was a professor at the University. For my father, he was a kooky shyster and perhaps the worst person I could be dating. My mother was perhaps somewhat more tolerant in that she had most likely had an affair with one of her college professors, who was a fairly well-known poet and quite probably a bohemian.

My relationship lasted less than a year and eventually ended quietly. In some ways, I was glad to be out of the relationship, though, as the drinking got a bit too much for me, believe it or not. Someone else could take care of him. Indeed, later on, I heard that the psychologist was dating an artist. So, there you go; I imagine they did fine together. As for me, I also didn't like the fact that my father was so upset about the relationship. The bottom line was that I respected my father's judgment.

Even with dating having its ups and downs, work continued going well. I enjoyed the OT Clinic, did diagnostic activity batteries, and was able to do a number of other things.

One of the nurses and I ran psychodrama. We usually screened people for the sessions, making a good guess who was well enough to abstract and not get confused as to what was real and not real, that is, we tried to screen out people who were psychotic. One day we were not on top of it for a young man who had apparently not been in the hospital that long. We chose to focus on family members, especially mothers, and work on how to relate to them in a healthier manner. When it was his turn, so to speak, he mooned the group. This was quite a surprise to all, including the therapists. There was not too much damage done, though, and it was very informative as to what might need to get some attention in his therapy.

Building from these experiences, I decided to do a play with the patients. They wrote it, and I got the in-service training program to lend us a video guy who taped the play. The patients named the play "A Day on the Psycho Ward". A number of staff members were clearly portrayed, and it was actually a fairly good play and those who saw it liked it. The patients had a good sense of humor, and so did most staff, thankfully.

Beyond these Occupational Therapy approaches, I also did standard group therapy, family therapy, and couples' therapy with a co-therapist. Over time and with good supervision, I learned a great deal and began to develop confidence in the work that I was doing.

A new psychiatrist came on staff; and, although I didn't know it right away, he and my roommate began to date secretly without me knowing. I thought he was a little egotistical, though, and partly because I didn't know that he was involved with my friend, I made fun of him at home several times.

One day, my roommate decided to be honest with me. "Jim and I have been dating secretly," she told me, "and he's going to move in. So, you'll need to find another place to live."

I was ok with moving but quite embarrassed about making fun of him not knowing they were involved. The whole thing was not good for our friendship; and, although we remained friends, it wasn't ever the same.

THE NEW APARTMENT

BACK TO LIVING ALONE, I FOUND A GREAT APARTMENT located near the hospital in a nice neighborhood. That particular apartment had a fireplace, which I loved. It was a cozy little place and close to my psychodrama co-therapist's house. She had four children, including a pair of twins. They were great kids, and I spent quite a bit of time with them and their mother.

But my friendship with her was one in which we had also been drinking buddies for some time. One day, we decided to do something a little different in our drinking activities. We both got small notebooks and took them with us to the bar. Then we ordered drinks for a couple of men and waited to see what happened.

Of course, they came to our table, and we told them that we were sociology students at the University, and we were doing a study to see how men responded to behaviors that were most often aimed at women. We would then interview them on how it felt to have women buy them drinks, all while taking notes and asking more questions. In most cases, we would end up going somewhere else with them and take the evening from there. By the time we'd finish the interviews, we'd both be half loaded, as, experiment or not, they had, by then, bought the drinks.

One day we decided to have an "unbirthday" party for the kids. My sister and her husband had moved to Bellevue, near Seattle. Despite the move, though, I didn't see them often and had not spent much time with my nephew, Fred, who was five years old. The twins were his age, so I invited my nephew to bring a friend and come. We made unbirthday hats that were quite elaborate and then wore them as we marched down the street to Baskin and Robbins for ice cream. When we got back to the house the kids went upstairs to the attic that had been turned into a rather cool kids' room. It was carpeted and had a lot of great kid things, including a pet white rat.

When I got home, I gave my sister a call to see if my nephew had a good time. Her response, though, was not at all what I'd hoped. She was hysterical and said they were just going out the door to the emergency room because I had let the boys play with a rat in the attic.

"Stop!" I said. "It was a pet store white rat and the attic is a very nice kid's room. I hope Fred's friend is not about to go to the ER."

I was becoming quite aware of how my sister viewed my abilities to deal with my nephew. It was over for me and Freddy, and I was deeply saddened by that. That brief occasion would be the last time that I would be with my nephew without his parents present.

Even worse, Carolyn's hostility was becoming more blatant now, in general; and it was not going to get much better. There was nothing I could do about that, though, so I just had to let it go when she was hostile. Our difficulties would not get better with time. I will say that I was not too fond of her anymore; but she was my sister. The future of our relationship was going to be tricky and quite apparently dependent on how far I was willing to tolerate her offending me. Lucky for both of us, I had a lot of therapy under my belt and I knew that I didn't want to give up contact with her entirely, so I would have to figure that out, and I did. Even so, I was sad to not have Freddy in my life, as he was a little wild one in a good way, full of spunk and lots of questions. I would have loved to get to know him better when he was young. We would have had a great time.

Sadly, though, my nephew never knew his Aunt Janny as a child. Much more recently, we've gotten to know each other a bit talking on the phone about how my sister was doing and texting about the Seahawks. He is fifty years old now, and we've been keeping in better touch, even though he lives near Washington DC, a long way from Seattle. He and his husband work for the government and are very busy. We have invited each other to come visit, but that does not happen easily.

RITA

In 1972, I joined NOW (the National Organization for Women) and met my friend Rita. I remembered the warning of the staff at the psychiatric ward in NYC and decided they were ridiculous about not participating in politics. Rita was a Trotskyist and invited me to a meeting of the Socialist Workers Party. (SWP)

Rita had joined the party when she was fourteen years old. She felt that her parents, who were practicing Jews, had misrepresented to her the reasons behind giving financial support to the Zionists for the fight with the Palestinians in Israel. Standing firm, she knew her position as to the nature of that fight and decided that she disagreed with them. From a very early age, clearly, she was motivated and determined to live by her political principles.

So, Rita had become active in the SWP when she was young. When I asked, she told me a story about how her parents found her books and burned them. After that, she left home and joined the party; and she also told me that, once she came of age, she married one of the leaders of the party.

At some point, they moved to New York City, where the national headquarters were located. They had a son and a daughter who were a few years apart, though the children were quite young during the years when they lived in New York. Ed, her husband, traveled a good deal, and Rita was often left at home and had to deal with working, taking care of two young children and participating in the Party. These were difficult years for Rita. Rightfully, she had some resentments about it.

They came to Seattle in the early 70's in order to strengthen the party here. By then, the kids were teenagers. Not terribly long after the move, Rita and her husband separated. Ed left Seattle, and Rita and the kids stayed. When I met her, she was a leader in NOW. Rita worked for the railroad for many years and was very active in the union and in the SWP. She was particularly active with the feminist movement and the struggle for the Equal Rights Amendment. Indeed, she was a talented leader and a skilled coalition builder and was instrumental in bringing the women from both ends of the ERA spectrum, the Seattle Business Women's Association and Radical Women, together to work on the common issues involved in the ERA Coalition.

Partly through Rita's influence, I started attending some lectures and events at the SWP. I was beginning to understand their positions and was interested in learning more, so I got involved as a supporter. Certainly, I wasn't sophisticated in political theory, but over time, I began to know more. I learned a lot from Rita politically though she always thought I was a light weight, and she was right. It did not matter to me as our friendship was personal. I also got to know people in the party, as well as more of Rita's friends. So, in mid-1974, I decided that I wanted to join the SWP, as I agreed with the basic things that they were promoting.

A year later, in 1975, Rita met a woman named Joan. They would be together for a good forty years. So, I got to know Joan, as well, and became fond of her, too. Those two women were very caring and generous to me over the years. Even Rita's two teenagers, Wilma and Matt, came to feel like family. For many years, I would celebrate holidays with them, and I spent time with Rita and Joan regularly.

THE FOSTER DAUGHTER

ONE DAY IN 1974, RITA CALLED ME and asked me if I would be willing to take in a fifteen-year-old girl as a foster child. At just about that time, I'd been going through a period of thinking that I wanted a child in my life; and I had gone so far as to have an interview with an adoption agency. I decided considering the fact that I had to work and was getting involved politically, I didn't pursue the matter further. I had both my drinking buddies' kids in my life; and now Rita's kids were around, too. So, it seemed to me that I had what I needed.

Perhaps a little surprisingly, though, Rita thought that my taking in this teenager might be something I would like to do. She was essentially homeless and had been living in a boy's group home where her brother lived. This was not a good situation, so I met her and thought it had a good chance to work out. So, we went to see her social worker, and I became her foster mother.

What does a good mother do? Well, one of the first things I did was take her to JC Penny's to buy her some much-needed clothes. She'd need them for school, and that was part of the deal. A few things came out of her money from the state, and beyond that I bought her more as the state funds didn't pay for much. I wanted her to feel comfortable at school.

It was quite a new thing figuring out how to mother someone, especially a teenager. So, I thought about other things or experiences that might be useful to her, and I ended up getting her a job at University Hospital as a candy striper, and she would ride to work with me. The first day, though, I got a phone call at work saying I needed to come to meet with the volunteer people right away. My foster daughter had somehow gotten a large number of safety pins and had shortened her skirt to a point far past decency. The safety pins were removed, and I think because I worked at the hospital, they gave her a second chance. A few weeks later, though, there was another call to say I needed to come get her, as she was found in bed with a man in traction. So, we went home, and I asked her what was going on. She said she was just trying to be nice. I knew we were in trouble.

She was behind in school so I decided that I would try to get her into Roosevelt High School's special education program. She got in and had an excellent teacher, whom she liked. So, I felt good about that. I took her with me when I went to the SWP Hall and she would get together with Rita's daughter. She did date a few boys from school, and then I noticed there were a few older ones and I began to notice that she came home with new jewelry a few times.

At this time the World's Fair was in Spokane, so I took her to it, and we stayed with my parents. When we first walked into the house, my father reacted in an unusual way which I figured out had to do with my foster daughter's very seductive manner. I had not realized just how easy it was to see. We went to the Fair the next day. My parents did not come. While we were gone, the phone rang several times, and men were calling for my foster daughter. She had somehow gotten my parents' phone number, and when she excused herself to go to the ladies' room, she had gotten the number to several men. My parents picked up on what was going on, but said nothing, though I knew what was going on, and I knew that they knew.

One day, my foster daughter told me that there were two places she liked to be. One was juvenile detention and the other was at my house. When I asked why, she said that in both places, she knew exactly what the rules were. Based on comments like that, I thought things were going well enough. By then, she'd been with me for about five months. Then my neighbor asked me if I knew what was going on at my apartment when I was at work. My heart stopped, and I said I did not. She said that my foster daughter was prostituting out of my apartment. I thought hard about what to do. She had turned sixteen recently, so I decided to go see the social worker and to recommend we emancipate her, and that was what happened.

My foster daughter was happy about that and so was I. I knew she was a survivor and would be fine. I heard a year later from Wilma, Rita's daughter, that she was living with her boyfriend and that they had a baby and she was happy. I was glad she was happy.

One day soon after the trip to Spokane, I got a note from my father. For some years, he had put me on his board and had let me have a car, though I had to pay for the insurance. Somehow, being on the board allowed me to have the car. The note, though, stated that people who were socialists and foster mothers could not be on the board. In response, I went to a Ford dealership, where a man who had worked for my father now worked. I did not have a lot of money to put into a car, but I did have enough for a Pinto, the model that exploded if rear-ended. So, I got a friend to drive the Pinto, and I drove my father's car over to Spokane and turned his car back over to him. He walked around the Pinto and kicked the tires and said nothing. But our relationship changed, actually for the better. I think I gained some respect for me for my returning the car and standing by my principles. I never was sure why the foster mother was part of it, but I did understand the Socialism thing.

DIAGNOSIS CONFIRMED

IN THE FALL OF 1974, I HAD WORKED AT THE UW for just under four years, and I was starting to get manic. Early on, the way I was feeling reminded me of how I felt after giving birth. *I was euphoric.*

But then, it began to escalate. *I began to talk fast and a lot, going from one subject to another, and I understood clearly that this was like the episode in New York some four years before. I found that things had symbolic meanings and seemed connected to other thoughts. There was definitely a "high" feeling and again a low simmering fear. I knew again that I was in trouble.*

In Seattle at the UW Hospital, I had attended some classes that were taught by well-trained psychiatrists who knew about working with manic patients. The classes were open to staff, so I went. A major emphasis was that bipolar disorder was *treatable with the right medication and therapy. I learned that there could be good remission between episodes and that people could lead fairly normal and productive lives. In retrospect, I think I was in one of those remissions since my first episode. If I had been on the correct medication, it is doubtful that I would have been sick again.*

Fortunately for me, I wasn't the only one at the time who recognized that I was in trouble. My good friend and drinking buddy knew that I was not stable and that I was frightened, so she had me stay with her for the night. I had feelings that I might commit suicide or that others wanted me to, and I did not want to do that. *I felt helpless and out of control.*

My friend didn't want me to go to work the next day, but I insisted. Again, *my judgment was bad. A few hours into the morning, I was escalating, talking fast again with "flight of ideas," while I was in a meeting with staff. I started to rant about doctors who wore white coats to boost their egos, and I knew that I was not making sense, so I excused myself and went into my office, where the head psychiatrist found me.*

"You know what you are, don't you?" he asked me.

"Yes," I told him. "I think I'm manic."

"Do you want me to treat you?" he asked, and I answered that I did.

His name was Bob Friedel, and he was a very good psychiatrist and very kind and sensitive with patients.

"You need to go into the hospital," he told me. "I can arrange for you to be admitted where people you work with will not know." Instantly, I could see how thoughtful he was. In that same moment, he also made sure that I had some medication to start me and he gave me his phone number, "Here is some trilafon," he handed it to me "It's an anti-psychotic, and it will help you slow down. Take it until I can find you a bed," he instructed. I was familiar with trilafon and knew it was effective. We used to call it "Try Laughin."

So, I did what he told me, accepting his phone number and heading back to Rita's house. She was working, but one of her friends agreed to stay with me. I felt myself escalating and took more trilafon than was prescribed. I decided I could not wait to go to the hospital. I'd called an ambulance and asked them to take me to Harborview, because in my mania I saw it as "The People's Hospital." Then I called Friedel and told him I was going. The University ran Harborview, so he didn't really want to see me there, as some of my co-workers were bound to see me, and he was seeking a bed in a hospital that would provide me more privacy. He would have preferred that I had waited, but he was ok with it. I told him that I wanted to be on Lithium, and he agreed.

Rita's friend was a little bit unstable herself, but she was dear and did her best. She had been singing and playing her guitar in an attempt to help me stay calm and brought it with us in the ambulance. I was with it enough to think the ambulance people might have trouble figuring out which of us was the patient. Finally, though, when we got there, I told them that I'd taken more medication than was prescribed, and they thought about pumping my stomach.

In the end, though, they didn't as I convinced them that it had only been a few more than prescribed. The psychiatrist who admitted me diagnosed me as Borderline. Perhaps he'd thought my taking the extra pills was a manipulative suicide attempt.

"I'm manic," I corrected him, "and Dr. Friedel knows that I'm manic."

The idea that I would not get the proper treatment frightened me, but fortunately, Friedel arrived when I was on the unit, and he straightened things out. The admitting doctor was a resident, and Friedel was his boss, so I calmed down.

By this time, I was pretty sick, and I don't have much memory of that night. I know that someone put me in seclusion because I was singing revolutionary songs. I'd also used the bed as a trampoline, and she didn't care for that, either. So, I calmed myself down. For a short time, before the medication kicked in, I thought I had died and was struggling to come back. Again, it was very frightening and painful, as I did have a sense I was not in touch with reality. I was struggling hard and not getting back.

My stay at Harborview lasted for two weeks, during which time Dr. Friedel asked my parents to come for a family session, which they did. My father was very nice about it. What I had put together by then was that my mother had had a 10-year untreated depression and my Aunt Freida was very likely manic-depressive. I thought, too, about my grandmother, who had spent a year at the mountain cabin. The whole family drank a lot, and we used to use alcoholism in the family history as a red flag for manic-depression. It seemed clear that it was most probably on both sides of my family. Dr. Friedel was very good with my parents and told them that I was going to be ok. They liked him, and my father did not call him a shyster.

Once I was doing better, my sister came from Bellevue to visit me, too. I could tell she was quite frightened and uncomfortable. I was still manic enough to tell her that one of the patients was a staff member and asked her to come sit with us. The woman was delusional and was convinced that she was the second coming of Christ, and this time, it was a woman because of the feminist movement. I knew she would tell Carolyn this, which she did. I let Carolyn continue to think the woman was staff. When she got home, though, she told Dick, her husband, about the staff person who seemed crazy too. Dick laughed at her and explained that I had tricked her. Carolyn really resented that and carried that resentment for years. In my opinion, she should have factored in that I was manic; and, for my part, I should have known better than to do that. Often, my sister didn't get jokes. Years later, though, she still remembered that one and brought it up to me and I did apologize, but I don't think she accepted my apology.

HOME FROM THE HOSPITAL

SOON AFTER THIS, I GOT OUT OF THE HOSPITAL and went home to my apartment. I was on Lithium and trilafon, and I was doing well. The medication was of maximum importance, and my hospital stay was followed up with an appointment with Dr. Friedel. Days later, I was still a little shaky, but very much in touch with what was happening around me. When I sat down in his office and was talking about how I was doing, he was more than supportive.

He reminded me that, *"You know that if you do what we tell you, take your medicine and have a psychiatrist follow you, you can lead a normal life. There is no reason that you cannot work in psychiatry."*

This was hugely important to me, and I have never missed a dose of my medication. I was determined to return to working in mental health. *This was perhaps the most important and hopeful thing that anyone could have said to me at the time.* I remember his words still, as though I had first heard them just yesterday. In working with other bipolar people, I always remembered the strength of this encouragement and when I thought they were able to hear it, would give them a similar message.

I was having a hard time and was shaky, so I decided to go stay with my parents for a week or so just to get on my feet. I was feeling uneasy and had some thoughts of suicide, which I knew I would not do, but having the thoughts frightened me. Mother picked me up from the plane, and I told her that one reason I had come to visit was that I was having suicidal thoughts that frightened me. She responded, "That is too bad, as Fred was to the doctor yesterday and was diagnosed with cancer." He was actually at the doctor as we were driving home. "I am not able to deal with your suicidal thoughts and that too," she told me bluntly.

And indeed, I felt so selfish. So, I straightened up and we talked about my father. I was upset about him, too, as he was very special to me, and I felt terribly sad for my mother. Dad came home and said that he was scheduled for surgery the next week. I stayed only a few days and went home. I wanted to get out of their way.

Once I got back home, I was glad that I had spent time with Fred. Of course, I was still very upset about my father, but I knew that I had to get back on track. *I had that almost predictable depression after the high.* I knew that I needed to address it and set up a system so that I wouldn't give in to it and just stay in bed. *I was so glad that I knew a good deal about my diagnosis, and I decided that I would be alright if I was careful.*

So, I set my alarm for 8:00 a.m. every morning and made myself get up and have coffee and take my meds. Then I set the alarm for 10:00 a.m. and sat and let myself wallow in the depression. At 10:00 a.m., the alarm would go off, and I had to get dressed and go somewhere out of my apartment. I could go see a friend, go to the store, go run an errand, to the library or anywhere out of my apartment. I could only stand the wallowing for two weeks and was able to delete it. It was just essential that I stay somewhat busy each day. Soon, I was able to start to do things that I had liked in the past. I recommend this kind of regimen for people who are depressed and able to follow it. It is particularly important to wallow and then break from it and get moving, even when you do not feel like it.

Until he left the university, I stayed in therapy with Dr. Friedel. Before he left, it occurred to me that I should somehow let the adoptive parents of my daughter know about my diagnosis since *it is so clearly genetic.* I talked to Dr. Friedel and we decided to contact the doctor who arranged the adoption and delivered my baby and ask him to pass the information on to the parents. Dr. Friedel wrote a letter, and I felt I had done what I could and hoped that my baby escaped from bipolar disorder.

I now knew I needed to be involved in something and that I needed to stay busy. I went to the SWP meetings and began to attend study meetings and to help with events and other activities. I even sold Militant Newspapers on the street, which was a trip. I spent time with my old drinking buddy and with other friends including Rita. I did the Huntley Drinkley thing nightly and did not tell Dr. Friedel about that. Soon, I started to think about getting back to work and checked the papers for jobs just to get a sense of things, though I was not ready to interview for a few months.

Today, I look back on this time and realize that I am still a person who needs the structure of work or a project to feel productive and therefore happy. I have always managed to find this kind of activity and during my recovery from this last episode until I could go back to work in mental health, political involvement gave me that. This is not to say that I "used" the Party for that, though. I did believe at this time the Party was doing important work. I was happy to do what I could.

GARY

I MET A MAN TEN YEARS YOUNGER THAN ME. He was attractive to me and he was a member of the SWP. He seemed bright regarding politics and was an amateur astronomer which I found very interesting. When I mentioned him to my friend Rita, though, I couldn't help but mention that he was younger.

"What's wrong," she responded. "Are you an ageist?"

He was quite appealing to me, so maybe I needed to get over myself about the age difference. Gary, after all, was handsome, six feet tall with dark, shoulder-length hair, a groomed beard, and deep brown eyes. He was from an Italian American middle-class family who were somewhat supportive of his politics. His father was an accountant and sometimes went to demonstrations. That kind of support was not that usual within families at this time. Gary dressed casually, though in an attractive way. He also had a great sense of humor that was a little unusual in some ways, not cynical, but with a little twist that I found entertaining. It was a bit different. We laughed a lot. He was a good companion.

Within a month of when our conversations began, we were living together at my apartment. The day he came to stay, I remember, was March 1, 1975. Often, we played a game of "What were you doing when …?" One of the times we compared was when Kennedy was shot. Gary was in 5th grade, taught by nuns who were quite upset by the news. I, on the other hand, was at the HUB at the U of W using a pay phone to call my mother. So, we had different experiences. We found these comparisons to be interesting and at times humorous in a strange way. His presence helped me particularly during my recovery from the episode.

Gary had no idea, though, what he had gotten himself into regarding my drinking. Before long, he began to get uncomfortable watching me drink every night. We quite often went to social events with the SWP. The problem, though, was that as I had for years, I usually had a couple of drinks before I left, as never knew how much liquor would be available there. This is not uncommon with alcoholics, as we need to be sure we have enough liquor available. This habit really bothered Gary, though it didn't stop me. I kept drinking, and I always got drunk. That meant that I often said things that embarrassed Gary. In fact, I often thought it was my duty to tell people what I thought of them. This was at times embarrassing for Gary.

WORKING IN A FACTORY

THE PARTY WANTED MEMBERS TO WORK IN PLACES that had unions and co-workers with the potential to be recruited to the party. Since I was not feeling ready to return to working in mental health, I agreed to get a job in a sporting goods factory, even though I knew that, in the interview, I would be asked to sew something. I knew the commercial machines were nothing like the one I had at home.

I was right. A woman in the party told me that the machines were powerful and fast, and I would need to be careful operating them. I did not have access to one to try before I went to apply and when I got there and was asked to sew, I saw that the machines were huge and ugly. When I put the material under the needle and put down the foot, I stepped on the pedal, and the material shot across the room and bounced off the wall. So, instead, they offered me a job as an inspector, which did not involve sewing, and I took it.

That factory job was like nothing else I'd ever done. My co-workers were primarily refugees from Cambodia, which was confusing because it didn't quite make sense to me that they would want to join a party that was communist, a regime from which they had fled. Also, most did not speak English. I didn't know why the Party thought this would be a good place to work in order to recruit new members and I never got an answer that made sense. I was there about a month and a half when I witnessed a supervisor slap a worker across the face. I reported it to the Union only to learn that they did not want to hear it and that my supervisor did not like it either. It seemed time to leave, and also to call the whole thing a mistake for me and to find something in mental health.

Fortunately for me, I found something fairly easily that was related to my training, getting hired on at Seattle Central Community College to work with blind students. At Columbia I had studied working with the blind. This job involved getting them accommodation in classes, working with them on daily living skills and how to manage living on their own in the community. Most of them had come from a State school for the blind and had never lived on their own. I really liked the work, the other staff and the clients.

A VISIT WITH MY FATHER

As TIME WENT ON, I WAS DOING WELL and managing my bipolar condition, though other things within my family were still a concern. My father, for instance, was doing well after his surgery but was not cancer free. He also had a colostomy, which was very hard for him. As a fastidious person, this was really difficult. Still, he returned to work and my mother cared for him while they kept up the activities that they enjoyed together. This included Huntley Drinkley, which by then included playing a card game called "Spite and Malaise." It was competitive game, and they kept score.

There was still community in Spokane, too. They saw their friends, and Fred remained fairly active with the business. One time, he went to a conference that included a few hours lay over in Seattle before the plane for Spokane, and he called me and asked me to meet him at the airport so we could have a visit. I was delighted and our visit went very well. I really loved my father and knew that the remaining time was not going to be easy for him...or my mother, my sister, and me. Time with him was very, very precious now.

In the fall of 1975, I got a call from my sister that I should come right away if I wanted to see Fred again. She and her husband and my nephew had moved to Spokane from California. Of course, I went right away. Carolyn had overheard staff talking and misunderstood what they were saying, and she panicked and called everyone to come immediately.

When I went in to see Fred, he asked, "Why is there this stream of people coming through to see me? I'm not ready to die yet. Was this Carolyn's doing?"

It was quite typical of things that she would do such as misunderstand the situation and go into action prematurely. She meant well, though. Fred lived another three months.

My nephew Freddy had come with his father with Dad's black lab, Ringo, to stand below the window of Fred's room. Ringo was a very good hunting dog and my father was very fond of him. He also loved Freddy, who was his namesake. I helped Dad to the window, and we stood there, waving down to them for a few minutes, as long as Fred could stand at the window. Fleeting though it was, that was a precious moment, and when I got back to Seattle I painted a small picture of Freddy and his father and Ringo looking up. I sent it to Fred, who kept it beside his bed. It was hard to see him so very ill, but he did still have some spunk left in him.

Spunk or not, though, the insurance company wanted to transfer him to some place that had hospice care, even though he wanted to stay at the hospital. This decision on the insurance company's part wasn't the wisest, though, because my father had generated a lot of business for them over the years. For instance, Fred had told the other dealers in town about the health insurance company, which he used for his employees and felt they were reasonable and had a good program. A number of the other dealers had changed to this company and had big accounts. When they heard about the insurance denying Fred his request, they got together and went to the company, threatening to move to another company if they did not honor Fred's request to stay at the hospital. The company relented, believing that the threat was real, which it probably was. So, Fred stayed where he wanted to be. It was clear people really cared about my father.

BACK TO SEATTLE

LIFE IN SEATTLE WENT ON. I continued to work at the college, and Gary and I remained active with the SWP. The major issues were the Vietnam War, as well as the feminist movement and the small ambition to replace Capitalism with Socialism.

Gary and I continued to enjoy each other's company. His sense of humor was wonderful, and we had a number of good friends together, often spending time with them outside of Party activities. We also did political activities most weekends, which got me doing several previously unfamiliar things, like selling "The Militant" newspaper on the street corner, handing out informational leaflets, and trying to work in a factory. We were involved in coalitions that built and participated in political events involving educationals and demonstrations. Committed to non-violence, we often served as security at events where we watched out for and intervened with people who appeared to want to make trouble.

During this time there were a lot of political events in Seattle. The Stalinists hated the Trotskyists both historically and in the 70's in Seattle. Stalinists indeed did assassinate Trotsky when he was in exile in Mexico. They killed him with an ice pick. There were times at events when Stalinists would sit behind us and we would hear them whisper, "Ice pick, ice pick, ice pick..."

At one SWP party, I was doing the bump with one of our friends, and we bumped too hard. I fell and broke my leg in two places and tore out my knee. Of course, I had been drunk at the time. Gary and the man I had been dancing with put me in the back of my Pinto and took me to the ER. The ER staff asked how much I had had to drink, and I said "three," even when I had no idea how much. They messed with my leg and put on a cast and told me they were glad I had three drinks as they had just set my leg with no anesthetic. Gary was pretty disgusted with me, though he took good care of me, anyway. This was lucky, because the recovery was tedious, forcing me to stay home until I'd graduated to crutches and off pain meds. Now, most people would stop drinking after a trial like that, but not an alcoholic like me. I continued to do Huntley Drinkley every evening and drank at parties, too.

One night I wanted to drink, but was out of liquor, which was unusual. Gary would not go get liquor for me. I was mad and left on my crutches which might not have been bad except there was a snow storm. I went off hobbling on the crutches with a cast from hip to ankle to my drinking buddy's house five blocks away. I did what I had to, because that is what alcoholics do to get their liquor. We had a number of drinks and then she drove me home. Gary was not happy but said nothing.

In time, though, I recovered from the broken leg and continued to work with the blind students. There was a set of twins who both had been over oxygenated soon after they were born. This caused one to be totally blind and the other to have only a small amount of vision. One day when I was with the blind twin, for some reason we went to my apartment to get something. Gary was in the shower, heard me come in and stepped out of the bathroom naked. He was freaked out when he saw my student, not knowing that she was totally blind. Once she said hello, though, he realized that she didn't see him and gathered his wits about himself to say hello back.

Around eight months later, the program that I was working in was closed. I was very disappointed. I had very much liked working with the blind students and had felt that we'd done them a great service. Luckily, though, I was swiftly offered a job with the Women's Studies Department at the college, which I accepted and worked at for about three months. It was an interesting change, and I think I did fine as was by now a fairly well-educated feminist. It was good politically, but it just wasn't mental health.

So, I began looking for another job and found one in a small town South of Seattle. It was about a 40-minute commute on the freeway. It was a good clinic and I was to develop a day program for the chronically mentally ill. I was confident that I could do it well and arranged for an interview. And indeed, I got the job.

After the interview, I left the clinic and was later told by one of my co-workers that one of the staff members came in to see the director.

"You have just hired a bipolar person," he told her.

She responded by letting him know that, "At least she knows *her* diagnosis."

I liked the director, as she was a strong and wise woman who had many years' experience; and I liked what she had told that nasty man. I was to start on the first working day of January which was the same day I had started working at Bellevue Hospital in New York City.

FRED DIES

AS GOOD THINGS CAME MY WAY, though, sad ones did, too, so I wasn't able to begin that job immediately, as my father died a few days before. It was early

January of 1976, and Gary and I went to Spokane for the funeral. Mother was not pleased with my choice of a revolutionary for a partner and arranged for Gary and me to stay with family friends. She also did not like that we slept together and certainly didn't want that at her house. The couple we stayed with had been very close to my father, and they were kind to us.

Our next-door neighbor, my orthodontist and father of Carolyn's High School boyfriend, was very close to my father and came to visit. He and I got into a discussion and somehow the feminist movement came up. I don't remember the exact context in which we had a disagreement. I remember it was in passing and not a big deal to me at the time. He must have felt bad that he had disagreed with me when my father had just died. A few weeks after I returned to Seattle, I received a tube in the mail with four prints of Gibson Girls from him. Charles Dana Gibson was an artist from the late 19th and early 20th century and his drawings of women personified the ideal women of that era. The prints were depicting the Girls in roles not usual at the time for women. Gibson had drawn the women with tongue in cheek.

One was with a woman as a preacher; one was of a team of rugby players; another of women around a conference table entitled "The Cabinet Meeting"; and the final one was of women in military uniforms—all things not unusual for women of today. They were wonderful. They are hanging in my living room. They were my neighbor's apology for what he viewed as an inappropriate comment. To this day, they are precious to me.

At the time, though, I was very much in mourning for Fred, and I knew that my mother was, too, so I said nothing about her not wanting Gary and me to stay at the house. It just wasn't that important, and we had been treated very well where we did stay so it was not worth making a fuss. I knew that I would miss my father terribly, and I do to this day. His pedestal still gets taller with memories of what a wonderful man he was, and how lucky I was to have him as a father.

VALLEY CITIES MENTAL HEALTH

AFTER THE FUNERAL, WE RETURNED TO SEATTLE, and I got back into my working life, beginning the new job. At that time, there was a big push nationally for clinics to have out-patient programs for the severely mentally ill. The hope was this would reduce the need for beds in the state hospitals and allow patients to live in the community with less expensive treatment. The agency, too, wanted the day program as it was probable we would increase the number of clients they served by offering a solid program to the chronic population. That also meant that the clients for our program would come into the clinic at the back door directly into the program area and bypass the waiting room, where less severely ill waited for their appointments. This was typical at that time, but it made me angry. That kind of behavior always annoyed me, as I saw it as discriminatory. Did people think they might catch the more serious mental illness like a cold? It just fed into the stigma around the issue of mental illness.

When we started the program, it consisted of six middle-aged women, some with persistent depression and the others with major diagnoses. Fairly quickly, the program grew to include a wider age range and most clients with major mental health issues. We hired a few new staff and began to introduce activities into the program. We also had a kitchen and started preparing lunch with the clients. A few clients who wanted to cook with us took the certification exam and passed it easily. For those who wanted to do other things, we had several specific activity sessions, including various crafts, outings, and group therapy. We also began a medication group that the psychiatrist ran and staff attended, as we monitored medications and needed to know what was prescribed. So, the program began to have a schedule and variety and grew to cover around twenty-five. I carried a small case load of individual clients outside of the day program.

So, I liked my new job, though I began to realize that my drinking every night wasn't such a good thing. Up to that point, I'd still held onto the goofy theory that since I had to try harder when hung over, I actually did better than I would have without the hangover. But, my drinking was worrying me now, and I began to feel like death was stalking me, which was probably true.

Shortly after going to work at the new clinic, Gary and I had the opportunity to rent a house that belonged to a couple who were going to live in Italy for two years and wanted to rent it while they were gone. It was a nice two-story house with some character and gave us much more room than we had in the apartment. It was in a good neighborhood called Wallingford and was convenient for my commute to work. The house was also fairly close to the SWP hall. It was big enough to have people over and to have parties, so we went ahead and rented it. I enjoyed putting our things together and getting a few additional pieces that were nice. I recovered our couch which was quite a project, but which turned out well. I felt fortunate to have the house for the next two years.

Even more delightful was the fact that the back yard was fenced, and we decided to get a puppy. At the pound, we picked out a little terrier: an adorable little guy with an attitude. We named him "Rhubarb II" in honor of Rhubarb I, but also because he was a little fight about to happen, as in baseball. He was very good with us, but a vet and a groomer each asked us not to bring him back. We had a good friend who was a traveling vet and said Rhubarb's snout was too small for a regular commercial muzzle. She measured his snout and had a special muzzle made for him for those events in which he might be trouble.

I continued to do Huntley Drinkley and Gary continued to feel concerned about it but said little. Moreover, I was a bit brazen about it, keeping my bottle of scotch on the kitchen counter, as did not care who saw it. Usually, I would check it in the morning to see how much I had to drink the night before. Gary noted this practice, and when I wasn't home, he would pour out a bit so I would think that I'd had more the night before than I really did. I did once in a while determine to cut back, but this never quite happened, as once I had the first drink, I was always off and running.

About this time, Gary started calling "Dial a Bottle," which was the alcohol help line, telling them about my drinking. They would tell him that I was a late stage alcoholic, and he should leave me. I came to believe that I would never be able to stop drinking; so eventually, I stopped trying. This went on for another year.

Resigned to my fate, I began going down the road from work at noon most days and having two martinis for lunch. I'd be shaking so much, I couldn't pick up my glass, so I'd just slide down in my seat, putting the glass close to the edge of the table, check to see if anyone was looking, and take a few sips in order to calm my shakes and not spill when I picked up the glass. I knew this was getting down the line and that I needed to stop drinking, as might lose my job. But then, on my way home from work, I would have panic attacks while driving on the freeway and would pop Xanax to calm myself. Xanax is like alcohol in pill form. By the time I'd get home, I could hardly wait to get a drink. Later, I would realize that these "panic attacks" were withdrawal and having a drink or a Xanex was the cure.

I was very close to one of my co-workers, Rick. He'd joined the clinic shortly after I did and became interested in the day program and had asked to work with us. He was a social worker and a very good man and a good therapist. During my early days working with him, I was still drinking a lot, and I took him with me once for my martini lunch. He knew little about drinking, though, and just thought my having two martinis at lunch was a little weird. He never said anything to anyone about it.

We needed to hire a nurse and I remembered a friend of mine, Lynn, whom I had known at the university when we both worked there. She was a psychiatric nurse. I sent Rick out to talk with her and she came to work with us. Apparently, my match-making skills were working well because they were immediately attracted to each other and eventually ended up getting married. At their wedding, I was given a special corsage as "mother of the relationship." They were wonderful, and recently I have renewed contact with them. Lynn and I ran into each other downtown one day and I went to visit some months ago and have talked with them several times recently. The years have brought us both some difficult times but apparently that is just part of life. Rick has had MS since some years ago and both he and Lynn are still active in a private practice doing therapy. It is good to be in touch again.

THE JIG IS UP

I CAME HOME FROM WORK ONE DAY TO FIND GARY waiting for me at the back door. He told me that he was leaving, that he couldn't watch me kill myself with alcohol any longer. And he left. I remember that feeling so well, standing there and thinking, this was the best and most important relationship I ever had, and I have ruined it with my alcoholism.

As soon as his tail lights were around the corner, I was in my car on my way to the liquor store. I bought $75 worth of hard liquor, in jugs with handles. This was back in 1977, and $75 worth of liquor was a lot. Then I went home and got drunk because that is what alcoholics do. I stayed drunk most of the weekend, though somehow I managed to go to work Monday and Tuesday, coming home and drinking both evenings.

On Wednesday, I came home to find a strange man on my doorstep.

I asked him, "Who are you and what do you want?"

He told me, "I talked to you last night for forty-five minutes, and you agreed to go with me to a meeting."

Clearly, I had called in a black out.

Insisting, though, he asked, "Will you still go to a meeting with me?"

I would, I promised, "But I have to feed my cats first."

That was true, though it also gave me a little time to deal with what I call "white fear," meaning very intense fear. But I did it. I fed the cats and then got in his car and went to a meeting. I will always remember that day because it was June 9th, 1977, and I have never had a drink since.

It was probably just my perception then, but I thought that the meeting was huge. This is a disease of distorted perceptions and it was just a large room with tables in a rectangular formation filled with probably thirty or so people. I sat there, shaking like a leaf from not having drinks that night. I kept thinking, "Can I give up my Scotch?" Then, I listened, and people were talking about what it was like before they got sober. Many of the tales were quite funny, and I thought some were worse than what I was like. Later I would realize I was pretty bad, myself. I thought that if these people can do it, I should be able to do it, too. I didn't know that sharing as they did is how people in the program respond to new people. The good news is, it worked for me.

I was very thankful, because things had really gotten quite bad. After all, it was wild that I had gotten myself to the Program in a blackout! Moreover, I was an atheist, as Trotskyists do not have Higher Powers, so I did not attribute my situation to anything spiritual. But I was thinking that Gary left, I was close to losing my job, I was overweight, and I felt horrible physically most of the time. And I knew without a doubt it was due to my alcoholism. This was the first step to sobriety.

The nice man who had picked me up for the meeting went home with me and helped me pour the rest of that $75 worth of booze down the drain. We also flushed a bottle of Xanax down the toilet. It was a miracle that I didn't have DTs or a seizure from going cold turkey off the Xanax and the liquor. It was pretty lonely at my house, but I had mustered some determination not to drink and I felt good about it. I had no idea about the journey that lay ahead. At work the next day I told my supervisor that I had gotten into recovery.

"Thank God," she answered. "I was going to have to talk to you about that."

It looked like I was right that I was about to lose my job. So, I'd quit drinking just in the nick of time.

I BEGIN THE PROGRAM

I WAS NOW IN THE PROGRAM FOR RECOVERY. and taking it seriously. Soon, I found a sponsor. She was someone who had been sober for some years and was a woman with a great sense of humor. I started to go to meetings once a day and did most of what I was told to do, except to stop being an Atheist. That was something that I just wouldn't do.

For quite a while, I was still pretty toxic. Gary was seeing another woman, and I was furious. She was a worse alcoholic than I was, but I just had to ignore it, which didn't entirely work. I began to ruminate about it and did not like what I was thinking, so I called someone from the hall where I had been going to meetings and told him that I was angry and wanted to go shoot her.

"Do you have a gun?" he asked me.

"No," I said. "Do you know how to get one?"

"Meet me at the meeting hall in ten minutes," he told me, and I did. He took one look at me and said, "You are really crazy, you are not going to shoot anyone."

But of course, I already knew that. I went to the meeting and forgot all about it, though that was pretty crazy, as sometimes happens when you are still toxic and still withdrawing early on. So, I was grateful to him for being there and grateful that the people in meetings knew what it was like to be early in sobriety.

At this early point in my sobriety I needed to do abstinence one day at a time. I also needed to find a way to always remind myself of this in some way as thinking I would never drink again was not helpful, indeed, it made it harder. So, for the first three months of my sobriety I personified my addiction and invented an imaginary little blue man who looked like a smurf and had a shit eating grin. He sat on my right shoulder and was always there. He would say to me, "Wouldn't a scotch on the rocks be good right now?" And my response was always, "Not today."

Beyond all of this major life change, I was busy with work, with going to meetings and meeting with my Sponsor. I also remained in therapy. Dr. Friedel had moved to Virginia in 1975 and had turned me over to someone else whom I also really liked. His name was Nick Ward. I worked well with him, and he was my rock for the next twenty-six years. I was still drinking for the first two of those years with him and, of course, did not tell him. When I saw him after I started the Program, I did finally confess to him that I had been drinking alcoholically for many years and for those previous two years while in treatment with him. I shared the story of the strange man on my doorstep and that I was finally in recovery. It was good to no longer hold onto my lie of omission.

Three weeks into my sobriety, Gary heard that I was sober and asked to come back. I had missed him and was glad he wanted to come back, which he did, and we would be together for the next eighteen years. By then, I'd left the SWP because, once sober, I didn't feel comfortable around all that drinking. Gary was still active in the party, though, which was fine. I remained friendly and supportive of the party and fairly soon felt comfortable at social events.

Another benefit of sobriety is that I began to feel better physically, and I lost thirty pounds within two months. So, life began to settle down, I began to work the program, getting to know people there better. They were all supportive of my sobriety, even if I stood solid on the "no God" stuff. I felt there were other approaches to things. At the same time, I began to know a woman who was very spiritual. She had problems but was always able to overcome them through her Higher Power. I was a bit fascinated by her, as she was so calm and had a glow about her, though I chased away an idea that I admired and would like to be like her, but the seed was planted. Her name was Noreen.

Work was good, too, when I stopped drinking. For one thing, I was more present. When I think of what I must have been like as a therapist when I was drinking, it is not a good thought. I had been busy thinking about when I would get my next drink, so being present was not easy.

The Day Treatment Program I had started was doing well, and I enjoyed the work. I still saw patients in counseling and that was going well, with the exception of the one day when I was held at gunpoint by a very sick woman. The worst part of that experience was the fact that no one noticed that both of us were there in my office for over two hours. Finally, I talked her down, and she put the gun back in her purse and left. I don't remember what we did about it but think we notified the police, but nothing was done. She never came back to the clinic.

That episode was the closest that I ever would come to being in danger from a client. It was not good, but I survived it and was not hurt. There was no way anyone could have known the woman was armed. Someone, however, should have noted I was missing in action and I was not happy about that. Nevertheless, I still loved my work and the population I had chosen to work with.

Soon after this incident and some months after Fred died, Mother came to visit us. By then, I was sober and doing well in my career. We were going out to dinner with her one evening, and I remember that I was ironing a dress that I was going to wear. I was in a room on the first floor and Gary was upstairs getting dressed. Suddenly, I felt a presence in the room and saw what looked like molecules moving about six feet tall in an oblong shape. I was not a very spiritual person at this time, but I was sure that it was my father, letting me know that he was proud of me for being sober and doing well in my career. An instant later, Gary called down the stairs, asking who was there. So, he felt a presence, too. That's when I knew that it was a real experience of a visit and I was sure it was from Fred. It was very powerful and totally unexpected and certainly unusual for me, as I had never thought such things really happened. Because Gary had been aware of something going on, I shared with him what I believed had just taken place, but I didn't tell others, as I had never believed people when they talked of such things. My mother was one person I did not tell, as I knew she would be a doubter. So, it became an experience private to me and Gary for some time to come.

SOME CHANGES

THE COUPLE WHO OWNED THE HOUSE that we were living in came back from Italy in 1978. A woman in recovery owned a house down the street and offered to rent it to us. It was a well-kept and attractive two-bedroom bungalow. I made one bedroom my office and put out the word that I was taking private practice clients and specialized in counseling for bipolar people. Several were referred to me from the University of Washington.

I stayed in touch with Maxine who by now was doing quite well. She was still playing in her trio, was regularly playing bridge with women friends and continued to be an avid reader and crossword puzzle addict. She also continued to do Huntley Drinkley each evening, though without anyone saying, "Now Maxie, I think you've had enough," Carolyn and Dick were not doing well. They had decided to move to Spokane. I never knew why Dick wanted to move, but knew Carolyn wanted to be near mother. They too were doing Huntley Drinkley each evening. Carolyn wanted to divorce, but my mother told her not to do it. Their relationship was still symbiotic. Carolyn often turned to our mother for advice she seldom took. She divorced Dick.

My own mental health was doing well. *I had responded well to lithium and I was now quite stable, and I was also convinced that my sobriety was another important part of my stability. It was important that I was totally aware that I needed medication and sobriety.* I knew that sobriety would not keep my mental health issues from raising their ugly head because serious mental health issues still need to be treated with medication. *Thankfully, the correct medication for bipolar disorder is not addictive, which is an important fact to know.* There are sometimes people in the program who advise newcomers to stop their meds as they think they are "mind altering." *People are bipolar because they have a bio-chemical imbalance and the medication addresses that. It also does not make people high.* Telling them to stop their medication is a dangerous thing to do, as I have known people who become psychotic again and I have known a few who became suicidal.. *Most importantly, a member of the Program who is not a doctor has no business interfering with someone's medical treatment.*

During this time, I went to Spokane to visit my mother. Afterward, I'd decided to come home a few hours earlier than planned, though, and came home to surprise Gary and his best friend in bed together. There was plenty to be upset about, though I was not really bothered by the gay activity as much as I was upset about the disloyalty involved. I had known that Gary had been bisexual prior to our getting together. He'd convinced me that he had not been actively gay since we got together and that they were only experimenting. So, I tucked the gay issue in the back of my head. What more was there to think about? This was a few years before AIDS became an issue.

So, Gary's sexual identity did become an issue, as if he was unhappy in our relationship I did not want to continue it. We had discussions in which he assured me he wanted to stay together. Things went well for another year and a half and I decided I wanted more official stability and Gary said he understood that. Gary and I got married in 1979. We found a judge near our house who married people, and so we gathered our very small wedding party and got an appointment. My old roommate was my witness, and Gary's was an old friend who was a woman pregnant at the time. I am sure the judge thought we were weird. The judge, of course, thought at first that she was the bride. But then again, he was a weird judge and did the ceremony in a kind of chanting fashion. We had a hard time trying not to laugh. Finally, it was a short but official ceremony, so that was good enough for us. Afterward, we went on a honeymoon to Cannon Beach in Oregon, which was lovely. In those days, we were getting along well enough and I did like the idea of having a stable relationship with an official mutual commitment.

On some level, though, I didn't think being married would change much in the relationship. As I look at it now, I realize that I somehow felt that to be married might mean that Gary would not cheat on me again, "experimenting" with his friend or anyone else. Although I was right that it didn't happen again, that mindset I'd had is what I call "magical thinking," and it was unlikely that just thinking something would make it true. As best as I know, Gary did no more experimenting with anyone. The fact was that if Gary wanted to be gay it would have been ok with me, and I would have stepped aside.

Also, in 1979, it became clear to me I should find another job. A union, SEIU, started to organize the clinic and, of course, I got involved. Even so, I knew that it was not a popular thing for me to do, and I felt that my time in my job was limited once again. Certainly, my alcohol history could not have been terribly helpful, either. So, I began looking for work elsewhere and found that the Mental Health Agency on Whidbey Island was looking for someone to start a day program for people with major mental health problems. This was right up my alley, so I applied and got it. That job, though, meant a move to the island, which was a big commitment. As I had always been the main breadwinner and Gary had never developed any real skills, he also faced a tough choice. We discussed the fact that the move would take him away from the Party, but still he agreed to it. It was a big decision, and, in retrospect, I don't think that I was terribly sensitive about it all.

By then, I was not going to many meetings; and, when I look back, I see the signs that I was becoming a "dry drunk." That is, without active involvement with recovery, without meetings and fellow alcoholics to relate to, and without a sponsor and doing service for others, one's behavior begins to revert to the unattractive, controlling, self-centered patterns from previous times. The decision to move to the island was controlling and selfish. I did need to work but certainly could have found work in Seattle. Moving to the island seemed exciting and adventurous to me, though, I think not to Gary, who was already somewhat depressed.

WHIDBEY ISLAND

THE ISLAND IS BEAUTIFUL and living there was an adventure. The clinic was in Coopeville, in the middle of the island, and we found a very cute little house near Langley on the South end. It was close enough to the clinic for a reasonable commute and also close to the ferry to get to Seattle.

At the end of the road where I turned onto the main highway, was a farm where they raised West Highland cattle. They are beautiful with long shaggy hair and look like a cattle-sized shaggy dog. I enjoyed seeing them every day. The drive up the island was pleasant, with farms and fields and forest. There were also some water views, and Coupeville was a pretty little town on the water at Penn Cove, well known for the muscles they raise and harvest there. Life was tranquil, and there was essentially no traffic on the island roads.

The house near Langley had a big yard where I would put a garden. There was a great fireplace and good kitchen. The house had been built about five years before and was in good condition, somewhat isolated, though, with few neighbors close by. The house was painted red and had red carpets and was essentially surrounded by woods on three sides. There were deer and rabbits who would have to be dealt with when I built a garden. We still had Rhubarb II, who was still a snarky little guy. He was good with us, and he and Gary would walk the woods almost daily.

The town of Langley was quite special, in my opinion. It was on the water and had little shops for the tourists, some good restaurants, and, my favorite, a general store that had a wide variety of things from groceries to hardware to clothing. There were bins of bulk foods like flour and granola, and nuts, not often found in Seattle at the time. I always found it a treat to shop there. There were also some very good craftsmen and artists who sold their work out of little shops, and also quite a few hippie types.

We were viewed as newcomers by the Islanders, those who had been there for many years or even born there. You had to earn your place, and my co-workers and I were not only new comers, we were mental health people, especially viewed with suspicion. No one came to our door with a freshly baked pie of welcome.

On the other hand, the staff at the clinic were welcoming and appreciated the fact that I was starting the program. In addition, I did individual counseling and was a county- designated mental health professional, meaning that I evaluated people for commitment. On Whidbey, there was a person who had done that work for a long time who trained me. It wasn't rocket science, but it did involve knowing the commitment laws and diagnoses, including having a sense if a person might be dangerous to self or others. Doing that work meant that I was on call a bit, though, fortunately, there were three of us who rotated doing this.

The major part of my work was at the clinic. I have always loved developing programs and was not short on knowing what to do. I hired a good staff who liked working with our population and were willing to actively participate in activities with the clients.

In this work, though, the island presented a few unusual circumstances. One issue was the fact that commitment calls often involved finding the subject in the woods somewhere. We usually knew the person we were looking for as the Island is a small community and the mental health community smaller. If we knew the client, the older MHP was a nurse and would bring a loaded syringe with her. She always asked them to let her give them the shot and they most often agreed. They usually knew it helped to calm them. If they did not agree, of course, she did not give it to them.

Another difference was that the police often went with us in order to bring the client to the hospital when they would not cooperate. When I first arrived, there were a few times they would enter the house ahead of me with guns drawn. This was most often unnecessary and only scared the client (and me). So, we began to work with them to better understand what to expect from clients in crisis and how this was not needed. It was evident they appreciated our suggestions and were cooperative. We began to work more closely with them, and things got much better.

There were other limitations, too. For instance, the hospital in Coupeville didn't have a psychiatric ward, but it did have a room that was padded where we could hospitalize patients for a few days until they were more stable. How they came up with the padded room I don't know, and I wasn't ever sure it was that good of an idea. It was big and empty and not exactly what I would consider calming.

Another thing that was special about the island was a particular field near Coopeville that was full of "magic" mushrooms. When it was in bloom, the number of patients attending the program diminished for a time. We always knew when the field was blooming.

In the meantime, Gary was having a hard time. In 1979 there was a recession and many small businesses on the island closed. This phenomenon was frustrating to us personally because Gary would get a job, and then where he was working would close. This happened three times in the first six months that we were there. That lack of stability certainly was difficult for Gary.

Also, by this time Gary had officially left the Party, and we were no longer under discipline, which meant that we could smoke pot, which we did very quietly and privately. I did not connect it to my sobriety. When we first arrived on the Island, I found a meeting close to our house and went to meetings once a week. It was hard because I was used to Seattle meetings and they did them a little differently on the Island. I thought it would be good to share with them how we did things in Seattle which absolutely did not go over well. So, I didn't do that again. Soon after we'd arrived, I stopped going to many meetings, as I was feeling like my life was full and was going well. This is a big mistake that too many people make, and it often leads to drinking again. In my case, I didn't drink; I just used pot. I had no trouble not drinking, but I was missing a lot about recovery.

I wasn't the only one with a problem. Soon, I realized that Gary was smoking daily while I was gone to work. He would walk the dog in the woods and be a house husband. Now, I'm not great with cooking, so I liked the house husband thing, as it was nice to have dinner waiting for me in the evenings, plus, he did a good job of keeping up the house. At first, I wasn't concerned with how he spent his time, but as time went on, I began to realize that he was getting more and more depressed. He didn't complain, but he also did not get out often to look for work. Most of all, he wasn't that happy; and, because I was basically self-centered, it took a while for me to recognize how miserable he was. I was happy with my work and liked the island. At that time, too, I was doing fine with my mental health. Clearly, I had become more stable with sobriety, and I felt good, with barely detectable mood swings; and when I did have a little depression, a small dose of an anti-psychotic like trilafon for a short time got me back on track. For Gary, though, things weren't going as well; I just didn't see it as soon as I should have.

One of my co-workers and her partner raised Golden Retrievers. They had just had puppies about three months before. One puppy was left, and they were thinking of taking him to a pet store. I wanted to do something for Gary for his birthday and said that I would like to see him. He was lovely, so I bought him, and Gary loved him. We named him Zackery. He was a great puppy, got along well with Rhubarb, and fit right into our family. So, Gary had a puppy to raise.

Time went on, and work went well. The day program was growing, and the staff were getting seasoned and doing a good job. One of the best staff members had a baby and was going to stay home but wanted to keep working. So, I saw no reason for her not to bring the baby to work. We had enough room to keep the baby in the staff room and there was most often someone not with the clients who could keep an eye on things. So, the baby joined us, and the administration went along with it. I began to feel a little maternal, so I took baby shifts now and then and actually enjoyed it, though I became very aware that I was not that comfortable because I had never been around babies. I never changed diapers but rocked and sang to the baby and even would sing some of the revolutionary songs that I knew.

I decided that I wanted to grow a garden and took a class that covered things to know about doing it on the island. So, I learned how to "double dig" to form raised beds, what to do to keep the deer and rabbits out. For deer, it was important to get someone to pee around the perimeter of the garden, and for rabbits, we put four feet of wire fencing and buried a good foot with the rest on top of the ground. I also learned what grew best on the island. My garden had both vegetables and flowers. It was a great hobby and I remembered Uncle Kip and his gardening. On May 19, 1980 I was in the garden and felt like I had suddenly been pushed by something. I went inside to tell Gary about it, and he told me that Mt. St. Helens had just blown. That was what pushed me, and it seemed very strange that I felt it from there, though I met others who were outside and felt it too.

By this time, I was watching Gary and clearly saw he was not happy. I knew he needed to be in Seattle, so I decided to commute. After a year on the island, we moved back to Seattle, to the north part of the city, which helped with my commute. The place we lived, though, was not an attractive house; it was pretty much a big box divided into unimaginative rooms.

But, we were back in the city, so Gary could go back into the SWP. He stopped doing pot, then, and I did too. That was fine with me, and I didn't really miss it. Gary got a job at a cable company, and it appeared to go well. He made friends there and clearly appreciated being off the island. I was glad that I figured that out but kind of missed the island myself. Things seemed simpler there, and I missed my garden. So, I put in a small one at the new house. We fenced the back yard for the dogs and walked them on a beach on the Sound near the house.

Zackary could really run. He did not retrieve, though we tried to teach him. After a while, we gave up and called him a Golden Receiver. He was a very dear dog, loving and wanting to please. He and Rhubarb II got along well. The walks were good for them as well as us and were very pleasant. Things were going well between us.

My commute was forty minutes on the ferry and another fifteen to twenty minutes up to Coupeville. I learned quickly to use the ferry ride for reading or writing and relaxing. The drive up the island was lovely, so I made the best of it. The only problem I had with the commute was that one day as I passed by the farm with the West Highland cattle, there was one hanging by the side of the road waiting to be butchered. I was sad, but I realized that it was a reality of farming. Still, for several years after that, it was hard to eat red meat.

The program at the clinic was going well, and I decided to use an idea from a program that had originated in New York City that was built around a vocational theme. We put together a used book store. The idea was for the clients to do the work with guidance from staff. The hardest part was to keep staff from taking over, though we did our best. Together with the clients, we built shelves and got a desk for the front of the store for ringing up sales and answering questions.

The clients participated in getting word out to the community that we needed books donated. We put an ad in the Whidbey paper, made and posted flyers around town and solicited staff to donate old books. It soon started working. People would come in and purchase books and then bring them back as donations after they read them and purchase more.

The clients were very proud of what we had done. We needed to keep some therapy groups and some counseling going and had room for that separate from the book store. We also had a lunch room and kitchen that had always been there, so we did serve a simple lunch that we prepared with the clients. I was very happy and saw clients learn to function in the environment of clearly productive activity.

Some of the administration did not get it, though, and wanted us to make a profit. Our profit was small as we would put some of it back in to help cover the food and the few other supplies we needed for the store. I had to defend it frequently, which began to wear on me. The program still brought in fees for client treatment, so that was nothing different regarding income. I fought that good fight for a while, staying at the clinic for a total of three years.

A while after I left, I heard that the bookstore was closed, which of course made me sad. We had established an environment in which our patients could experience productivity with some pride in their part in a real work place. I had watched them grow individually, learning to cooperate and working together with others to achieve common goals. It made me angry to see others could not appreciate the value of allowing the clients to explore their own talents and skills and put them into practice.

BACK TO SEATTLE AND GROUP HOMES

AFTER NEARLY TWO YEARS OF IT, THOUGH, I got tired of the commute; and, in 1982, I found a new job running two group homes in Seattle. As I got started at the houses, I asked a psychiatrist whom I'd known over the years to consult with me and the staff regarding diagnosis and medications. He was a real character, and at times would challenge me on my knowledge about medications. At the same time, he was fun to work with, and I was likewise confident in his abilities as a prescribing psychiatrist. One of the houses specialized in serving veterans, and the other had a mixed population. Both were small, though, and only served around fifteen people, so it was manageable. Moreover, most of them had been in the mental health system for years, so they knew the system. Some went to community mental health centers or the VA for treatment programs. Bedrooms were shared and the lack of privacy and the fact that this population does not always get along with each other was an issue, and I felt private space was seriously missing for the residents.

Whatever their mental health background, people end up at group homes for various reasons. In our case, many of the people were there due to problems with taking meds. A nurse on staff for both houses gave out the medications, and we monitored people to make sure they took them. We also had several activities at the houses in which staff participated and assisted when needed. All told, they were a good staff, and I worked closely with them to make sure that ours was a good place to work.

So, I did my best for others, though that job was not always a good place for me to work, as they were privately owned by people who were in the business to make money, and the budget was not geared toward good client care. The food budget meant a lot of carbohydrates. I did draw the line when I saw "tater tot casserole" on the menu. It was starch and fat only and served alone. I seldom intervened with the cook as detected it was clearly not a good idea, and some of the residents liked it, of course. But I pulled it.

By that time, Gary was doing a bit better about working. Going back into the SWP and becoming active again had helped a lot. Within a short period of time, he began to be happier, partly due to the anti-depressants which he had begun taking. They clearly made a difference. Moreover, he'd gotten a job at a cable company, and that helped financially. We were getting along fairly well at that time, and he remained very supportive of my sobriety. I did not go to recovery meetings regularly but went now and then, especially if I had a "drinking dream." That is one in which you break your sobriety and wake up thinking you had. It is a very real feeling. When the cobwebs clear, you realize that it was just a dream and probably a signal to get to some meetings.

Even though I went to meetings, I did not have a home group or a sponsor. Nor did I have a Higher Power, as Trotskyists don't. In retrospect, I was quite controlling in our relationship, though was not all that aware of it at the time. I wanted to have my own way about most things. I was fast becoming a "Dry Drunk."

After some time, the SWP moved its headquarters to the south end of Seattle to Columbia City. So, we found a house nearby and moved from our house in the north end. The new house was old and had mold on the walls. Apparently, there was a stream running under the house which was the guess of one of the neighbors who also had mold. We did what we called mold patrol, to go around the house with Clorox and water, wiping down the walls every two weeks. That helped a little, but the house was quite old and damp, and my asthma was on the increase.

Still, we tried to make that place a home. I fixed it up as best I could, making blinds and putting down some Chinese rugs that I'd gotten from my mother. We also had two cats from the same litter. They were part Siamese, and the female looked it, while the male was pure black. Rhubarb II and Zachery got along with them. The house was often cold, and the cats would sleep on the hot water heater. I couldn't blame them. That house was underwhelming to say the least, but I wasn't earning enough at the time to pay for the oil for the furnace. So, my mother loaned us enough to fill the tank, and we made ends meet after that because, thankfully, Gary was working again. Indeed, I had gotten tired of the financial pressure of being the only breadwinner.

We'd lived in that house for just a few months when the black cat got very sick. The vet said he would put him down, but I thought he would probably do better at home. So, I took him home and sat with him on my lap watching TV for many hours. Coincidently, I had agreed to have a "medication vacation" for two weeks. This was something they were doing at the time to "clear your system." I had been skeptical about doing it but went along with it. I have not heard of them asking patients to do that anymore.

Then the news came on, and I heard that Maurice Bishop, the leader of the Granada revolution, had been assassinated by the Stalinists. My cat died on my lap an hour later, and I will never take an animal that needs to be put down home to die again. I called Dr. Ward and said that I was going back on my medication. I had been a fan of Maurice Bishop, as he was a humane and caring leader, as I understood it, and my decision about the cat was a bad one, so yes, system clearing be damned.

I worked a year with the Group Homes and decided that I could not or would not continue, as I had conflicting feelings about how they were being run mostly for profit, with poor attention to the needs of the residents. So, instead, in 1983 I found a job at Eastside Mental Health in Bellevue.

EASTSIDE MENTAL HEALTH

IT WAS GOOD TO BE BACK WORKING where clinical issues were important. My job included working in a program for mentally ill with physical disabilities. I had a good supervisor who was a very nice boss, and I worked with a psychiatrist who knew a lot about our particular population. Once again, I was able to utilize my training in medical issues and found the job was a good fit for an Occupational Therapist. Through that time, I learned a lot and felt good about my contributions. We saw people in counseling at the clinic and helped run a residential program that was an apartment building with staff. Some of the clients were developmentally delayed, as well as having physical and mental health issues.

I had worked at Eastside for a little over a year, when our supervisor returned from a conference in New York City. When he returned to Seattle, he was diagnosed with HIV. That was in 1984 and was early in the epidemic. Medication was not very effective yet, and his condition converted quickly to AIDS; and he died within six months. It was a huge loss for all of us, and his partner kindly offered a number of things to the staff to remember him by. I took some day lilies that I still have in my gardens, to remind me of him, the first person whom I'd known fairly well who died of AIDS. Sadly, though, there were to be many more.

TWO GROUP HOMES

AFTER SOME TIME, THE MAN WHO HAD HIRED ME for the group homes contacted me to ask me to come back to work for him managing two large group homes in Auburn. He was offering me good money, and it was clear that he appreciated my work. Moreover, in order to ensure that I would be able to focus on the work instead of the business side of things, he assured me that he would be involved as a liaison with the owners, so I accepted the job.

By that time, Gary was not working again, and I didn't want another long commute, so we found a house in Sumner, near the group homes. It was clean and dry and warm, though otherwise was a very uninteresting rectangular box, and we suspected it was one that was a prefabricated house. It was a beautiful area, though, which helped make up for the house. As I drove home from work, I went up a long hill with Mt. Rainier looming up in front of me.

I attended some recovery meetings in the area which were good with devoted people who also had several social events. But as I got more involved at work my attendance dwindled and eventually ended.

The group homes were almost worse than the previous ones, so I had to commit to a lot of work training the staff. They did well but had little previous experience working with the severely mentally ill. The support of my boss was helpful, though there were some things that did not come to his attention in time to avoid some big problems mostly related to budget. The worst was with the upkeep of the facility. Sometimes, we had to take drastic action to protect the well-being of the residents.

From time to time, there were soiled mattresses that we would burn in a field along with a phone call to the owners that we needed new ones immediately as the County was due to come make their regular inspections. The mattresses were replaced immediately, though, so that we'd be in a position to pass the frequent inspections that we were subject to. Most often the inspectors were not really expected but it got the mattresses replaced quickly.

Sometimes, the problems were beyond our ability to remedy such as holes in walls that emitted an unpleasant smell due to rot inside the walls. There were several times the County did come to inspect. They would insist such things that presented health hazards be repaired, and they usually were bad enough that they got repaired fairly soon, but the County did little more than note the problems. As it is still true today, there was a shortage of beds for the mentally ill, so they were reticent to close any down.

One day someone dumped a puppy on the front lawn of one of the houses. I thought it would be great to have a house dog. It did not last long, though, as he "soiled" one of the resident's rooms, and she had a fit, rightfully so. Instead, I took him home to train him. Rhubarb II had grown old and had a stoke that he had survived at first, though he was disabled, and we'd put him down. So, there was room at our house. We named the little new one Chartley after the Group Home. He trained fairly quickly, but the staff and I decided that he should stay with us. He grew to be a funny looking dog with essentially no confirmation. He was like a big walking lump and not real smart, but we loved him anyway.

We had problems with drug dealers preying on the residents taking stereos and other saleable items as payment. Street drugs did interfere with treatment and presented a serious threat to the residents, so we went to the local police and the drug dealers disappeared.

After two years of things only slightly improving, I left again, getting another a job with a Community Mental Health Center. As a parting gesture, I called the local TV station, who did special programs exposing bad situations in the area. I told my new job about what I had done, and they were neutral about it, only saying so in guarded terms, and told me not to appear on TV. I didn't, but I very much enjoyed watching the airing of the program that was put on the air a few weeks later. The reporters honored my request not to mention my name or photograph me. This was back in 1986, and it would be fifteen more years before the group home was closed by the county.

At this point, Gary got a job in a residential care facility that treated adults with major mental illness who also had need for care for various physical health issues. His job was to run the activities program. My impression was that he was doing well and liked it. A few months in, the administration asked him to raise money for supplies for his program by having a car wash with patients doing the work. Gary felt this was exploitive of the patients and quit. This would be a pattern with several jobs during this period of time.

HIGHLINE WEST SEATTLE MENTAL HEALTH

MY NEW JOB WAS A TURNING POINT IN MY CAREER. It was with an agency that participated in a national research program on "intensive case management" with adult chronic patients. The program had originated in Wisconsin and was quite successful with good outcomes. The clients did better at living in the community and tended to clearly improve their quality of life. There was better medication compliance with more frequent contacts and help from the case managers and at times, a few rescues from scrapes within the community. The amount of contact with clients was significantly more than it was with other approaches.

I liked the supervisor of the program and the staff. I had done similar work at Bellevue Hospital in New York, where I'd work with the patient in the community to facilitate a successful return home post discharge. In my new job, we went to the patients in the community to promote success living as independently as possible. We monitored their medications, helped them when necessary to deal with daily life and guided them in what they needed to know about basic daily living skills. As we did this, we built relationships with them, and soon I realized that this was the most effective approach for this population that I had seen.

In the meantime, we moved back to Seattle. I went house hunting and came upon a cute little house in the south end near Seward Park and Columbia City, which would be close to the SWP office for Gary. He was active again and happy. We went together to see the house and decided to rent it. It was on top of the hill from Seward Park, a wonderful park which is an old growth forest on a peninsula into Lake Washington. It was great for walking the dogs. It was also close to an entrance to the freeway for my commute.

By then, it was 1987, and I had decided to begin a master's program in Public Administration at Seattle University. The program was friendly to people who were working full time. I enjoyed being in an academic environment and did well.

OPENING THE AGENCY, BUYING A HOUSE

ALONGSIDE MY STUDIES, I STAYED at the Case Management program for two years and learned a great deal. One of the guardians for two of my clients got to know me and encouraged me to develop a private program, as he felt that my work was good, and by now I had some ideas about how to do that work better if it was private pay and not tied to government funding, which limited the intensity of treatment. I also believed that this type of program should be more open to work with families, which the public programs did very little about and I thought were missing an important piece of treatment. It is very difficult to have a mentally ill person in the family, and support and consultation would be very helpful. I also had some opinions about how staff were an important asset and how I could deal with that. So, I opened my own agency on September 1, 1988. I'd had to quit the master's program to focus on the agency, but it was worth it.

Indeed, it was an all-encompassing project. Gary helped, too, especially because he wasn't working at the time, so he became the office manager. That, however, turned out not to be the best idea, as we had disagreements on how to run the agency. He seemed not to have enough experience to do the job, and we were both unhappy, so he suggested that he be a house husband again, and I agreed—a decision that led us both to being happier.

Also, in 1988, the owners of the house that we were renting let us know that they were selling the house. I knew that the major things in the house worked well, and it had a double lot. I asked how much they wanted for it, and they said $55,000, so I said I'd buy it. And, just like that, we became home owners! We did not know a lot about buying a house, and it's possible that we paid too much for it and indeed we were caught short, as didn't know about closing costs. So, we had to borrow that portion of the money from Gary's father.

Once the house was ours, we began looking at what we might do to make it better, including putting in a gas furnace and all of the rest we kept dreaming about. That house was big enough for the two of us and the dogs and the cat, and it was a good feeling to own it and not have to rent or move again. In thirty years, I have never moved again, and I have never regretted that decision. Slowly, we began to do things to make the house more livable and to improve its value.

In retrospect, by now, with no recovery program, I had become quite controlling when it came to the agency and probably things at home too. For instance, I remember that we decided to get a new couch, and Gary asked if he could pick it out "for a change." I felt a little ashamed of myself and that he cared enough about not making many decisions that he brought it up, so I backed off. It wasn't easy, and no doubt not too successful, but I did try. I wasn't fond of the couch that he picked but accepted it and kept quiet.

So, over time, the house husband thing wore itself out, as I was tired of being the only one earning the income; and, after a number of months, I asked Gary to get a job. I was working very hard getting the agency going and building the case load, carrying my own case load as well, and I was getting worn down.

ABOUT THE AGENCY

THE CASELOADS VARIED, AS SOME came in new and others left. It was not going to work to have people on salaries as when caseloads were low so was income.

So, I began doing revenue share. The clinicians get one third of what they bring in, which greatly stabilized things and fairly soon it meant staff could make more money than at other agencies. It was also good incentive to do good work and do better at keeping clients.

Our staff needed to be comfortable with being fairly independent in their work, as they set their own schedules that were compatible for the clients as well as them. We invited families to participate as part of the treatment team, and clients were asked to sign releases so that we could talk to the families about their care and advocate for clients in the family setting. We did, of course, keep confidentiality, though, regarding clients' therapy issues and let clients know when we felt it would be good to talk to family members and respected their wishes about this. We established our own crises line that was available to families and significant others. Staff rotated on call, for which they were paid, and we also charged for travel time and mileage, as it is part of the work.

So, I was making an effort to create a fair and positive place to work, and also to maintain a strong team dynamic. Twice each month, we had clinical staff meetings with discussions of approaches and peer consultation. Staff have always supported each other and work as a team. My training as an Occupational Therapist has impacted the work we do, and we were never hesitant to "do things" with the clients. The population we serve tend to feel more comfortable talking about things while walking or having coffee or having a picnic on a beach somewhere.

Over the years, we have worked with many clients, and I could tell many stories, but that is not what this writing is about. They all are important to us, and most of them have improved under our care. At the very least, their quality of life does, perhaps because of this their symptoms decrease, and they do better living where they are in the community either independently or in supervised settings. Because of this the stresses of running the agency have always seemed worth it.

Along the way, we also watch for side effects and the effectiveness of their medications and work with their doctors around these issues. We listen to them and consult families or significant others about what had been helpful or meaningful in the past and recognize the fact that most patients need stimulation beyond what they are getting and take them on outings and/or do activities with them where they live. Moreover, as we work with them, therapeutic relationships develop between us and the client, which spurs motivation to listen to our suggestions and follow through.

About a year after I opened the agency, the clinic where I had worked before closed my former program. Having finished the original grant, the organizers didn't feel that the program brought in enough of a profit. Moreover, their mandate was no longer for private pay clients. So, I got a call from the staff who had been laid off, asking if they could come and bring their clients, for a total of two staff and fifteen clients. I knew most all of the clients and having the sudden change would be a challenge but was ultimately good for us, so I agreed.

So, the agency was coming right along. The offices of the Guardian who had mentored me to open the agency moved to another building, and we moved to their office space, which was larger and was in the same building, located on Broadway on Capitol Hill. This office was not ideal, as was separated into partitions rather than closed rooms. The majority of clients have always been seen in the community, but when we needed to meet with someone in the office, it was a problem.

About this time, we changed the agency name from Case Management Services to Affiliated Mental Health Programs. We were beginning to do more counseling and family work, so it was no longer only case management. I managed to maintain the basic principles, though, for which I had originally opened the agency: providing a supportive environment for the staff, providing quality treatment, and including families in the treatment team.

And things just kept rolling along. A year later, a real estate agent from the Group Health Credit Union came to see me. They were remodeling the second floor of their building on 15th on Capitol Hill. Due to the economic recession, tenants were hard to find. The rent was reasonable for the space that we would have, and the location was excellent, so I went for it. Moreover, they let me work with their architect to design the space itself, which was a great opportunity overall.

That new office space, though, was actually larger than we really needed, so I leased two large offices to a chemical dependency outpatient program, which worked well and helped greatly with supplementing the rent. The owner of the program, Chuck, was a character, and I enjoyed having him around. Even better, we had plenty of things in common because he was also in the recovery program. At the time, he was riding high, having his own agency and doing quite well in business and in life. Sadly, though, his run of luck didn't last forever, as, several years later, he had trouble with his business partner, and he closed his agency. After that, I didn't see him for some years, though about four years ago he showed up in a meeting of the program, and he had changed, having lived in Mexico for a number of years. During that time, he'd left the program for a while, and he'd had some difficult times. Now, he was back in the program, and I found it good to see him. He seemed to be doing well again. To this day, he brings wisdom to the meetings and is an example of how sobriety gets us through troubled times. I am quite fond of him and enjoy knowing him again. We both have changed, and it is interesting to see how we have both grown in sobriety.

The office was convenient to the freeways and to the greater Seattle Area. We were in the Group Health space for the next sixteen years, during which the case load grew, along with the staff.

In looking back, there were times that the stress of the agency took its toll on me, though I always made it through. It had been a good idea, was working and providing good care and it became my baby. And, like all children, it could, sometimes, be a financial drain. There were challenging moments, but I managed to keep the doors open. The other difficulties from time to time was it was sometimes hard to evaluate potential staff as in interviews people are always on their best behavior. I began to get other staff to sit in on interviews, so I had several opinions. This was indeed helpful.

CAROLYN AND ALCOHOL

By now, my sister had been drinking alcoholically for many years. When I visited Spokane several times each year, I witnessed unquestionable incidents of her being obviously rude with others, especially those who were not in a position to retaliate, like clerks and other people who she felt were not providing the service as she wanted. Her drinking was taking a toll, and she was laid off work due to "being too frail." I suspected they were aware of her alcoholism. They just did not address it openly.

It was also true, though, that she was frail due to her obsession with being overweight. Moreover, she had developed serious digestive problems and claimed that she wasn't digesting food and that she had developed new food allergies. This was no doubt exacerbated by her drinking, and I also knew that she was anorexic because she would look in the mirror and talk about having a fat stomach, even though she was 5' 6" and weighed less than 100 pounds. By then, my sister was a very sick person indeed. She'd found a doctor who prescribed her anti-anxiety medications that did not mix well with alcohol—in fact the combination was dangerous. But, her son Fred didn't know what to do, and anything I said to her was summarily dismissed.

Since not working, Carolyn was spending more time with Maxine, although their relationship was not a healthy one. It still happened that Carolyn would ask our mother for advice and then find reasons not to take it. This wore on Maxine, who could be quite cruel. For instance, Carolyn reported to me that she had told our mother the she loved her, and our mother's response was, "Don't ever say that to me again."

It seemed to me that Carolyn would increase her efforts to get our mother's approval, which just did not come. All the same, I was careful not to get involved. Gradually with no job Carolyn began to drink more often. I had concerns, but there was nothing to do. I made an attempt at an intervention, but she was drunker than I realized, and it only made her angry. So, my visits became more infrequent.

The one thing I could do was stay in touch by phone. Clearly, Carolyn wasn't comfortable with my physical presence, but she would answer my calls. I began to call her about every ten days as I suspected that, aside from her son, few if any other people were calling her and she was lonely.

The calls themselves weren't pleasant, as she would do what I called "throw zingers", or insults. As best I could, I just didn't respond. Apparently, my sister began sleeping during the day and staying up in the night. She was also a Fox News devotee, and I knew that it would be trouble if I disagreed with her politically, so I suggested that we not talk about it. If politics did come up, I would remind her of our agreement.

Usually, her response was, "Well, you brought it up."

And, I did my best not to argue, but would rather just change the subject. It would have been the Fox News versus the old Trotskyist which could only be a disaster.

COMMUNITY SERVICE

BEFORE DIVORCING GARY, I HAD BECOME very involved with work and was also doing community service around mental health. Over the next years, I served on several committees and boards advocating for the mentally ill and with other disabilities. I became the chairman for an ADA committee with King County, which advocated for the disabled, for which we encouraged people with disabilities to be on the committee. I got to know several people with closed head injuries and learned a good deal from them on how difficult life could be having something that was not visible to others but was quite debilitating. This committee was advisory to the King County Executive and eventually participated in the formation of the Civil Rights Commission for King County, so I became a County Commissioner.

I also joined a committee that advocated for the mentally ill with the King County Mental Health Council and had the pleasure of working as co-chair with the woman who had helped develop NAMI (National Alliance on Mental Illness), both nationally and in the state of Washington. I also served a term on the Eastside NAMI Board. All told, these activities were quite satisfying, though sadly, at home, things were not.

TENSION AT HOME

ALTHOUGH GARY WAS SUPPORTIVE OF MY SOBRIETY, he continued complaining about how often I was not home because of my time with work and related activities in the community. Despite his complaints, though, I wasn't willing to give anything up. So, there began to be tensions between us. Perhaps, I thought, we just needed to try doing something together and an opportunity arose when Gary and I were both invited to join a group that studied Ikebana (Japanese flower arranging). I really wanted to do it, but Gary was not pleased, so I declined, as I thought it might be the last straw.

Compromises or no, by 1992, Gary and I were not doing well. He continued having difficulty finding work or keeping jobs, and he would get angry about the "ethics" of the people he worked for and would act about it either by quitting or getting fired. For instance, he was working at Starbucks in the roasting plant when he got involved in organizing a union which failed, and he got fired. It was a good evening if when I got home from work and he still had a job.

This became a big point of tension, and we went for counseling. The therapist asked what traits in the other one bothered us the most.

I answered, "Gary not working."

And Gary said, "She swallows loud."

I realized that this was not going to go anywhere, and the issue of his employment was not solvable. He was getting angrier, so I asked him to go to his own therapist. I also arranged for a safe place to go, in the event that his anger got any worse; and I began to realize that this is what happens when you marry a revolutionary who has not developed any work skills and becomes frustrated. I also wondered if he was in the closet and needed to be free to be gay. When I asked him about it, though, he adamantly denied it. So, what could I do? I decided to give the relationship time.

All the same, I remember thinking about what it would be like with him gone. Could I be ok cooking for myself? Would I be able to fix things around the house? Could I find time to walk the dogs? Would our mutual friends stick around? And then I realized that I was just trying to avoid what I needed to do.

So, in 1995, I went to a lawyer and filed for divorce. I'd found the lawyer through a friend who'd used him for her 7th divorce. He was a bit strange and arranged divorces with a judge in another county for only $150. But, I made sure that his work was legitimate, and it was. The only stipulation was that it could not be contested, and I knew ours would not be. There was little to contest.

So, I moved enough clothes to last me awhile, left a letter letting Gary know that he could stay in the house for a month to have time to get things together, and I moved in with Rita and Joan for the month. I told him where I would be but asked him please not to try to come to see me. He tried only once, and when he called to say that he was coming, Rita told him not to come as she had her shotgun resting on the mantel in the living room. Even though that wasn't true, he didn't try to come over again. Sadly, during that month, I truly forgot that the day I'd left was the 20th anniversary of our being together. I did feel bad when I realized that. It was indicative of how I had already left the relationship.

When the month was up, I moved back into the house, as Gary had moved back in with his parents for a time. His mother called me and asked if I would take him back, but I declined, Once I'd returned to the house, I thoroughly enjoyed being there alone. I had the two dogs and my cat Jerome, a black and white fellow who looked to be wearing a tuxedo. Gary and I were able to stay in touch and I agreed that he could have a key to the house so that he could walk the dogs. A number of months later, I discovered, though, that he was going through my things, so I took the key back and changed the lock. I was proud of myself, as I had been concerned about whether I'd be able to do those kinds of tasks around the house. Five months after I'd moved back into the house, Gary came out as gay. I was glad that he was free to do that.

Not everyone's response to the divorce, though, was what I expected. When I called my mother to tell her I was divorcing Gary, for instance, there was a silence on the line.

Then she asked me, "Did you stop your Lithium?"

I answered, "No."

She had experienced the aftermath of two episodes, and I knew that this kind of reaction was typical of families who have been through that.

Then she asked, "Have you become a lesbian?"

And I told her, "No."

That second question surprised me, not only because I had given thought to that at the height of the feminist movement, and it was clear that I was not a lesbian. Even so, my sister had come up with a number of weird accusations about me, so I expected that she had come up with that and told mother. I would hear about it later, so when it came up again from her directly, I knew that it had come from her back then.

IKEBANA (JAPANESE FLOWER ARRANGING)

AFTER THE DIVORCE IN 1995, one of the first things that I added to my life was Ikebana. It has become an important part of my routine and has been very good way for me to develop an artistic skill. *As a bipolar person, I find it important to have creative outlets.* I have continued to study it to this day.

In Japan, for centuries, flower arranging, and the tea ceremony were believed to be and remain important in the development of character and good etiquette. In Japan, women and men study and become proficient in these arts. Ikebana is taught to girls in secondary and higher schools.

Early flower arranging came to Japan from China during the reign of Shotoku from 573 -621 A.D., with the introduction of Buddhism. It was from this time and over several subsequent centuries that traditions for flower arranging were established. Over time, flower arranging came into home decoration in addition to its original use in homage to Buddha.

In modern times there are many schools of Ikebana, although all of them follow the established principles and traditions of flower arranging. The school of Ikebana that I belong to is the Senke School. In the mid-1500s, a priest and famous tea master, Sen no Rikkyu, made the first and important improvements in Ikebana that formed the basis of the Senke School. Up to that point, the containers used for Ikebana were elaborate and made of expensive materials like bronze, which made the art available to only the wealthy. In keeping with the aesthetics of tea ceremony, Sen no Rikkyu began using flower containers made of rustic materials like sections of tree bamboo. This meant that others, like the merchant class, in addition to the wealthy, began to do flower arranging.

Senke is one of the more traditional schools, with a very specific structure used for arrangements in the classical style. We also do contemporary style arrangements that retain the clean lines of the classical form while allowing for the artist's spontaneous response to the floral material. By now, I feel confident in my ability to improve my skills, and I participate in shows and have gotten to know my teacher, who is a lovely and interesting person, as is her husband. I have become appreciative of how developing skill in an art form can enrich life significantly. Accomplishing further abilities by inventing something unique that is still consistent with the principles of traditional Japanese flower arranging, is very rewarding. Every now and then, my teacher and I will do an arrangement together that maintains the basic forms but are a little inventive. I now have a certificate for "Instructor," and I am qualified to teach. Happily, in all of these ways, Ikebana has become a regular part of my life.

AIDS AND MENTAL HEALTH

IN THE EARLY 1990'S, I BECAME INVOLVED in mental health treatment for people with AIDS, as there were few resources for them elsewhere. This work began because I had worked with a client who was the first mentally ill AIDS patient to be hospitalized at Harborview. Working with a group of social workers at the hospital, we decided to form a coalition to advocate for the mentally ill with AIDS. At this time, there were few doctors who were willing to take AIDS patients. What would it be like to find medical treatment for the mentally ill with AIDS? My staff often accompany our clients to doctor's appointments as some doctors and/or their staff were uncomfortable with them.

I offered pro bono treatment at the agency for the AIDS clients, which meant that I did most of the work, as could not ask my staff to provide free services. Within a year and a half, though, a public clinic was opened for the mentally ill with AIDS, so there was no need to continue this work.

We began to realize that there was a great need to do AIDS prevention work with the mental health community. I thought about how to do this. Many of them watched TV all day so a video was not going to catch their attention. Lectures were not going to do it. Eventually I decided a way to get and hold their attention to a scary subject was to develop a program that presented live plays on the subject. I knew that live plays held my attention and would most often be a new experience for the clients, so I began to develop what would become "The AIDS Prevention Theatre Troupe."

Our organization needed to be a non-profit so that we could accept contributions. So, I buckled my seat belt and learned how to establish a 501c3 organization, consulting a lawyer for the legal issues but doing the rest on my own. What I learned was that it would be best to avoid doing this in the future unless it was absolutely necessary. It was a tedious task. Finding funding was not going to be easy, but I was determined. The mentally ill were a disenfranchised population, and the topic was one the general public still preferred to ignore. Some people didn't think that the mentally ill had sex, but that perception is very wrong. Not only that, but it was not unheard of that they were sometimes easy targets for molestation.

So, I began to look around for a philanthropic organization that might be appropriate to approach for funding. Coincidently, I happened to be looking for a new insurance company for my malpractice insurance. One competitor was Aetna. As part of their sales pitch, they talked about all the philanthropic projects they funded, so I seized the opportunity to tell them about the theater troupe that I was starting, and they responded by giving a grant to support it. I could now hire actors and a playwright and director. And yes, I did use Aetna for the insurance.

The first play, *The Story of Bruce*, was written by the cast and, with the permission of his parents, was based on the story of my patient who had been hospitalized about a year before. He had died soon after that hospitalization. We developed portable sets that we could use to take the plays to the clients in group homes and treatment programs and into hospitals.

We also heard that Canada was having an AIDS Week, and we applied to participate. We were accepted, so we went to Vancouver and performed the play five times over the weekend. It was an exhausting but good experience, and we did well.

I did not often go out with the troupe but on one occasion I did. It was to the institution where Bruce had gone after the hospital and served mentally ill individuals with physical illness. The troupe began the play, and a few minutes into it, a young woman in the audience got up and joined the actors. They were on top of it, and with some extremely talented improvisation brought her into the play. I was so glad I had gone that time. It was amazing.

Soon after this, I hired a very talented playwright who agreed to do her research about severely mentally ill clients and wrote a wonderful script for a play with a sequel. It was about a young couple who were in the mental health system. They lived together in an abandoned garage. They collected found objects and made art out of them. He was HIV positive, and the story was about their struggle around that fact and what they had to deal with not only to keep her safe but also how they faced his death. It was well written and poignant, and the message was clear.

The Troupe continued on with the help of various grants including a number from Northwest AIDS Foundation in Seattle and one from someone who was wealthy and was encouraged by his guardian to begin to make charitable contributions. We toured the Seattle Area a number of times and went into several in-patient programs. Toward the end of tour, we performed for several community colleges. The mentally ill were not the only population who thought "it will never happen to me."

One day the cast came to my office and said they were tired and needed to quit. I had lost track of time. The troupe had lasted eleven years, which they informed me was longer than any troupe they had ever known. It had been a good run. I was sorry we did not have the resources to research the effectiveness of the project.

MOTHER MOVES TO WATERFORD

FOR ANOTHER FOURTEEN YEARS AFTER HE'D DIED, my mother stayed in the house that Fred had built. At that point, many of her friends had moved into retirement communities; and, in 1990, she signed up for one called Waterford, not far from the house. My mother missed my father but otherwise was doing fairly well. She was playing bridge regularly and was still playing the flute in her trio. Many of my parent's friends remained close and included her in many of their parties, and she did things with some of the women who had been friends for many years. About the time that she was to move, though, she became ill and had also begun falling.

One day, not long after the move, Carolyn called me and told me that I needed to come to Spokane and help with our mother. When I arrived in Spokane shortly thereafter, though, Carolyn was not in any shape to help, so I was on my own. I went to see Maxine and knew that I could not give her the care she needed. If she fell, I couldn't pick her up. Plus, she had other things going on that she needed help with for her basic health as well. I called the people at Waterford and told them that she needed to go into assisted living and not into independent living and that she needed to go right away. They balked at first, but I insisted, and they relented. Then, I called Carolyn to come help me get her there, which she did. So, Mother entered Waterford and Carolyn and I were left to deal with the house. Fortunately, Carolyn called her son, Fred, who agreed to come help.

Fred came and the three of us began dealing with the house. Carolyn helped for a few days and we went through mother's personal things and sorted them for what she would want to keep and decided what to do with the rest. Mother had never accepted gifts with grace and often just handed them back stating she would never use it or did not want it. So, we decided to get her things we liked in the event we would get them back. We found a number of things she did accept in the back of drawers and other remote places. The deal was that if you gave it, you got it back.

Overall, my mother's behavior around receiving gifts has taught me a good lesson. Just as it is a gracious thing to give gifts when appropriate, it is also a matter of grace to receive gifts. I realize that many people feel good when they can give to others and refusing to be a part of this at the other end is inconsiderate.

Carolyn did not come back after two days, as she'd gone to bed with a bottle of vodka. So, Fred and I kept on working on the house. We had gotten a big dumpster and began going through things. My mother lived in that house for close to forty years. Although she certainly wasn't a hoarder, she had just accumulated a lot of things. Some of the things were indeed a little unusual, like a can of pickled asparagus that was close to twenty-five years old. There were a number of such things throughout the house.

So, it was somewhat slow work, but Fred and I got to talk a lot. He was full of questions about the family, and I realized that Carolyn had never shared much about it. I did, though, and we began to get to know each other a bit better. We hadn't spent much time with each other because as he was growing up, I was viewed as a communist, and the time with the rat in the attic was not helpful. So, Fred got to hear about the family, and I liked telling him about it.

Then, every day at three o'clock, we would take a break, go to Baskin and Robins for ice cream, and then get back to work. With this pacing, we got through it all in about a week, as I recall.

By the end, the dumpster was full, as was the storage unit, and all that was left were big items like furniture and rugs and drapes. So, we let the trust know. The house was going up for sale. The bank sent two men, who were quite obnoxious and talked about mother's things as if we weren't there. They talked about taking some things for themselves which was just plain rude and unprofessional. Several things were those Carolyn or Fred had plans to keep and we told them they could not be taking things for themselves. I made note in terms of trusting the bank after that.

Once again, I returned to Seattle and picked up my life. I was glad I worked for myself as it seemed a long time to be gone and I did not have to answer to anyone about it.

Still, I heard the updates by phone and was glad to know that Mother recovered quite quickly in the assisted living facility. One day, however, she noted that one of the staff had tried to give her the wrong medication and she decided that she'd had enough of assistance and marched into the office and told them she was ready for independent living. She didn't have to wait long and got a lovely apartment with one bedroom, a den, a living room, and a kitchen, which opened into the living room. Because Fred happened to be in town, he took Maxine shopping for the furniture she needed and got her all set up.

So, my mother was quite comfortable. The apartment was lovely, and she was happy to be independent. She had quite a few friends at Waterford and was playing bridge up to three times a week. She had her car when she needed it and was able to get out. I also discovered that if I called her before 5:00 p.m. the calls went better because after that, she tended to be a little drunk and would become more critical, and her usual good humor was absent. If I caught her before Huntley Drinkley, things went well.

Mother, though, was not terribly pleased with the amount of attention Carolyn paid to her. Rather than giving attention, Carolyn mostly needed attention, which annoyed my mother. This meant that Carolyn just tried harder to get Maxine's approval. And on and on it went. The two of them were all tangled together. As always, I felt sorry about their relationship, but tried not to react, as it had never been helpful, and I wanted no part of it. It's interesting how when you have been trained in mental health and have had a good deal of therapy yourself, your own family is perhaps sicker than you would have ever realized. At least that was true for me by then.

A BUSY LIFE

By that time, I had a relatively busy life. The agency was doing well regarding the effectiveness of the treatment we offered, though there had always been financial stress. I managed it and kept the doors open. A major amount of time went into it, but it was always worth it. I have always felt fortunate to love my work, and the agency was my baby. I had more than I really needed in terms of material things and felt fortunate, though was not getting rich. And, finally, somehow I developed a tolerance for the financial pressure.

After all that had happened, I wasn't very involved in active recovery at that time. Now and then, I would go to a meeting, but I wasn't really participating. I no longer felt a need to drink and was happy with being sober, though I was really more just "dry." Certainly, I was controlling in much of my life and only became aware of it if that didn't work. But mostly, it did. I had friends that I felt good about, some of whom are still in my life. Rita and Joan were very much in my life, and I spent most holidays with them and their family. I felt very much a part of their family, and that is still true today. I feel very fortunate and have enjoyed watching Wilma and Matt grow, become responsible adults, and succeed. They both have two children, and two of them got married this year.

BREEZY

IN 1997 I TRIPPED OVER A FOOT STOOL in my living room and landed on my tail bone, which caused significant damage. It was very painful, and I was told there was nothing to do but let it heal and not to carry much weight. Zackery, the Golden Receiver had died in 1995 at the age of sixteen, and I had gotten a Bearded Collie. She was beautiful with flowing hair, so I'd named her Breezy. She was very smart, out smarting me at times. I loved her spirit. When I was told I could not carry weight, my occupational therapy brain kicked into gear, and I decided to go to service dog school with Breezy. There was a great place nearby called "Pawsabilities" that was run by a couple who were very good at training the owners. Breezy and I trained up in eight weeks.

Thereafter, she went to work with me, carrying a pack that held all the things that I needed. She also helped me with my balance, which by now was determined to be poor. She had a harness that I could hold on to with my left hand, and I used a cane on the right side for more balance. She was always with me, and we bonded more than before. Sometimes she did things that were not service dog acceptable, and when I scolded her, she would sulk often turning her head away from me. Then I would pet her, and she would forgive me and did not do that bad thing again. Don't tell me dogs don't have emotions.

She did her job well and was right there for me. She required grooming every day which just became a part of our morning routine. The only bad thing about her service dog duties was she was extremely cute and people who were not familiar with service animal rules (Do Not Pet while working) always wanted to pet her.

I often think about Breezy and how special she became as my service dog. She was very patient with me and all my demands upon her, even though she surely must have gotten tired of wearing the pack she carried for me. She also put up with being groomed daily. She did like being with me all the time, though, and I think she also liked riding in the car. I always put a seat belt through her harness, and she rode in the passenger seat of my car. I'd never thought of it before, but it must have been quite a sight with her incredible flowing hair and her regal head sitting there as we went by. All my dogs have been special in their own way. She was indeed of service, and in this way a different kind of special.

SOBRIETY FOR TWO

IN AUGUST OF 1998, CAROLYN CALLED and asked me to come with her to the hospital where she was scheduled to have a heart procedure. Mother had refused to go with her. I found that really sad. I knew that Carolyn was afraid and did need support, so I went. As I was driving, I said a prayer that I could be of help to her. This was the first prayer that I had said in many, many years.

When I got to Spokane, Carolyn looked terrible. She still weighed less than 100 pounds. Her legs and arms were alarmingly thin, and her liver was swollen and protruding. I knew she was in danger from drinking and knew that I should at least try to get her help. She was clearly anorexic as would stand in front of a mirror and pat her protruding stomach and say she really needed to get rid of that. It was indeed protruding as her liver was swollen due to her drinking. Her observation was totally ignoring how thin her arms and legs were. Her perception of her body was truly distorted.

At the hospital, I began talking about my sobriety and how much better my life was since I stopped drinking. I prayed to know what to do that would not offend her but might get her help. She told me that since she'd stopped working, she was drinking through the day.

She had a screw driver for breakfast and a Bloody Mary for lunch and drank wine throughout the day, still doing Huntley Drinkley to top it all off every evening with Scotch or gin. She also disclosed that she was on an inordinate dose of Ativan, taking eighteen milligrams per day. She must have been confused about the dosage, as I've never heard of such a high dose. Honestly, I didn't know how the Ativan added to all that liquor hadn't killed her already, and I wondered what kind of doctors she had, as I knew that she went to a number of them, and frequently.

Gradually, though, it dawned on me that she didn't have access to either alcohol or the high dose of Ativan while in the hospital, and that she hadn't been honest with the staff. She was in danger of seizing from withdrawal, and nobody knew it. So, on my way out of the hospital, I went to the nursing station and told them what I had just figured out. I knew that she hadn't told them that she was taking far more Ativan than she had revealed, and she certainly hadn't told them how much she was drinking. They thanked me for the information and said they would attend to it.

I thought about what else I could realistically do, as knew that she would dismiss any advice I suggested. I remembered that surgeons usually came out of the procedures and spoke to the family who were waiting to hear how it went. I also knew the doctor had only seen Carolyn once before the procedure and that he would not be offended if I told him of my grave concern. So, that is what I did the next day.

The procedure had been successful, so I told the doctor that I needed to talk to him, and he heard me. I told him that my sister wouldn't listen to me but always listened to doctors and would he be willing to do something. He said he would run a liver test and if it was bad, he would talk with her. I wasn't concerned about the outcome of the liver test. So, I went to her room and waited with Carolyn for the doctor to come in to see her. He was wonderful.

"I saved your heart," he told her, "but it makes me very sad to know that you will go home and kill yourself with alcohol. Would you like to go to treatment?"

And miraculously, she answered, "Yes."

So, we wheeled her from the cardiac unit down to the Recovery Program in the hospital.

After I left Carolyn at the Treatment Program, I went to Carolyn's house, and with her permission, began to get her liquor out of her house. She lived alone but had hidden bottles all over the house. I found that really strange. I knew where I would have hidden things, probably on the kitchen counter. But

Carolyn had told me where to look, and between that information and my intuition, I found most, if not all, of what she had hidden, and I poured all that liquor down the kitchen sink. It smelled disgusting to me. There was so much that it took an hour and a half to get it all down the drain. While doing it, I suddenly realized that I had not truly been sober for twenty-one years because I had smoked pot. I truly had not connected those things before, and I decided that if I was going to introduce my sister to the Program, I had better be on the up and up myself.

About a year ago, I learned that Carolyn had never told Fred that I had come to Spokane and helped her to get into treatment and had gone back a month later to take her to the Program. He'd thought she'd just done this on her own. This surprised me, not because I needed credit, but because I hadn't realized how much she resented my rescues.

MY RETURN TO THE PROGRAM

I RETURNED TO SEATTLE HAPPY that things had turned out so well. Getting Carolyn help was clearly an answer to my prayer. Things had happened as was needed to get her help. It had just rolled out with answers coming to guide me. In retrospect, I felt like a spiritual intervention had happened, which included the realization that I needed to go back to the Program and change my sober date and begin to work on my spiritual awareness. I began to acknowledge a Higher Power. For this, I will give the experience, and in that sense, Carolyn's rescue, the credit. I also remembered Noreen from years past and knew that seed had finally sprouted.

In thinking back, after Gary left, I continued to smoke pot, but not at all as frequently. Nevertheless, it eventually affected my work, as my short-term memory clearly took a hit. One day my business manager said to me, "It is not easy to work for you as you often forget what you have said." So, I'd quit using pot immediately. That was in April of 1998. I never got another comment after that, and I'm fairly sure that I was doing better. Fortunately, I also didn't feel any withdrawal, and I didn't really miss it at all. It wasn't, after all, my "drug of choice." Scotch clearly was. I was still in therapy with Nick Ward. When I told him about the pot, he wanted me to participate in a study that he was doing about chronic marijuana use. I declined, though, due to pride and a concern about my reputation.

It has now become clear to me that using pot as an escape had interfered with me getting the Program. I can testify that a sincere and active Program works much better than pot does to fill that hole that nags at you and to live a more fulfilling life. I cannot say that my life is stress free, but I have no doubt an active spiritual base has changed my life immensely for the better. I begin each morning with a quiet and prayerful time that stays with me for the rest of the day.

When I started attending the program again, I changed my anniversary date and realized that I had finally been honest with myself, which I believe has had an effect in all areas of my life and feels very good. I changed my date to May 1st, 1998 ,as could not remember exactly when I stopped smoking in April.

I found a sponsor and began working the Program in earnest. This time, I worked on the spiritual issues that I'd refused previously and finally got it that this was the basis of the Program. I went to a meeting a day for three months and worked with my sponsor who was a very spiritual person and gave me guidance in the program. I liked the importance of helping other alcoholics and began sponsoring other women, something I had rejected before because I was a therapist and did not think I needed that. I was very wrong, though, as sponsoring strengthened my own program and was inspiring. Watching another woman achieve sobriety is a very special experience.

It is clear to me that a clean and sober base in my life has strengthened my stability with my mental health. I also noted that other people in the program who have mental health issues benefit if they understand that you cannot stay sober if you do not attend to mental health and are not nearly as stable mentally if you do not work a good sobriety program. One supports the other.

When Carolyn finished treatment in one month, I returned to Spokane to take her to meetings in her community. I had talked to one member of my group who knew members in Spokane, and I contacted them explaining my situation. They were very welcoming and said that they would direct me to some good meetings. I took Carolyn to one or two meetings every day that I was with her, and she liked them. Of course, people were very welcoming to her. She found a sponsor and began working the steps. I was hopeful the Program would be helpful in changing some of her behavior. Expectations are not good in situations like this or perhaps in general. Very often, they lead to disappointment.

Carolyn's withdrawal from the Ativan, though, was difficult and took nine months. I was able to be supportive by phone, and she was determined and did get through it. It was hard for her to accept the Program, and she seemed to repeat with her sponsor much of the behavior that she'd had with our mother. She left the program after two and a half years because her sponsor didn't call her. In the Program, you call the sponsor, not the other way around.

She also began to have an elitist attitude about the fact that there were people in the Program who had been in prison, and she didn't want to be in meetings with people like that. I believe that the Program was too intimate for her. People share openly and deeply about very personal things. Most meetings are quite diverse, with people with many different backgrounds, and all are welcome and accepted. Carolyn had always had trouble with intimacy and making and keeping friends. She often spoke about her deep anger, and people do get tired of that.

MY RELATIONSHIP WITH MAXINE

IN 1999 I WAS AT A POINT IN MY PROGRAM that I needed to deal with my relationship with my mother. I suspected that if I approached her directly and said that I needed to make amends for my sobriety, she would have said with some disgust, "Oh for Christ's sake!" So, I decided that I would do it in a "living" approach. She was now about to turn eighty-nine, an age when reminiscing is common and often pleasant. So, I began talking to her about things I remembered as good times we had when I was younger. These were the things I was quite sure she would enjoy remembering together.

They were things like picking huckleberries at Priest Lake and baking pies, gathering wild flowers in the woods by our house in Spokane, identifying and pressing them for keeping, that were nice memories. It had also been special playing Bach on the flute and piano together. We laughed about how she would call from the kitchen when I would make a mistake when practicing the piano. She would say things like, "You'd better go over that again!"

We also talked about how my father would give her different demonstrators to drive, changing them quite frequently. She would go downtown, and park then not remember what color car she was driving. It became a joke at the dealership among employees when she would call to find out which car she had. Fred had thought it was very funny.

This reminiscing went on for four years and greatly changed our relationship for the better. The day came when she told me she loved me and was proud of the work I was doing and the fact I owned my own agency. This was close to a miracle. She became demented when she was ninety-three. I was so grateful that we'd been able to reminisce for those years before her dementia came on.

THE PROGRAM CONVENTION

IN 2000, THERE WAS A NATIONAL CONVENTION for the Program. I thought it would be nice if Carolyn and I went together. She had been asked to be a participant on a panel discussion as someone who came to the Program at a later age. Carolyn had been fifty-nine when she went into treatment and then joined the Program. So, we decided to go. By then, she had been sober for about a year and a half, and I had expectations that I would finally have a nice sister back. Indeed, I had written an article for the Program's magazine about her sobriety giving me back a sister and had led to my developing a higher power. Carolyn had been about six months sober at the time I wrote the article. It was published in March of 2000.

When we got to Minneapolis, where they held the convention, though, it was dreadful for me. To start with, Carolyn was flirtatious with the bell boys, which was embarrassing. She was also demanding and attention seeking in restaurants and was not willing to go to the convention events. At one point, I took a "time out," and as I was waiting for an elevator, an old friend from my early days in the Program came out of the elevator. We gave big hugs and I told him about my situation with Carolyn. He asked me to go to dinner, and I accepted.

That little "time out" helped. I had forgotten how Carolyn could be such a trial. I had very unrealistic expectations of what she would learn in the Program, and when I returned to Seattle, I began going to another Program for friends and family members of alcoholics. I needed it, as I began to be angry that she was not working her program like I worked mine, and I knew that this was not rational. Everyone is entitled to their own program, and I needed to let go and yet still remain in a relationship with her. This Program was very helpful.

After she left the Program, I began to wonder if my sister was an untreated Borderline with significant depression. Carolyn had struggled with depression all her life and had never been happy. There were periods of time she related fairly well to others, but that would switch to pulling back and being somewhat mean, especially with her son, Fred, who was trying hard to help her. Neither was she nice to me, especially if I was with her in person. In her withdrawal from Ativan, I was able to be supportive by phone, and was glad that I could do that. After that, I tried visiting her only a few more times and realized that she would get paranoid when I was present, so I greatly reduced visits and related to her primarily by phone, which went much better.

I suspected that Carolyn would anticipate my calls and would start thinking about me. She would "run movies in her head" and think up scenarios about me. There were a number of them, the most consistent and repeated one was that I used cocaine and was a lesbian. She accused me of these on several occasions, usually saying someone was at a party with me where I used cocaine.

She had witnessed me being friendly to and including a woman to join us for lunch at a Program event in Spokane. The woman was the speaker at the event, and when lunch time came, no one invited her to lunch, so I did. The woman was openly lesbian. She was also African American, two strikes against her that apparently left her out of an invitation to lunch by the Spokane people running the event. I just could not believe that no one included her. When she returned to Seattle, there was a short period of time that we attempted to get together to do something, but it never worked out. I suspected this was the basis for Carolyn's accusations about me being a lesbian. The fact was that neither was true, but Carolyn had made up her mind. She did this with several other ideas she got about me, and I don't doubt that she really believed them.

FINDING MEXICO

IN THE WINTER OF 2000, MY OLD DRINKING BUDDY invited me to go to Mexico with her. She had been going to Puerto Vallarta for some years. I had not traveled much and decided that it would be good for me to go, even though I wasn't great with flying, as I hadn't done much since the time when I'd lived in New York. Our flight to Mexico was relatively long, but the destination sounded great—and it was.

On a trip like that, I felt solid in my sobriety, even knowing that others whom I would be with were drinkers. These were a number of people who had been meeting in Puerta Vallarta over many years. They were into the art, music, food, and the people of Mexico. They were respectful toward the Mexican people, and they knew the city and the restaurants, the beaches and the customs. They also knew how to barter down prices to buy things within reason from the people selling their products, so I had a good time with them. We went to charity events, too, and art shows and galleries and to the sunset each evening. I drank a lot of "limonatas," which were essentially virgin Margaritas.

I loved it all, especially the music and the art, and decided to return the following year. So, once again, in 2001, I arrived to stay with my drinking buddy in Mexico, and some people who knew that we were coming stood waiting for my arrival with a little dog they had rescued from being chained to a roof. She was one year old and was most likely part Havanese and another small, long-haired breed. They knew I was a sucker for dogs and were convinced that I would agree to take her home with me.

Once again, Puerto Vallarta was wonderful with its food, music, art and people. I couldn't have a dog where I was staying with my friend, so the people who rescued her kept her until it was time for me to go home. Some of my time on this visit was spent with her, and she proved to be very sweet and good. I took her to a vet, who proclaimed her healthy and gave her needed shots and papers to get through customs. After paying fifty dollars for her plane ticket, I was able to take her home with me three weeks later, all the way back to Seattle. She was small enough that I could keep her under the seat in a crate inside the cabin of the plane, and she was absolutely quiet the whole trip. When we got to Seattle, we went through "Agriculture" at customs, and all went well. Her name was Duchesa, which I kept, and indeed, she now had the life of a Duchess.

She got along with Breezy, too, so Duchesa joined us on our walks in Seward Park where Breezy would often swim. It was quite a sight as Breezy's long hair would float, and she looked like a weird kind of water creature. Duchesa would go in the shallow water and get her belly wet. Clearly, she loved the park as much as Breezy and I did.

In 2002, I decided to go on my own to Mexico, as going with my friend was not going to work. By then, I had some friends who lived in Puerto Vallarta; and, when I decided to go back on my own, they helped me find a condo to rent in Old Town. It was close to the things that I wanted to be nearby, and it had a swimming pool. It was in a Mexican neighborhood, high up a big hill with a climb up fifty stairs, which was good for me. There was an English-speaking meeting of the Program there in which I had participated, so I felt that I had everything I needed. One of the things that I liked about the neighborhood was the Mexican people whom I would see as I walked to the beach.

There was a woman who was a little person who was also a leader in the neighborhood. She sold used clothes on a clothes line at the sidewalk. She also made a wonderful sweet corn drink that I usually got when I walked back to the condo. I heard that some drug dealers moved in at the end of the street and she complained to the police it was a family neighborhood and not a place they should be. She was tough and not going to put up with that. They left due to her protests. She was a brave woman.

There was also a man who sold coconuts on a corner in front of a juice bar run by his wife and another woman. One day on my way home from the store I tripped, and the women came out and helped me get up. I spilled the milk when I fell, and they were upset about that. They took me inside and bandaged my skinned knee. The next day, I brought them a bouquet of flowers that they set on the counter of their shop for several weeks way past the time of their wilting. The coconut man would talk to me in Spanish, and I would try with my horrible Spanish to answer him. He would often laugh, but I knew that he appreciated that I was trying.

I always bought foreign service for my cell phone to stay in touch with work and the people who stayed at my house and took care of my dogs. So, for the next eight years, each February, which is my birthday month, I rented the condo. I invited friends to join me for a week at a time with a deal of some help with the rent.

We most often went out to eat but also went to the open market and bought food to fix dinner at the condo occasionally. I began to buy art, clothes, and some jewelry over the years all of which I still have. I always invited an old friend from our revolutionary days to come. She lives in Milwaukee and loves the water, and therefore the beach and the pool. I also invited a number of other close friends from the Program and my Ikebana teacher and her husband, Michael. Rita and Joan came to stay. We always had a wonderful time, and I very much enjoyed sharing what I saw as my good fortune with others.

A very special person in my life during this time was a woman named Shirley. She was a dear friend for several years and then became my service sponsor when I began to do District level service in the Program. She was an amazing expert on the inner workings of the Program and taught me so very much.

A number of years into our friendship, Shirley was diagnosed with end-stage lung cancer. She had been with me in Mexico when she began having a dry cough. I'd had another friend who had lung cancer that started with a dry cough, so I was worried. I knew that Shirley had been a heavy smoker many years before but had quit when she got into the Program. I was concerned, and she did go to the doctor when she returned.

So, the next year, when she was at the end of chemo, she got permission from her doctor and came with me again to Mexico. I remember watching her eyebrows grow back which we checked every day. Sadly, though, she died later that year with much support from family and friends and with tremendous grace. I still miss her and think of her often and always will want to do service in the Program as she taught me well.

I couldn't keep up with the Mexico visits, though; and, after a hiatus of nine years, I really have missed it. I know it would not be the same if I went, as the people that I knew there are off to other places, and I am not sure that the condo is still available. I am also very comfortable with my life here in Seattle, though, and my old revolutionary friend is still in touch and may come out next spring to visit. Most of the people that I'd spent time with there are here, and I see them frequently, so that's all right. For a time, my trips to Mexico were a good experience, and I treasure the memories. But, life goes on and changes, and it seems most often for the better.

MAY OF 2001,
A BIG CHANGE

NOT ALL CHANGES ARE EASY, and in late February of 2001, I became very ill. I would become chilled and very shaky, and I thought it was different than the flu. Finally, I got to the doctor who tested me to discover I was septic from a bladder infection, so I was hospitalized immediately, and they treated it. It was then determined I had a mass on my right kidney. I was told that most likely I had kidney cancer and would need surgery to remove the mass. They told me that there was a 5% chance it was not cancer, and this would not be determined until they did the surgery. It would be a very new technique that they could not do for several months as were booked until then.

So, I went home to wait, holding onto the idea I had cancer and could possibly die soon, though I assumed that they felt like I would last until the surgery. I knew I couldn't sit around thinking about this for several months, so my wonderful sponsor worked with me around it all. I began to think that I now had a Higher Power and that I had been convinced it was powerful with my sister's recovery. It had been responsive with other incidents too. I no longer worried about death, as that Higher Power had always been kind and loving and why would that not be true with death. This thought stays with me still.

Finally, I had the surgery and found out that, miraculously, the mass was not malignant. Even so, I did lose a third of my right kidney, and there was damage to the other one. The surgery was extensive and the recovery painful and draining, so I hired a medical attendant to be with me for a day and a night when I returned home from the hospital. I remember how she rubbed my back to help me deal with the pain. And, little by little, I got through it.

The kidney damage was due to my being toxic from Lithium. It turned out that I had not been tested as regularly as I should have been, so Dr. Ward had changed me to another medication. At the time, I was not aware of how serious it was and remember being worried as I had been very stable on the Lithium and was nervous about a medication change. I trusted Dr. Ward, as I knew that he had written a well-used book on psychiatric medications. He put me on Neurontin, a drug that was not hard on kidneys, and I made the change, with some trepidation.

When I was in the hospital, one day after the surgery, I got a phone call from someone in the Psychiatric Department at the University of Washington. He told me that Dr. Ward was on permanent medical leave, and I needed to find a new psychiatrist. I got in touch with a colleague who worked at Harborview, where Dr. Ward had worked and where residents trained. I knew that the staff there were familiar with many of the residents who came through and would know who was good and who wasn't. I trusted them as had worked at the university myself and knew that this was obvious. She did not hesitate to recommend a man named Grant Haven. I contacted him, explained what had happened, and he agreed to see me when I was well enough to come to his office.

I was stunned this was happening and how I had found out, just when I was fresh out of surgery. I had great difficulty with the fact Dr. Ward was so sick and had been told that he had an early onset dementia, which was extremely sad. He was only fifty-three. He had been my rock for twenty-six years. I did remember that in a recent session I was talking about my family and he appeared to not remember extensive work we had done regarding them. For a brief moment, my head swam, but I'd put it out of mind, as it was really weird, and I did not want to deal with it. In talking to my friend regarding this she told me he had been showing signs of the dementia for a significant amount of time. So apparently, it had been hard for them to grasp too. The residents he was training noted it and insisted the department intervene. I wasn't angry, just sad.

I remember I had my third anniversary of recovery from alcohol about three weeks after the surgery and with support and a little help from my sponsor I made it to the monthly anniversary celebration. I had a hard time walking from where I was sitting to get to the podium to speak, but I made it and did give a little talk, which is the tradition.

As I recovered and got back to work, I did get angry and decided to see a lawyer. The first one I saw told me since I was not dead and would only have to deal with a special diet I did not have a case. I did not accept this and saw another lawyer who had a different reason not to take the case. I did not give up as I thought I did have a case and the reasons I was being given did not sound reasonable. I had been damaged by medical incompetence and the U had not intervened in time for me. I consulted with three more lawyers and the last one said to me, "Don't you know why no one will take your case as you do have a good one?" I said no and he said "No one is willing to go up against the U, at least not here in Seattle as they are very powerful here. If you went to New York or even to Portland a lawyer would take your case."

I thought about it a while and decided that if this was going to be so difficult to get a lawyer to take the case, it was probably my will pushing aside reason and was not meant to happen. Besides, it might be very difficult for me, as there is no question that they would bring up every bit of dirt on me. This was not a pleasant prospect and might be bad for my career, so I dropped it. I have always thought that when I want to do something, and it has many roadblocks, it is perhaps my self-will that is the problem, and I should pay attention to that.

My new psychiatrist was wonderful helping me to deal with losing Dr. Ward and the anger that I was feeling by then. He changed my medication, being careful that it was something that would be effective and not hurt my kidneys. He gave little opinion about a law suit, which was good, as I needed to be the one to make the decision. Also, he had trained at the University. When I finally gave it up and moved on, it was a good thing, as I had much to deal with. And for many years, I was able to keep the kidney disease essentially stable. I have a great nephrologist and always look forward to going to see him, as he is kind and supportive and honest, telling me things I do not want to hear like lose weight, and exercise and follow your diet better, all with some humor but I know he is serious.

I learned a lot coming through the kidney experience and losing my psychiatrist. Most importantly I strengthened my relationship with my Higher Power and dealt with issues around my own mortality. I got through a difficult physical experience, which I felt somehow strengthened me physically and emotionally and spiritually. Today, though I certainly would not want it to happen again, I realize I grew a good deal because of this experience. I feel very fortunate to have found my current psychiatrist.

BACK TO WORK
AND BEING A BOSS

THE AGENCY WENT WELL IN MY ABSENCE. I had a good clinical director and a very good business manager. Sometimes, being the boss is not easy, and actually it was a nice little break to be away even in bad circumstances. This does not mean that I didn't like my work, because I did. It was just good to have a break. Like most people, I want to be liked, and sometimes that doesn't happen when you're the boss. And when I have to do things that I need to do for the good of the agency, I always remembered what Fred told me.

"If you are liked by everybody," he used to say, "you are probably doing something wrong."

Nevertheless, I had opened the agency partly to provide a pleasant and respectful place to work. Since I'd gotten sober and worked the Program, I began to consider more carefully what I was going to say before I said it. I would ask myself, "Is this a necessary thing to say?" Or "Would this be hurtful to someone?" Or, "Why am I being so judgmental?" In the past *I had pretty much said what I was thinking without thinking, something I felt related to both being bipolar and alcoholic.* I did get better about it, and I was feeling more comfortable with myself.

During the post-surgery period, I was grateful that Dr. Haven was skilled and helpful. For one thing, I no longer had any lies of omission as I had for many years before I got sober. I felt very comfortable with him and he was helpful with the sadness and the anger I initially had. I had learned in the Program it is not good to carry resentments and that helped too. I still see him and appreciate his wisdom and skill. I like my sessions, as I always leave with something helpful and worth more contemplation.

I was not interested in dating and didn't. Adjusting to what I came to call "tricky kidneys," I had enough to deal with. Also, since my divorce, I viewed relationships as a lot of work. I saw women who were what I call "male dependent." I enjoyed my independence too much to arrange my life around another person at the time or perhaps ever. I had a number of men who were good friends. I also just did not feel that attracted to anyone either. So, at the time this was not an issue. There was still financial pressure at the agency. By now, I enjoyed my own company and rather liked time alone by myself. I considered this a gift from sobriety. I was still doing Ikebana and some service work in the community. I had a number of good friends, my sponsor and some women I was sponsoring. It was all good.

BREEZY DIES

BREEZY WAS MY SERVICE DOG FOR CLOSE TO FOUR YEARS, but in 2002, she became ill. Her adrenal glands were over producing and causing problems. I agreed to give her a medication daily that slowed this process, though it had side effects that slowed her down, too. So, I retired her from service. I had healed enough to deal with carrying things myself, and I gave her the medication for a bit over one more year and watched her decline. Finally, she lost her quality of life, and I had to be honest about why I kept up the treatment. So, one day she was doing worse, and I took her to the vet and put her down. It was very hard, and I was horribly sad.

Duchesa also was clearly mourning. I waited a few weeks and called my first sponsor who had a wonderful poodle and we went to her breeder. I fell in love with a darling black puppy with beautiful eyes and a loving disposition. He was an odd size that excluded him from show. He did not have a poodle cut but did have a mustache. He is smaller than a Standard Poodle and bigger than a miniature. He has grown to a perfect size of twenty-five pounds. Duchesa bonded with him quickly, and we all began to heal. His name is Charlie.

He is one of the smartest dogs I have had. I see him problem solve and do somewhat naughty things at times. Sometimes when he gets a treat, he goes to find the other dog and brings her to whoever gave the treat so she would get one and more importantly, he gets a second one. If candy is left out at all, he will snitch it and unwrap it if wrapped and it is gone. We call him a "scallywag," meaning that he is full of mischief. He loves toys, has his favorites, and carries them around proudly. He buries specific ones in the garden in a special place so many have been through the wash more than once.

A bit over a year ago, Charlie was diagnosed with congestive heart failure. We have been diligent in treating it and he has done well much longer than expected. He takes eight pills twice a day and is very good about it. He still has good quality of life, though when he gets excited or overexerts, he coughs, sometimes somewhat uncontrollably. Once he calms down, he seems to do fine. We are very careful about his quality of life. He is still active with Coco. He has a dog friend next door named Gracie who stands on her deck, and Charlie on his and they bark and wag their tails. He eats and drinks and all functions work. We are surprised that he has done this well for this long. He is, however, beginning to slow down some. He is sixteen years old, and such a great dog. We know we will lose him fairly soon, so I just try to love him a lot. We out live our dogs and have to accept that.

A DIFFICULT CASE
FOR THE THERAPIST

IN 2002, A CLIENT WAS REFERRED TO ME from one of the psychiatric hospitals in Seattle. He had been hospitalized for a serious depression following a manic episode and was in need of our services upon discharge. He was also a famous artist. Our agency is private pay, and we often see our clients in their homes. This offers more confidentiality than a hospital ward or clinic with patients from the community. Confidentiality was a big issue for this client. The referral resource knew my work, and I took the case myself upon their request.

I greatly admired his work and was hopeful I could help him. On rare occasions I will self-disclose that I am bipolar, and this was one. He was still struggling with the depression but was somewhat better, better enough to agree to follow through with my suggestions. I bring this up not to write about the client but to write about the effect this had on me. I became aware that I was attracted to him and knew that I would need some expert supervision and guidance in my work with him. He certainly did not need his life to become more complicated than it already was. It was also important that he could trust me. I had to take my feelings elsewhere.

I am absolutely aware that this happens to other therapists and that I was not unique. But that was not helpful. I took it into my own therapy and Dr. Haven was very helpful. I believe I served the client much better than I would have without doing this. And my work was clean and rewarding.

I was comfortable in how I dealt with it and appreciated my psychiatrist for mentoring me through it. It was a pleasure knowing the client and I will always appreciate what I learned. The client still does his work and is active with new shows which on several occasions I have attended.

MOTHER GOES
TO SKILLED NURSING

IN 2002, MOTHER WAS DOING WELL and was playing bridge three times a week. One day, however, she had some intense pain and asked Carolyn to take her to the emergency room. I had a call from Carolyn early in the day and had flown over to Spokane to be with her. It was determined that she had gall stones. She was given a light anesthesia to deal with the problem. She was ninety-two years old, and when she came out of the groggy state, she was having trouble with her memory. It was clear there was a change. The doctor felt she should not live independently and needed to go to skilled nursing. This was what she had always dreaded, but it did seem what needed to happen.

She still knew who Carolyn and I were but seemed disoriented as to where she was and how she got there. One of my concerns was she would need help with her medication. Waterford had graduated care which, included skilled nursing, so, we offered to get her a private room in skilled nursing, but she rejected that. I think she didn't want to be alone. So, she didn't go back to her apartment but instead went into the skilled nursing unit. I was impressed with the excellent care she got there and how good the staff was. I helped sort through mother's things in the apartment. We put much in storage and some went to Carolyn's attic and a few things to me. I returned to Seattle feeling assured Maxine was in good hands and where she needed to be. She had severe osteoarthritis and would benefit from special help in dealing with that. In fact, not too much later she became less able to walk and in more back pain which they managed well.

Overnight, Mother became very sweet and not demanding. My suspicion was that she was not sure who she was dealing with at any given moment and knew she was dependent on their care. It would be important not to offend anyone. So, she was nice. She kept her sense of humor in her dementia. One day when I was visiting, I arrived to find her reading the paper.

I asked her "What's in the news today?"

She put the paper down, looked me in the eye, blinked and smiled.

She said, "I have no idea!"

Carolyn became the family person to watch over mother's care and watch she did. She was Maxine's Power of Attorney which meant to Carolyn she was in charge. Indeed, she was to deal with the Bank Trust to pay mother's bills which was fine with me at the time. And, ironically, the Trust Officer was the man who was living in the apartment near the Delta Gamma house where I would go for respite my freshman year at the U. I was comfortable things were in good hands.

Soon, I found out that Carolyn went to be with mother every day, sitting at her bedside. She would decide that the staff were not responding to Maxine quickly enough and would let them know. She would put up signs on the wall with instructions to the staff to "do this" or "not do that." Apparently, she would not be quiet about it. I would learn later that the Head Nurse was assigned to keeping Carolyn calm and not create a scene.

She began to interfere with mother's medical care and not let them do something she thought was wrong. The problem, though, was Carolyn was not a doctor. Mother was on pain medication, and it was not agreeing with her, so the doctor wanted to put her on Methadone. Carolyn refused to allow it because she thought it was a street drug when it is also a drug of choice for severe pain.

Addiction is hardly an issue with a bed-ridden 93-year-old and keeping her comfortable was the issue. I found out about this when I asked why mother had not been put on Methadone and the head nurse took me to the nursing station and showed me the chart around this issue.

Another time, there was a shortage of flu shots. I knew that the nursing homes would be first in line for the serum when it became available. But, although I told Carolyn this, she took Mother to a public health clinic to get a shot. Mother was in a wheel chair, and I remember that Carolyn was highly offended when she was made to wait in line with everyone else as apparently felt mother was entitled to that over the other people there. Carolyn felt entitled about most everything. So of course, against my advice, she exposed Maxine to the flu far more than it would have been at the skilled nursing unit where the vaccine became available the next day.

Mother did not like Carolyn's constant presence and would ask the staff to tell her not to come every day. They would explain they could not do that because Carolyn was her POA and she could do what she pleased. I wondered if this wasn't fate paying Maxine back for refusing to give Carolyn her acceptance. I'm sure that Carolyn's motive was once again to get acceptance, but it once again did not work. It was very much a part of the sick relationship of years past. Still, I have no doubt that Carolyn was trying to be the best daughter she could by being there to supervise mother's care. Carolyn just never got it; and as usual, Maxine was annoyed. I thought they were both getting their just desserts.

Then I found out that Carolyn was paying herself for supervising mother's care, for which we were paying seven thousand a month. She also was using trust money for things that she had decided Mother would have helped her with financially. One day she offered me $3000 to make things even as "Mother had helped her with something," and it would make things even. But more frightening, on one of my visits, Carolyn greeted me in a designer outfit. This did not make sense since she was on Social Security Disability. I did not care if she was taking a reasonable amount for taking care of mother, but designer clothes were not my idea of reasonable. It also revealed the fact that Carolyn had Maxine's Nordstrom credit card and was using it for her own purchases and paid for it out of the trust. That was the last straw, and I told the bank that they would have to take the card. Later, though, I would realize that she had just paid for the clothes directly from the Trust after that and continued to spend down the trust.

By then, I had been calling Carolyn regularly about every ten days. I knew she had only one friend who would go out to lunch with her about once a month. I knew she did not get along with her neighbors, or with grocery store clerks or the man at the hardware store because she told me so. She'd informed me that when I came to visit Mother, I couldn't stay at her house because she knew I was a lesbian and I might come on to her. I told her that I was not a lesbian but would stay elsewhere, anyway.

Sometime later, she called and told me that Waterford had told her if she did not take unneeded items out of mother's room, they would not keep mother any longer. She said I needed to come get things out of Mother's room. So, I went and found magazines stacked three feet high on a long ledge under the window. Her wardrobe was absolutely crammed with clothes. Mother was bed ridden by now and usually wore velour pants and matching tops when she did dress. Some of Mother's clothes were being kept in wardrobes that were for her roommate. There were wire clothes hangers cascading from the top of one wardrobe, down the side and out onto the floor.

Her drawers were full of more items than Mother could use. Clearly, Carolyn was hoarding for mother. I never did understand, though, about the clothes hangers.

It took me seven hours to clean out the trash, bag up the clothes that were in good shape, and put things neatly in mother's dresser and closet. One of the staff workers helped me put the things I needed to throw out in a dumpster. I had the staff check the room. Maxine was in the room while I worked and when she wasn't sleeping, we would visit. It occurred to me that it was a good thing that Carolyn wasn't present while I ruthlessly threw out things she was keeping. Hoarders do not do well with that.

Afterward, I called Carolyn to say I was bringing the bags of clothes to be stored at her house, but she told me, "I don't want them."

I clarified, "I will leave them in your driveway."

When I got there, the garage door was open, and I left them in the garage. Then I headed for I-90 and called Carolyn, telling her,, "I have finished and am headed home. Maxine can stay now."

"You just did that to make me look bad to the staff," she retorted.

"Whatever," I shrugged. "It's done now."

That's when I understood that Carolyn was sicker than I'd thought.

After that, I would go visit Mother about every six weeks for the next three years. I stayed at a delightful small hotel in downtown Spokane. I got a reduced rate because I came often and regularly. The fact that I stayed in a nice hotel angered Carolyn. She accused me of making my trips to see mother a vacation.

I began to think there might be a more likely reason that she didn't want me in her house and may have things belonging to Mother that she did not want me to see, or that she was hoarding—and it might be more designer outfits. Whatever it was, I much preferred the hotel where I was welcome. In addition, Carolyn had told me that she would not let me know when Mother was dying, so I made arrangements for Waterford to contact me.

I knew Carolyn had resentments, but this was more than I thought. I knew that she resented the rescues, and she'd always felt that our father favored me and that her relationship with mother was difficult. She never did get the love and acceptance that she sought from Mother. She also resented the fact that I had a career and that she never really did. She resented that she was the one who "took care of Mother," so now she would cut me off on information about mother. It was hard for her to do since I did visit regularly. I felt sad that she carried these resentments, which must have eaten her up inside. As always, I wanted to help her, but there was no way for me to do that and it was no longer an option. She was successful in getting back at me by collecting designer clothes through the Trust. The problem was that it probably hurt her son Fred more than me. But she resented him also, as after mother died, he became aware that Carolyn had gone through her inheritance. He bought her house so she could live in it until she died. To Carolyn's twisted thinking, he had stolen her house.

It was all very sad. I continued to call Carolyn every ten days, despite the fact that it was mostly unpleasant. We did have one phone call when we watched a dog show together while on the phone. That was both pleasant and fun. It never happened again, though, as there just are not that many dog shows or things like that to watch together.

MOTHER DIES IN 2005

MAXINE WAS IN SKILLED NURSING for nearly three years. She died in 2005 at the age of ninety-five. Waterford called me one afternoon to say that I needed to come if I wanted to see her before she died. Since my relationship with Carolyn was pretty damaged by then, my friend Rita had offered to go with me. Rita was a wizard at getting people to work together even with significant differences. She had been brilliant working with the ERA coalitions in Washington State as well as nationally. My tiny family would be a breeze. I picked her up and she came with me.

Mother was not conscious when we got there. Carolyn was sitting in the room with her. Rita sat with us. We took turns holding mother's hand and talking to her. A few hours later, her breathing became labored and louder. I knew that it was the death rattle. Carolyn went to find a nurse, though Rita and I told her that this is what happens when someone is dying. The nurse came and told her there was nothing to do and that it was a natural thing. The staff suggested that we go home, and they would let us know how she was doing.

The next morning, we found out that she died early in the morning. I always have thought that she was hanging on because of our presence and that our leaving released her. She had a good marriage, many friends, and her music. Her kids, maybe, were not so much of a blessing, though. One was difficult to love, and the other was a rebel. I had figured out that she had lived vicariously through me around some of the things I was able to do in New York City. She had wanted to go there when she graduated from college. And finally, in her last years before the dementia, I had found a way to share memories, which clearly did draw us closer.

FRED, CAROLYN, RITA AND ME

MY SPONSOR AT THE TIME THOUGHT that I should sue Carolyn and possibly the bank for abuse and irresponsibility with the trust. When we arrived in Spokane, I took one look at Carolyn and she was so sick both physically and mentally that I couldn't do that. She was extremely thin and drawn and shaky; and she had been decent to me on that visit. Rita worked her magic, and things went much better than I had hoped. Rita and I stayed at my favorite hotel, and one hotel staff person heard that my mother had died and gave me flowers.

Carolyn thought Rita was wonderful, and Fred appreciated the fact that she had come. A number of things went wrong, and we could not believe how dysfunctional the staff at the cemetery were. Mother, typical of her need for social approval, had written her own obituary. She had also chosen her container for her ashes and paid for all of it plus the plot. But, they lost the obituary, and, as I recall, her urn too. They had called in supervisors and other staff to right the situation and all had failed. My nephew offered to write a new obituary. We all ended up laughing hysterically as each disaster happened. We wondered what these people thought of us as we were supposed to be in mourning but of course, we didn't care.

Mother got a plot next to Fred, though she wanted to be inside his grave with him. We were told that that was not allowed. The service went well, and there were only a few others who came as mother did not have many friends who were still living. Then it dawned on me one day that I was an orphan. That felt strange, and probably it was stranger yet that I thought of it that way. I was glad that mother and I had mended our relationship before she had dementia and that it stayed good after that. I was especially glad I had a loving father who was so special to me.

As mothers are, she was a lot of things, at times humorous, at times wise, not so often loving, and to be admired for her accomplishments. And at the same time, she was a piece of work, clearly narcissistic which did not serve us well as her children. That meant that most of her decisions were based on what would be best for her, most often connected to her social standing.

At the same time, she did some good things for me. She taught me to love music, mostly classical music, but others also. She encouraged me to pursue my artistic talents. She significantly helped me through a serious manic episode, making good decisions in what she did. She also supported me through my pregnancy and advocated for me to get a good education at Columbia afterward. And she took good care of Fred, loved, and supported him in his work and his recreational pursuits. She was a good care giver to Fred. In that, she moved through her narcissism and was of service.

The financial things were settled sometime later. I knew what had been in the trust, and after accounting for Maxine's care, Carolyn had significantly reduced it. There were also a number of things that mother had wanted to go to me that somehow did not. This problem had begun before mother died. I was not into raising a fuss about most of it, though, as I have always thought it is sad how many families fight over material things and alienate each other beyond repair.

There was one thing, though, on which I stood my ground, and that was some art, that clearly was to come to me. These were three Chinese smoke prints of birds. There was also a lovely lithograph that we were to choose between. I let Carolyn choose first, and she chose the lithograph which left me the smoke prints. She told me they had been destroyed in storage. She had given them to Fred. I told him that he had to return them, which he did.

Whenever Carolyn took things, she apparently felt that there should be a reason and would call to tell me. These calls were always prefaced with "a terrible thing happened," and whatever it was had somehow been destroyed in storage or had disappeared mysteriously. I have to admit that I had resentments about that behavior, but I just didn't think it worth aggravating our relationship, which was tenuous at best.

WE INHERIT

THE TRUST WAS FINALLY SETTLED AROUND FIVE MONTHS after mother died. It was still a good amount. Carolyn had settled down some in our relationship, and I continued to call her regularly. However, I was careful not to visit in person with the exception of when I went to my 50th High School Reunion. When I did, I stayed at the hotel.

When we inherited, both of us put a significant amount into our houses. Carolyn sold the one she was living in and bought a new one that was being built when she bought it and was able to choose how it was finished. I did an extensive remodel on my little house that I had bought in 1988. As you may have noticed, houses are important to me, definitely something I got from my father.

THE REMODEL

THE REMODEL STARTED IN THE LATE FALL OF 2006 and was finished in the spring of 2007. I had a great architect whom I'd met some time before the remodel because I'd followed his career. His name is Greg Bader, and I contacted him, and then we met and discussed the things that I wanted to address in the remodel. He was very good about helping me to think in terms of my age and what my needs were currently and what they might become over the next years. That process went well, and I hired him. He and his wife have remained good friends since.

I wanted to add a master bedroom wing on the first floor, to improve the kitchen, and to put a fireplace in the living room. The living room also needed a special space for my piano which is a "parlor grand." bigger than a baby grand and smaller than a regular grand piano. It is six feet from keyboard to the end of the instrument. The kitchen was a galley kitchen, and since I am not much of a cook, I left it that size and just put in new appliances, new cupboards and counter tops. I wanted a formal dining space in the living area. I also wanted a fireplace in my bedroom and a washer and dryer in the bedroom wing. I wanted both a tub and a shower in the bathroom and a water closet for the toilet. The addition of the bedroom wing increased the space below and the total project increased the house from 1300 square feet to 2600 square feet.

The blue print looked great, it was time to hire a contractor. Greg brought one in who wanted to tear down the house and build from scratch, but I didn't want that. He recommended another one and I also consulted a neighbor who had remodeled recently. The one I found gave a lower bid. I was about to make a big mistake which turned the project into "The Nightmare Remodel."

I was determined to remain living at the house during the remodel. This was not a popular idea, but it would have been expensive to move for a short while and I had two dogs and a Maine Coon Cat that would not move well. I also wanted to keep an eye on things, which was most likely the reason the contractor did not want me around full time. He also raised a fuss about the architect coming around to check on things. I have since learned that many contractors don't want the architect around to be overseeing things. My second mistake was to succumb to this. Greg pointed out this was not a good sign. Could there have been a bigger clue that things were heading for more trouble?

Next, and probably the worst thing, was that I discovered that the workers were drinking on the job. I am a sober woman and absolutely did not want drunk men working on my precious house. I told the contractor that they could not continue to drink while at my house. I was not convinced that he would do anything about it or that he cared.

I remember the day the inspector came to approve the initial stages of construction. He said there was a lot of rebar in the foundation. It would be strong. I felt better to hear this and was happy Greg had put that in the plans. I relaxed a little.

One evening when I was home alone, I climbed onto the new part of the bedroom wing which was still open without an exterior wall. I sat there looking south. I was feeling better about things. and it felt great just to sit there for a while. This was all really happening, and it was exciting to just sit there and fantasize about the finished project.

There were a number of complaints that I was living there, which I ignored. I had moved my bedroom to the living room couch, as they were digging the new foundation and the bedroom was not habitable. There was a heavy rainstorm that night, and I was awakened by water gushing down the interior wall of the living room. I called the contractor, and he said it was ok because that wall would be replaced before long. It was not ok with me. The crew had done work that day and had not protected things when they were done. They had left the roof open to the rain. It was not long after that I became aware that they were not happy that the old section of the house was to be taken down to the studs and reconfigured. I think they had underbid the contract, but I was not sure.

More beer bottles were found in the house. This time the crew blamed it on the Mexican workers who had been there. I did not believe this and found it racist. I reconfirmed with the contractor that there was to be no drinking at the house.

The crew had been working on putting in the French doors from my new bedroom to the deck, and they were off center. I happened to come into the area where the contractor was talking to them on how he would "adjust things" so it did not show. I wanted to suggest they adjust their drinking schedule to take place after work, but I kept my mouth shut as things by now were getting a little dicey. When they saw me standing there the contractor said he would fix it and I would never notice. I don't but I do notice that one of the skylights is a little off kilter.

A number of other things were done without care, and I asked that they repair the heating pad under the tile floor in my bathroom. They removed the dial that controlled it while I was there, but I left minutes later, and it has never worked.

In March, a good friend of mine was diagnosed with lung cancer. We decided to have a fund raiser for him in mid-April at my house, which was scheduled to be done by then. I checked several times to be sure things would be finished and was reassured it would.

As the date approached, there was a severe rain storm and the bottom floor flooded. They had "failed" to install an essential drain under the patio, and the water came in under the French doors. That day I came home from work, and all the equipment and contractor and crew were gone. The people who were putting in the hardscape for the garden came to my rescue and helped me get the water out of the house. I was concerned about the fundraiser that was to take place in a wonderful newly remodeled house.

We decided to have the fundraiser at the house anyway. When it happened, no one cared that the house was not finished. My friend was a well-known local artist and had friends in a number of communities in the Seattle area. We estimated that somewhere near a hundred people came through the house and participated in the silent auction. I will always remember a friend of the artist was an opera singer and announced which sections of the auction were open in song. It got peoples' attention. We raised $12,000 dollars that night for our friend.

During the fund raiser, one of the guests asked me if I knew that the guest bathroom toilet water was hot. I checked it, and indeed it was hot—not just warm but hot. The drunken crew had plumbed the toilet to hot water.

Our artist friend had been commissioned to do a retrospective show of his work at the Frye Museum about a month later. It happened to open in the evening after he was seen for follow up from the surgery and he was declared cancer free. When I arrived for the show, he told a small group of us the news. I cried a bit as was totally joyful and it seemed fitting it was on the evening of the opening of his show.

I hired a number of people to come in and fix and finish things. When electricians came in they found live wires hanging in the attic next to piles of old insulation. There was no new insulation. I had heated an uninsulated house for six weeks. I later found out that the contractor had not paid the painters that he had brought in, as well as the people who had installed the garage door. I knew that I was responsible to pay them. I contacted a lawyer and did not get much help. I never had to pay the last bill of $17,000 and got the bond of $12,000. The repairs and unpaid bills came to far more than that, but the remodel was finally done.

THE FINISHED REMODEL

So, this was the "Nightmare Remodel." I know I am not the only person who has survived such an experience. In spite of it all there is a happy ending. In the end I was left with a very comfortable, attractive and functional house for which I am very grateful.

The front entry has a front porch and an entry hall both tiled with porcelain tile. The floors are bamboo and quite attractive but not too durable, at least not what I got from the contractor, who claimed they were high-end, and I am pretty sure they are not. The entrance goes into the living/dining area with the grand piano sitting against the wall. The fireplace is fairly large and is gas and turns on with a switch. I did not see myself splitting wood or cleaning up from wood in the house. There is a large bookcase on the wall next to the fireplace and a couch next to that. "My chair" sits next to the couch facing the fireplace with a large ottoman and tray in front of them. There is a large, once beautiful leather chair near the fireplace which has become the dogs' chair and allows them to watch out the window. It will one day need a new cushion. This area has a blue, red and beige oriental rug. There are no carpets in the house.

The dining table is on the opposite wall from the couch. There are French doors onto the deck and a big window next to them. The main area is painted taupe which works well for displaying paintings and other pieces of art. The kitchen is a galley kitchen. Had I known that Brent would be living here with all his cooking skills, I would had made it larger and opened it up more. That will be for another day. There is a nook with a small Mexican table and two chairs next to a window and a guest bathroom past that.

My master bedroom suite is in the new wing. It is connected to a hallway out of the living area with my laundry at the end behind a door. The bathroom is just down the hall and my bedroom is open at the end of the hall. It has skylights and at a certain time the full moon travels across them and sometimes gently wakes me. I have a French canopy bed, queen size, with a crystal chandelier at the end of the bed. I always wanted one, and it just didn't fit in the dining area, so I put it in the bedroom. There is a large Japanese tansu (chest) instead of a dresser on the interior wall and a small one next to the bed and a medium-sized tansu in the living room, too. These are a result of shopping at Japanese stores for Ikebana vases. The bedroom area is painted a color labeled "Chocolate" and is simply several tones darker than the taupe in the living area.

There are French doors onto the deck, and looking out of them is my writing table, which looks across the large patio to a side of the gardens. Sitting at my writing table, looking out to my right is a small patio with a table and red umbrella, an arbor behind it which today has red berries on the Heavenly Bamboo. Brent's garden is beautiful even in winter. Looking ahead are trees and bamboo and a territorial view to a ridge. There are often beautiful sunsets.

Brent's part of the house is below the living and bedroom areas. There are two large rooms, a bathroom and a storage room that I have not looked in for many months. It is plumed for water and gas and can become a kitchen if I ever need to make it a separate apartment. The main room has French doors onto the patio with the fountain and gardens. His area is quite separate from mine, which allows for good privacy for both of us, perhaps the secret to our compatible living arrangement.

The house is very welcoming, with many windows. It flows from one area to another and is large enough to comfortably accommodate up to fifteen people. My art collection fits in fine. A number of pieces are done by friends. Others are from Mexico and a few are Japanese. Some are things that have meaning for me or that I simply like. My art says to me this is my place to live and enjoy. I love to share my house with my roommate and with friends.

CHUCK

In 2006, close to the remodel being finished, I began dating, and I met a man named Chuck. He was an engineer who had graduated from Princeton and was recently retired. He was a free spirit who liked to play.

He had lived in Ballard, a residential neighborhood in Seattle and had built large metal sculptures, which he displayed in his yard. Some of the sculptures had moving parts. He lined the edges with a thick wick and would set them on fire, so that they were outlined with fire. The one I remember most was an eagle with moving wings. He would move the wings with an attached rope. The neighbors complained and the city told him to get rid of the sculptures. I believe it was the fire thing that the neighborhood objected to most.

Instead of getting rid of the sculptures, he found four acres of property north of Seattle and moved there with the sculptures, which he could display without trouble. His land had a rather rustic cabin that was near a deep pond fed by a stream that we swam in. Most of the property was wooded, but there were a number of other buildings. One was a bathroom in a small house like structure that was seventy yards from the cabin. There was also a building for a sauna that held up to twelve people comfortably. There was a large workshop, a guest house, and a yurt, all quite rustic to be polite. He had laid out a labyrinth on top of a hill a way up from the pond and cabin. He was a pagan.

I found it interesting and fun to go spend weekends. Everything was like a game that children would play. It was fun while it lasted, until I found out he was seeing other women (plural) while leading me to believe that he was only relating to me. This had gone on for nine months. When I found that out, I realized that there had been clues that I ignored. The dishonesty really bothered me. I was furious and hurt at first, until I realized that, once again, I was in love with the idea of the relationship and not with him. Looking back, I'd had a good time. I'm hopeful I've learned to stop being in love with relationships with not so lovable men. And I learned some things about Paganism, at least Paganism according to Chuck and friends.

BRENT

WHEN THE REMODEL WAS COMPLETED IN 2007, I lived in the house for a few months and began to feel it was too large for me to live in alone. I mentioned this to a friend who knew someone who wanted to move back to Seattle. He introduced us and we met and talked, and things felt right. His name is Brent. I invited him to move in, and he moved into the downstairs part of the house and we share the kitchen. There is good separation of the major living spaces and privacy is not a problem.

He agreed to help with the gardens as a part of his rent. Originally, I was to help with the gardens, but since then my balance has taken a hit and I tend to fall over when bending down or walking on uneven ground, so they have become Brent's gardens.

Brent is a real animal person and bonded quickly with Duquesa and Charlie. In fact, they soon were sleeping with him instead of me. He cheated a little by getting a heated mattress pad, which they loved. He took over grooming the dogs, as felt that what I was paying the groomer was outrageous. We wash them together, but he does the rest. He is here at the house most of the time and they follow him around. If I want to know where Brent is, I just find the dogs. They are incredibly attached to him.

Brent does other things that I did not include in the deal. He was a chef for a high-end restaurant for over seven years, so he does all the cooking and grocery shopping. His cooking is excellent and much appreciated. He keeps the kitchen up and sets up the coffee pot for the morning.

Brent has become a good companion, confidante, and advisor. He was helpful in supporting me in dealing with my sister and with things at the agency. He is gay so there is none of that sexual tension that can make relationships difficult. He is very helpful to me and now that I am not able to drive, he gives me rides when he can. Brent has contributed to our quality of life by his involvement in the gardens and the bird sanctuary and by caring for the dogs and me. I feel very fortunate to have Brent in my life, and I think we have a win-win living situation.

THE BIRD SANCTUARY

BRENT ALSO DEVELOPED A BIRD SANCTUARY that has matured over the years. The patio near the sanctuary has a good-sized Mexican fountain, which provides water for the birds to drink and bathe in. The patio is brick and flagstone, and there is sand between them which the birds need for digestion. I have noticed that several sparrows come and pick at a rope like fiber matt outside the door to the deck. They are pulling fibers they use in their nests. The Stellar Jays essentially destroyed some Tibetan flags we had, tearing strips off also for their nests.

We keep suet cages hanging in two places and spread their seed on the top of a retaining wall. The birds are tended year-round. There are also a number of plants in the gardens that they feed on. The humming birds have feeders and are quite competitive about them, chasing each other back and forth during the day. In the evening, they are calm and share for the last feeding before sundown. There are a number of bird houses for nests that are not as popular as they used to be. At dusk, the crows from the area fly south, hundreds of them, to nest for the night. Crows and starlings are not welcome in the sanctuary, as they are aggressive and have killed the young of the other birds. They seem to know this, and we seldom see them in the yard.

There is also a Paragon Falcon that hangs out periodically and every now and then snatches one of the birds, usually a fat sparrow. It has been around lately and according to Brent appeared today with a female. They have attitude and do not shoo off easily. We have to just accept this as part of the balance of nature. They are very beautiful, large and brown with speckled breast and light-colored chest. But they eat our babies. There is a long evergreen clematis that extends the length of the garden where the smaller birds hide when the Falcon comes. There are also nests in this sprawling heavy vine.

Most birds are seasonal, migrating to warmer climates in the fall and returning in the spring. There are some that do stay year-round. The birds help reduce the bugs in the garden. There are more types of birds than I realized that are native to Seattle. There are a number of different kinds of sparrows, chickadees, juncos, bush tits, towhees, robins, flickers, stellar jays and hummingbirds. I am partial to the flickers because of their beautiful color of orange underwings and to the stellar jays that are a beautiful dark blue and have attitude, often scolding whoever is around. Flickers are wood peckers, and I often hear them pecking on the house. There has never been any damage, just fewer bugs.

THE GARDENS

THE BACK GARDEN IS MATURE WITH PLANTS collected over the years. Brent has developed it and nurtured it since the remodel in 2007. He has planted food bearing plants among the ornamental. We have grapes, Italian plums, squashes, cucumbers, rhubarb, raspberries and tomatoes. There are towers that Brent built for green beans to climb. There is an Asian pear tree, a peach tree and a fig tree in the front garden.

In the back garden there are at least ten roses, just behind the retaining wall above the patio. When they are in bloom, the fragrance is lovely. The roses are not often used in Ikebana but wonderful for bouquets in the house. When they are in bloom, a vase with a variety of blooms may well just appear on the ottoman tray near my chair in the living room or on my writing table.

There are lilies, some a few feet tall and a fair number of a very tall and pungent variety that grow above the rose bushes. Brent has also planted a number of things that I use in Ikebana, such as Iris, gladiolas, dahlias and mums, peonies and hostas. There is a giant hosta with very wide leaves, too big for Ikebana, that grows in front of a large, bright red peony bush. It is one of my favorite spaces in the garden. There is also a large plant called "Bears Breeches," which has big leaves and flower stalks that are blue and white that loom up over the surrounding plants and can be seen from the deck and patio. It is not for picking but does add great interest. Another favorite of mine are different varieties of clematis. One called Montana Ruben is very full and needs pruning constantly. It has medium size pink flowers and spreads quickly into other plants. For this reason, it is not a favorite of Brent's, but it is beautiful. Another deep blue clematis grows on my bedroom exterior wall with relatively large blossoms. Below are somewhat unusual flowers called Fritillaria that Brent has propagated over a number of years. They are about three-feet high with bright red and orange blossoms. A prolific jasmine grows beside the stairs from the garden level to the deck and wafts wonderful fragrance when blooming. The evergreen clematis harbors the small birds, the flowers have small white blossoms and the fragrance is very pleasant and strong enough that it spreads through the garden and into the neighbor's yard, too.

By now, Brent's gardens are lovely, and we have a Garden Party every July. About forty people come and it is always a good time. We serve ribs and lasagna. Others bring pot luck that is always great food. There are some consistent desserts, Margi's coconut cake, Pat's brownies and Geri's lemon bars.

We put extra chairs and tables outside where people can eat and talk and move from group to group visiting. People eat grapes off the vine and plums off the tree. Some years there are smaller children who play with the water around the fountain. They fill up watering cans and water the plants or just play scooping the water and usually get pretty wet. Parents always stand by as the pond of the fountain is about two-and-a-half feet deep, and little kids need supervision.

RESCUE ATTEMPT FOR GARY

After the divorce from Gary, we had stayed in touch infrequently by phone and email. It sounded like things were going ok for him and he was involved with a gay community in Oregon. Soon after Brent moved in, though, Gary called to say that he was destitute in rural Oregon and needed help. He said that he had stopped drinking, which was a surprise, as I did not know that he had a problem. He was being evicted for not paying rent, had sold his car for food, and did not know what to do. Brent and I discussed it and decided that he could come stay with us for two weeks, provided that he would figure out housing and get on some kind of DSHS program. It was suggested that he do some kind of recovery program, too. I grabbed one of Brent's friends, and we headed out to pick him up. It was a 400-mile round trip.

When we got there, he was standing in the middle of a field with his dog. I would not have recognized him, as had not seen him in ten years, and he had put on a huge amount of weight, and his face had changed with signs of alcoholism. Both he and his dog needed a bath. He had few possessions but had a lap top. He and his dog were both depressed.

He agreed that he had two weeks to find a place to live. Brent and I filled out his application for welfare and medical coverage. I took him to the DSHS office near our house and he did get benefits. He displaced Brent from his living room and spent his days on his computer and watching TV. There was no progress for six weeks. He went to one Program meeting with me and refused to go to any more. As time went by, he began to get angry and rude toward me. While I was away from the house one day, Brent told him that he could not act like that and that he would need to leave. I came home and agreed. We gave him until noon the next day to have a place to go, and we would take him there. We left him the next day at a small hotel that took dogs. I put two days on my credit card with the promise that he would pay me back with his next check, which he did. He did connect with some old friends a day later and went to be with them. I got a few emails that were hostile and told him to stop, which he did. I didn't hear from him again.

MARGI

IN DECEMBER OF 2007, MARGI MOVED to the Seattle area. We became friends soon after she arrived. Eventually we began going to dinner and a movie most Saturdays when she is in town. Margi also came to Mexico on several visits.

On one visit we had a serious tropical storm. It was quite frightening, and water came gushing down a wall in one bathroom. The house was built of mostly concrete or stucco and came through the storm intact. I was a little worried, but we came through it intact too.

Margi and I share a good deal about our work and life in general. She is good company, and we have much in common regarding our past. Her father was an automobile dealer, as was mine. We both had similar escapades growing up. We often shop at similar stores and on a number of occasions have arrived at our destination in the same outfit without consulting. Margi has worked in the hair industry for many years. I, too, have had a long career. We both do a fair amount of service and consult with each other about it. Since late 2007, we have remained close friends.

Margi is a lovely and lively person, very congenial with good energy. She has a great sense of humor. She is a good speaker and runs workshops for her job. She puts energy and humor into what she presents. She is a very loyal friend, generous, caring and accepting. She is one of the people I know who is stable and with good mental health. She is liked by many people and has become very important in my life.

THE ATTEMPT TO RETIRE

IN 2008 ON THE 40TH ANNIVERSARY OF MY CAREER, I decided to retire. It gave me time to read, to get back to painting, and to visit more often with friends. I was thoroughly enjoying these things, especially painting. It was good not to have to rush to get to work on time in the morning. It was good to be able to watch some late-night TV.

I put Mary in charge of the agency. She had worked for me for three years as the Clinical Director, and I believed that she would be competent and adhere to the principals of the agency that I had established. I would meet with her at home once weekly for supervision. It was difficult, though, as she did not respect the feedback or direction I gave her. I later learned she would go back to the agency and declare that she would not do what I suggested and was going to run things as she wanted. Brent was often at the house when I met with her and heard our disagreements and told me to fire her. I was hesitant to do that, though, as I have trouble firing people and I did not know who could take over. I wanted to remain retired. My friends Shirley and Margi recommended I fire her too.

One day, I got a call from the Business Manager that I needed to come in, as they were significantly short on the money to do pay roll. I went in, found that a significant amount of money was missing and learned that the agency was a disaster. Mary had lost a number of good staff, had failed to do marketing, and had offended many of the referral resources that I had spent twenty years developing. The case load was very low. She had not marketed in many months. She had not been presenting the whole and realistic picture in supervision.

We knew that she would sue us when I fired her, as we had witnessed her sue a number of people over the time she had worked at the agency. I learned that she had been very critical of staff and disrespectful. Apparently, the first staff who got to the agency on a given day would let other staff know what her mood was so they could avoid her if possible.

So, I contacted a good lawyer, got my ducks in a row, and a short time later I fired her. She sued us relatively shortly after that. We went to court, and it was a grueling experience. I never want to do that again; but, we won, and I went back to work full time.

I began to contact the referral resources that she had offended and to say "She is gone. I am back, and we would like to work with you again." Some responded and we were careful to prove ourselves again. Things began to get back together. I put all my energy into repairing the damage and no longer did clinical work.

It would take me nine years to bring the agency back. We put together a good staff who liked working with our population and did a good job. The staff stabilized and we took a number of interns which always brings some energy to the agency. The Clinical Director semi-retired, and the new one is still there and doing well. We raised our rates, which helped the financial stress. This gave the staff raises since we revenue share.

WALKING IN SEWARD PARK

In 2010, I STARTED WALKING WITH TWO FRIENDS in Seward Park. We met every morning at 7:00 a.m., rain or shine including on the weekend. I have lived near Seward Park for thirty years. The park, along with a number of other parks in Seattle, were designed by the Olmsted Brothers in 1911. They designed Central Park in New York City, as well. Seward park is located on a peninsula that juts out into Lake Washington. The walking and running path around the water's edge is two and a half miles. There are a number of beaches along the way. There is a view of the city looking from the northwest side and a magnificent view of Mt. Rainier looking south. I have walked many dogs in the park over the years. I have three dogs' ashes under a clump of three trees near the pathway.

The eagles nest near the water and soar overhead and sometimes we would see them dive for fish. The cormorants rest on pilings out in the water watching for fish. They are voracious fishers and in Asia they band their long necks so they can't swallow the fish, reel them in and take the fish. Blue herons are large and beautiful and territorial. I became fascinated by coots, small dark birds that gather together closely on the water and when threatened move in closer to each other and stir up the water to confuse and turn the predator away. From above they must look like a very large thing. I have witnessed an eagle starting to go for a coot and then turn away when the water got turbulent. It was fascinating.

There was also a beaver who swam by some days. I took it as a sign that it would be a good day. The company of the other women was most pleasant. We talked about people we know in common, not gossiping of course, just sharing information, and about family members, and some about ourselves. The hour it took us to complete the walk set things up for the rest of the day. It was good exercise, and we continued to do it for over three years.

THE END OF WALKING THE PARK

Unfortunately, in 2013, while walking in the park one day, I did something to my right foot and was in severe pain. I went to my doctor who put me in a boot, but the pain increased. I was referred to PT; and, when there was no improvement, my PT gave me the name of an orthopedic surgeon.

I went to the surgeon, and he informed me that I had shredded the tendon that holds up the arch in the foot. I needed a form of surgery that would be quite complicated in order to rebuild my foot. I had five incisions and was not able to weight bear for over six long weeks. They put me on pain medicine that made me feel crazy, and I was glad when I didn't need it anymore. Some women from the Program brought several meetings to my house during the time that I could not get out.

Getting around was not easy, but I did get a knee scooter that allowed some mobility. A good friend who is a contractor built a ramp off the front porch. I thought I did well maneuver the scooter, though Brent did not agree and made fun of me. Whatever, I did get around. When it healed, the pain was gone, and I have been grateful. I would not walk the park again for a number of years and really missed it. The other women kept it up for some time then stopped also. We are all getting older.

PAT

PAT, WHO WAS ONE OF MY SEWARD PARK WALKING BUDDIES, and I have remained active friends. Pat seldom drives her car so I would give her rides to meetings. Since I stopped driving, we have several people who give us rides together. There are several who are reliable and take us to meetings regularly with several back up people.

Pat just turned eighty-five and, like me, is beginning to slow down physically, but not mentally. She does take regular walks near her house several times a week. She is well known in the Program and has many friends. Her husband died a few years ago, and she now is living with one of her daughters.

Pat loves to eat, though she is not overweight and must have the metabolism of a tiger. She loves pastries, and whenever Brent makes a pie, we always send her a quarter of it, which she eats in one sitting. She is partial to quantity though considers quality important too. Brent's pies are very excellent with great crusts.

She is great company and we talk often on the phone. We don't gossip, but just keep up on what's happening with everybody. She had many great stories of her past, and I find I laugh frequently when in her company. She is a favorite friend along with Margi and Joan, as those whom I see most regularly.

DUCHESA DIES

In 2011 Duchesa died when her throat closed up from an old injury. Charlie and I were walking with her. We were with a friend who was an Emergency Room nurse who talked an ambulance crew into letting us have a small tank of oxygen while we rushed Duchesa to the vet. My friend got the tank back to them the next time they came to where she worked. We got to the vet and they worked with her for three hours but could not save her. They let Charlie and me stay with her. They said Charlie needed to know what happened to her. It was hard because not only was she a dear little thing, she had been my Mexican rescue. She was eleven years old, and ten of those had been good with us.

Charlie, Brent, and I were in mourning, so one day I looked on line and found puppies for sale that were part King Charles Cavalier and Shia tzu, so I grabbed Margi, and we went to see them. It was a family with kids who had them, so I knew it wasn't a puppy mill. I picked the most curious one.

She was a little black and white fuzz ball and very cute. I named her Coco Chanel. Charlie was cheered up and they have been the best of friends. Coco has become truly bonded to Brent. She is smart and very sweet. She is definitely Brent's dog. She is also overweight which is difficult to work with when you have two dogs. But she is happy and lively.

THE 50ᵀᴴ HIGH SCHOOL REUNION

I had begun writing this Legacy in 2010 and had hit a block on my adolescence. In 2011, though, when my 50th high school reunion was about to happen, I decided that it might help me to continue writing, so I went.

To my surprise, it was a good experience. We had gone through Vietnam and the AIDS epidemic, so there were quite a few people who had died. The rest of us were just glad to see each other. The old competitions, resentments were gone, and it was very interesting to learn what each other had been up to all these years.

My old heart throb was there, and we spent some time together. He had become a farmer, a successful one. He was somewhat bald like most of the other men. The women seemed to age more gracefully. He drove a sports car. He also seemed a little uncomfortable that I was not drinking, as he and many others were certainly celebrating. I was happy to be sober. I got several drunken marriage proposals, which I declined graciously.

After the reunion, I got a number of calls from him and was suspicious that he was drunk and perhaps in blackout when he called. He would make a date to get together as was coming to Seattle to be with his kids and his grandchildren. He never followed through, and I did not take it personally as I too had made many phone calls in blackout, and I don't know what I said. It just made me a little sad.

I stayed at "my" hotel but took Carolyn out to dinner and invited her to come with me to our grade school luncheon. She clearly enjoyed this. She wore a short-sleeved blouse to the luncheon and her arms were not much more than bones. People were civil about it, but it was startling. This would be the last time I saw her in person. I would keep up the phone calls but not visit again in person.

I realized just how much my perceptions about myself at that age were distorted. I learned that I was liked by my peers and was much more popular than I had thought. There was much reminiscing that was enlightening and fun. People clearly liked the parties and other gatherings at my house. A few had water skied behind our boat on Priest Lake. They also really liked my parents, especially my father. We wore badges with our graduation pictures on them, and I was prettier than I had thought. I am glad that I don't have to do that again. Adolescence was hard.

A SAD PHONE CALL

In late 2011, I got a phone call from the Peirce County Coroner asking if I knew where they could get in touch with Gary's family. They had found him dead somewhere in Pierce County. They got in touch with me through a doctor, who had prescribed some anti-depressant pills that were in Gary's pocket. I had referred Gary to him many years ago when we were still married. I had gotten to know the doctor when I was dealing with the mentally ill with AIDS. The only family I knew who was still alive and in Seattle was Gary's brother-in-law, and I called and asked him to call the coroner, which he agreed to do. I never found out how Gary died. I tried to, but they would not tell me, since we were divorced. He must have been alone.

I'm glad that I had made the attempt to help him in 2007. It wasn't successful in many ways but I, or I should say "we" to include Brent, tried. You just cannot help people who are not willing to do the work needed. I can only assume that Gary died from something related to his alcoholism, and that it seems likely he was on the street—things that seem very tragic to me. I had been with him for twenty years, and I was shaken he had died with no one there who knew him.

MOVING THE AGENCY

The offices above the credit union became too expensive, and were now larger than we needed, so I found a business real estate person, who found us a new space in Madison Valley in 2012. It was once a little house, and is a bit funky, but fits us well, and we made it attractive enough. It is a nice neighborhood and has been pleasant.

My commute was wonderful. It started at the south end of Lake Washington Boulevard and went along the Boulevard to Madison across from where the Arboretum begins. There are no stop lights, and traffic is relatively light.

The boulevard runs along the lake most of the way and goes through several lovely and interesting neighborhoods. I was very grateful. It took me eighteen minutes from home to the office with few delays. Some of my friends and co-workers were taking up to an hour in their commutes.

I liked the new space, as it was small and just casual enough to make people comfortable. The old space was a good deal larger but had a somewhat corporate feel to it, and I feel like the little old house fits us better, and the price is right. We do struggle for parking, and we are without a kitchen, but we survive. I renewed the lease for another five years in 2017.

The agency still struggles, but somehow, we keep the doors open. I finally did retire in July of 2018 but still go in for staff meetings two days a month, which I intend to drop soon. I am available to the bookkeeper and my assistant by phone. The treatment we provide remains high in quality, and I am proud of that. The staff are devoted to their work and, as best as I can tell, are happy. I feel it is most important that we still welcome family involvement.

RITA IS DIAGNOSED

IN 2007 MY FRIEND RITA WAS DIAGNOSED WITH LUNG CANCER. She made it clear to everyone that she was not going to stop smoking. She told me that the urge to smoke was so strong and painful that she wasn't going to quit. So, I stopped bringing it up and just accepted that was clearly what she wanted. She would survive the next nine years.

Some of the political women in her life pursued archiving Rita's papers that related to her work with the Equal Rights Amendment in particular, in the State and nationally. They are now in Olympia in the State of Washington Archives.

Rita and Joan got married. A fairly large amount of people went, including me and Brent and all of Rita's children and grandchildren and many friends. Rita did fairly well for much of the nine years. Brent would smoke with her when they came to our house or we went to theirs, so Rita and Brent had many talks and were fond of each other. She and Joan had two large and important birthday parties, one for Joan's 75th and one for Rita's 80th. Many people came to both. People from all over the country came to Rita's celebration. She had worked politically for many years and had gotten to know many people.

She and Joan chose for her to stay home and got help with hospice care. When Rita died, it was a great loss to many people, including me, as for many years, she had been a big part of my life, had been very kind to me, had taken care of me in my last episode, and was always supportive and generous, along with Joan.

When Rita died, she left money to be used for the family to celebrate holidays together. We have done this for the last two Thanksgivings. There were twelve of us this year. This speaks to Rita's generosity and thoughtfulness of those of us who are part of the family. We all miss her very much.

Joan and I have, of course, remained friends since Rita's death. She is a sound person about many things, especially financial things. When I have consulted her, I take her advice seriously. We do get together regularly and still spend holidays together, most often with the family which has now grown to include twelve of us, including me. I am still in contact with Rita's daughter Wilma and her son, Matthew.

CAROLYN DIES

WHEN CAROLYN DIED IN JANUARY OF 2017 of a massive stroke, my first response was relief. I found it sad and uncomfortable that this was my first thought. Carolyn had really been so difficult. It made it very hard to mourn her. As a little time went by, I began to realize that I was having trouble with it because I had not forgiven her.

I thought about the relationship Maxine and Carolyn had and how mother became such an important and negative influence for her. When she was little, mother set Carolyn up with her teachers, the other mothers, and the kids telling all that she had a life-threatening condition. It was easy for them to view her with trepidation for fear she might die on their watch. It really was like she was a little time bomb. I do not think that Maxine thought of the impact that it would have on Carolyn with these people. Her major concern was to know that Carolyn was not wheezing. Might there have been a better way to let people know without making her a freak. It is possible mother had ambitions for Carolyn to be a concert pianist. She did push her to join a social club and music club and later the Junior League. I think that there was a part of Carolyn that liked this and did not view it as I did, which was to support Maxine's thing about social standing.

Our mother never did show much empathy for Carolyn, and not often for others, either. I will always remember my mother asking me with contempt, "How did I raise such a do-gooder?" I have no doubt she meant it negatively and was truly puzzled as she had little understanding for people who did things for others. Carolyn had real difficulty with intimacy and empathy for others, too. She tended to be judgmental and to avoid relating closely to others especially in the later years of her life. Also, she clearly felt entitled. She remained a Princess. She eventually became paranoid of her neighbors, and clearly of me. She was bitter about her life and that pretty much got displaced on the rest of the world which included me. I still believe if she could have related more closely with others in the Program her life in sobriety would have gone well. For instance, if she had helped others in the Program, she would have grown to better relate to people in general. There were signs of this happening when she was early in the Program.

When Carolyn died, Fred found three closets full of designer clothes with the tags still attached. I asked how many and his response was 100. I am not sure if it was really that many or it just seemed so. This business of designer clothes really bothered me, as I thought of how much they must have cost and how much of that money was supposed to go to me and eventually Fred. When Carolyn had gone through her inheritance, Fred bought her house for her so that she could live there for the rest of her life. I finally let the clothes thing go by thinking of them as her art collection.

Carolyn's unending quest for our mother's love was never fulfilled. Understanding mother's narcissism and lack of empathy was not easy, and I was able to do it only with some heavy therapy and work in recovery. Maxine's decisions were based on what would serve her well with little regard for others. Whenever there is hurt there is anger, but to be angry at mother was not an option for Carolyn. This anger spilled over onto many of us in her life. The relationship between mother and Carolyn had been so sick. How did mother become such an important and such a negative influence in Carolyn's life? For one thing, Carolyn allowed it.

I was able to mourn and be sad that her life had gone as it did. How lonely she must have been all those years. I was just glad that I had called her regularly and had let her know that I cared. Perhaps I forgave her before I was aware of it.

Fred, my nephew, wrote a wonderful obituary and organized the memorial service and a lovely luncheon afterward. The flowers for the grave and service were not delivered as promised, apparently because the van driver who was to bring them was not to be found. There was a white rose bouquet sent by a family who were friends of Fred. The service was attended by seven people plus Fred and his husband Adam and me. When Carolyn's ashes were in the grave. I threw in a white rose. as I have a special love of flowers.

As I entered the room for the luncheon, it dawned on me that all these people had been told tales of Fred and me. I was a cocaine snorting lesbian, and Fred was an ungrateful son who took her house. I knew that there had been more tales told, and I laughed silently to myself as I sat next to her best friend.

I said to her, "Contrary to what you may have been told I am not a cocaine snorting Lesbian." There was a little laugh.

The luncheon was lovely, and the guests seemed to enjoy it, sharing their memories with each other. As we were leaving, Carolyn's friend took my hand, "I am so glad we got to talk," she told me. "Now I can see you through my own eyes."

At dinner that night, Fred and Adam started laughing and told me that they thought the missing flowers may have been due to Carolyn's ghost doing its thing. Apparently, she had continued to celebrate her anniversary in sobriety, and they had sent her flowers in a Tiffany vase the last time. They did not hear from her so called to see if she had received the gift.

She said curtly, "I did, but the flowers were wilted."

So, they had sent another bouquet. Again, they hadn't heard from her, so they called again.

She told them, "The second flowers were also wilted. Don't ever send me flowers again."

And had I annoyed her by throwing the white rose into her grave? It certainly wilted soon after that.

NEW KNEES AND SHOULDERS

IN 2016 I HAD A KNEE REPLACEMENT, and Brent had shoulder surgery. Brent had hurt his shoulder and torn his bicep trimming the hedge in front of the house. Since then, I hire that done. Brent was persistent in working with his shoulder to get his range of motion back and seems fine now.

My knee was just old and full of arthritis. Prior to the knee surgery I mentioned to some of my women friends in the Program I might need some help when I got home. I did not want to impose on Brent but did not want to go to a nursing home for "rehab" when I knew I would do better at home. Twelve women responded, brought food, meetings and two stayed overnight with me when I was still on pain medication and might have had trouble falling. One stayed two nights in a row. This is how the women in the Program have each other's backs. I am very grateful and try to return the favor. The Program teaches that it is important to ask for help when we need it.

AGING GRACEFULLY

BY NOW I HAD TO LOOK AGING IN THE EYE. It was happening, and I wanted to do it gracefully. This was not always easy. I went through a period when I was falling. Falling is not graceful. I always fell forward and though I hit my head several times the doctor always minimized the damage. But they did not minimize the danger this presents. I was sent to PT to work on my balance, which I never felt was that effective, and I surrendered to using a cane as it was better than taking a chance of more falls. Using it is now second nature. I had kept some attractive canes I had after the fall and back injury some years ago but had not used them in many years. Now I do. And I am quite conscientious to be careful as falling is not a good experience. I wore an emergency call bracelet for a while, too, until I realized that my cell phone would do the same thing by calling 911 directly.

I have surrendered to wrinkles and wear them with pride as have earned them. I have surrendered to being paler than in my youth and just wear a bit of blush. I surrender to needing a new glasses prescription each year; and I surrender to needing reading glasses, which I really do not mind.

The hard one has been my decision to stop driving, as I have a scar on the macula of my right eye. It is obvious to me I do not have adequate depth perception in that eye. I have scraped too many things on the right-side mirror of my car, mostly in my narrow garage. I have had three flat tires from hitting curbs, always on the right side. The final straw was I came close to hitting a bicyclist. This was more than enough.

I needed to sell my car back to the dealer, and at first the dealer would not agree to do that. The car was a 2018 Toyota Camry with 2600 miles on it. I'd had it for six months and had not driven it much. It was in mint condition. When the dealer refused to deal with me, I got two doctor's letters and called Toyota Financial Services at the suggestion of my friend Pat. She had occasion recently to call about a problem she was having with a dealer and had gotten what she needed. I explained my medical condition, my age, and the fact that I had doctors' letters. Apparently, they didn't want people to think that they wouldn't help a little old lady who was going blind. So, I got a call from the dealer's public relations person soon thereafter. They were now willing to buy the car back. The car was leased, and I did have to pay a relatively small amount to close the lease. That change did remove payments and insurance from my budget, and that helps toward Uber expenses.

Not having a car is one of the hardest things I have had to do around this aging thing. Lucky for me, Program people are nice about giving rides to meetings, and in a pinch, Brent can give me a ride if I really need it to get something like a prescription or to get dropped off for a doctor's appointment. I am also very lucky that Uber was created, which I use when I have no other options. Though I have had two inappropriate drivers, most of the drivers are usually interesting to talk to and generally drive well. I am the one who made this decision for safety, setting aside pride and independence. I do feel good that it was my decision, and no one took the keys away from me.

CELEBRATION OF MILESTONES

TOWARD THE END OF JANUARY OF 2018, we had a party to celebrate three of my milestones, the 50th Anniversary of my Career working in Mental Health, my 75th Birthday and twenty years in Sobriety. Over sixty people came, many from the Program and others from work and other areas of my life, like Ikebana and a number of old friends.

Seven of my women friends in the Program took over organizing it. One friend put out the invitations, took care of the RSVPs, went to the store with me for supplies and essentially oversaw things during the party. They greeted people at the door, attended to the food, did dishes and in general allowed me to interact with the guests. I did not ask them to do this, they got together on their own. I was grateful and touched. Aurelio, my hair person, arranged beautiful, large and many bouquets and put them throughout the house.

That day, I was filled with gratitude for the life that I have had and mostly en-joyed, for the fact that I seem to be handling this aging thing relatively well, and for the Program and all that it has brought into my life. I am especially grateful that I have been successful in managing my bipolar disorder.

THE PROGRAM

I SHARE HOW THE PROGRAM HAS IMPROVED MY LIFE as an example of how it has helped me to do things that I would not have been inclined to do or know how to do. Everyone needs to make their own decision about recovery from addiction and for it to work you need to want it. We never push it on people but instead live an example of its benefits.

I am grateful that I have gotten in touch with a spiritual part in me. In retrospect, it was a lot of work to not recognize this aspect of life. I was deter-mined to remain an atheist. When I would be in a situation such as flying when there was turbulence, I would hold onto the arms on my seat and repeat to myself, "I'm not going to pray, I'm not going to pray," and then congratulate myself for not praying after we landed.

I believe my experience with my sister and getting her to treatment was a response to a prayer and got me to explore spirituality. Today, I have a spiritual practice every morning, which sets up my day and I start the day with gratitude and acceptance. My relationship with my Higher Power has helped through difficult times, and when I experience anxiety or fear, I say a little prayer that it goes away so that I may be open to do service. This usually has brought me some peace.

My Spiritual practice reminds me specifically of all I am grateful for, like my sobriety, my career, the agency, Brent and Margi, Pat and Joan and other good friends. I am grateful for things that are important to me and make life pleasant like my house and gardens, my dogs, Ikebana, writing and painting. Remembering this each day has helped my attitude generally. Some things I still need to work on, such as not being judgmental of others and acceptance of life as it happens probably just as it should.

I practice slowing down and thinking things through before acting or speaking. Sometimes, I catch myself and ask if what I am about to say is necessary, or insensitive to others. *I feel speaking out impulsively is one of those traits those of us with bipolar disorder need to slow down and work on. The Program helps me to do that.* It's an inspiring thing to watch others get sober. And there is satisfaction and happiness that comes with service to others that brings a decrease in selfishness and ego. The Program has also brought me some amazing friendships that will no doubt be life-long.

I believe that in order to sustain sobriety, one needs to be around and relate to others in recovery. I had those years when I did not do this, and I clearly became a dry drunk and, in my case, a person with an emptiness regarding spirituality. I did not drink, but I did use pot as a means of dealing with negative things in my life and in this way, and I didn't use a spiritual solution to help me through difficult times. I have found that a serious recovery Program works much better than pot. I am not anxiety or stress-free at all times, but when I utilize my recovery principles, I am able to function around the stress and before I know it, answers come, and I am able to get through it.

THERAPY

THERAPY HAS BROUGHT MANY REWARDS. I have been in therapy for a very long time and it has been very stabilizing. I first went into therapy as I believe, as did my teacher, to be a good therapist you need to know yourself well, be as stable as possible, be able to differentiate yourself from others and develop insight in order to help others do the same. *After my diagnosis as bipolar, I knew that I must stay in therapy, as I need someone to prescribe medication and to follow me to ensure its ongoing effectiveness.*

I have continued in therapy since 2001 with the same psychiatrist. He has been most helpful through all that has happened since then. The insight and self-confidence that it has brought me has been important. I have a doctor who is skilled in psychiatry who observes me and helps me deal with stress, any indication of mood swing, and can confront me when I need it. Therapy has taught me the value of allowing another person to know me extensively and to listen to their opinion when given. This has been freeing and is a part of what this is about for me.

MY CAREER

MY CAREER WAS A GOOD CHOICE FROM THE BEGINNING. I was so fortunate to find working in mental health. I found it before I was diagnosed as bipolar, and I do think that in some ways, being bipolar contributed to my ability to have something special to share, as I have related to others with mental health issues. That is not to say that one has to have experienced psychosis in order to be a good therapist. I just think having experienced that pain helped me to better understand what it was like for them. I have never been convinced many therapists realize just how painful psychosis can be.

For me, my career has been enjoyable, challenging and I have mostly good memories of people along the way. I have known some amazing people as clients and staff alike. And knowing that in the fifty years I worked there are many people who did benefit and have an improved quality of life. This is a big reward that has made it easier for me to retire. Having staff whose skills I trust has also made retiring easier. I was somewhat surprised when I realized that fifty years had gone by. That was a long time! I just did it a day at a time as I truly enjoyed my work, and time just happened.

TIME TO RETIRE

In 2018, I realized I was now seventy-five. and one day I thought, "I should act my age." So, I decided to retire.

It was not so easy as I had thought it would be. The Agency is my baby. I have worked a long time. It was not that I did not have things I wanted to do as I had Ikebana, writing, painting and the Program and friends to play with. I kept the Agency but had to teach people my job. Of course, I could never remember everything so I will always be available for consultation, but it took me a while to let go. Also, I had a bad experience when I had tried to retire once before. So, I mustered my courage and let go. It has been wonderful!

BRENT AND HOME GO WELL

Before I retired, I continued to put the agency back on track. There was financial pressure, but I came to take it in stride. It was easier when things were so good at home. I consider myself very fortunate as Brent does so much that makes my life easier. Things continue to work well for me, and I hope for him, too. We came to have things as a routine such as my calling him as I left work. After my call he put the kettle on to make a pot of French Press coffee, which is a good way to end the workday. Now that I am retired, we do coffee around 3:00 in the afternoon. This is perhaps a healthy Huntley Drinkley.

I currently spend a good deal of time writing. When I am not working on this, I am going to meetings, spending time with friends, doing Ikebana arrangements. I also enjoy working sudoku puzzles and playing mah jongg on my tablet. Brent is good company, though we do respect each other's private time. The dogs are around and come to see me for pats when I am writing. I usually watch the news some in the morning and evening. I do like to get out a bit and enjoy going on errands with Brent, though he usually will pick up things for me if I ask. I need to read more than I do and will work on that when I finish this project. I do talk with work more often than I thought I would, but that's fine as there are a few things going on right now that do need my attention. Life is relatively quiet, and I like that for now.

ON BEING BIPOLAR

In the preface, I stated that one reason I am writing this legacy is because I had a number of deaths within a relatively short period of time. When someone in our life dies, it brings up the issue of our own mortality. One function of this legacy is to help me to get in touch with what my life has been and what I have done worthwhile. In doing that I believe there has been a reason I am here. I think that most often, *those of us who are bipolar have a hard time dealing with losses.* By now, I had found a spiritual entity that I experienced as loving, protective, and kind. This helped me determine that death itself was probably nothing to fear, as why would that change? It also had led me to have a daily spiritual practice, to which I added a prayer for the souls of those who had died. It was my way to show respect and remembrance and to help bring closure to my mourning.

This helps me to be able to accept losses of things and of people not due to death but due to circumstances. If I have something to do with those circumstances, I try to learn how I might have had a part in it and if so, what can I learn from it. And this can apply to us especially because *we often lose people and things coming through manic episodes.*

Despite my diagnosis of bipolar I have had an interesting and full life. I have dealt with a number of difficult situations. I have done well as I have also built a good support system, and I have come through the hard times intact and learned a lot.

The reason I have done well is because I accepted my diagnosis and learned as much as I could about it and what I need to do to treat it. Denial is a big enemy for us. You cannot "fix" what you need to if you do not admit you have it. We are lucky it is as treatable as it is!

I was particularly lucky to have studied bipolar disorder before I was diagnosed with it. I encourage bipolar people to do their research and ask their doctor questions about things they need to know. How does the medicine work? Are there side effects? What might you do about it? What happens if you don't take your meds? What happens if you drink or take drugs? If you follow treatment what can you expect? If you do not follow treatment what can you expect? Are there certain behaviors to watch out for? The more you know, the better. Again, you will learn it is treatable, which is not true of some other mental disorders. Many successful people are bipolar, and if they treat it properly, they can do well and live full, rich lives.

There is one theory about which there is some controversy. It is called "kindling" and means that with each additional episode, it becomes more intense and is more difficult to treat. From what I have seen in my work, I believe that this is true. If you stop your medication, it is as good as guaranteed that you will have another episode.

When you are on medication and doing well, it does not mean that you can stop your medication. It means that the medication is working. The bipolar condition does not go away, but, if treated properly, we can be stable and function well. Sometimes, it takes a second episode to convince people that they are bipolar. No one wants to be bipolar, but some of us are. It does not, though, have to be a revolving door in and out of hospitals. If you learn how to take care of it, you have a good chance to have a good and even special life.

Most of us do humiliating things when we are manic. It might be a good thing to think about the humiliating things you did when manic. I have known people to do things like run through their neighborhood naked, take off their clothes in a public place, or jump into Puget Sound because they believed it was the fountain of youth, impulsively take airplanes to unfamiliar cities, buy expensive items they cannot afford like an upscale automobile, give money away to strangers, say inappropriate and embarrassing things to people you will need to deal with in the future, end up in jail when they should be in the hospital, and on and on it goes. *When I think of things I did while manic, I do not want to go there again.*

A good psychiatrist that you trust is so important as warning signs of judgment being off and mood swings are not always things we can see in ourselves. This inability is a part of mania. *Also, mania can be somewhat addictive because it can be fun. But too often, fun may be in poor judgment and have serious consequences. Or, what we think of as fun is not fun to others or to us when we are stable.*

Most of us who are bipolar do not like depression. *Depression almost always follows a manic episode. If you stay on your medication and work with your mood swings with your psychiatrist, chances are good your depression will be shorter in duration.* It is also very important to know that depression most often goes away. It just takes some time. *This is our dangerous period as it is when people get tired of the pain and give up and suicide. This is a terrible tragedy because we do get stable and can have a good life.*

I lost friends and a part of my purpose in work and politics in my first episode. In my second episode, I did lose my job but was able to resume my career because I was correctly medicated and followed recommended treatment. *Most importantly, I believed my psychiatrist when he told me that if I followed treatment I would be ok.* My life certainly has not been all roses, but I have been able to deal with a fairly high level of stress in my career and personal life. I have dealt with more than my share of losses.

I have been very fortunate to understand all this and to have had good psychiatrists to guide me regarding my choices in relation to my condition. Dealing with stress and difficult situations and developing some insight in dealing with my behavior, which is not always wise, is a big part of therapy for me. And being willing and honest about accepting help is not easy but is essential. *We are complicated people who need someone we trust to be honest with us about our behavior because a part of our disorder is not being so good about recognizing trouble coming by ourselves.*

And if we are alcoholic and/or addicted which many of us are, we need to be honest about this as well as it will make a big difference in stability and the effectiveness of the medication. Many of us do get addicted as we think alcohol and drugs make us feel better, which they may well do. I think alcohol calms mania to some extent. But it is temporary and eventually turns on us and often loses its good effect.

It also does interfere with the effectiveness of medication. Being active in recovery is good insurance for stability. I share this as I have learned this, not always easily. When I was first on lithium, I thought it was not helping that much. I stopped drinking soon after that and it worked quite well. I am not always perfect but when something fails, I have learned to look at it, take it into therapy and things usually turn around.

The rewards of being stable in our disorder are huge. Bipolar people are usually good at what we do, and we are usually quite talented and interesting, lovable people, when we are stable. We generally finish what we start, and most often get good results. We can be an asset at work and other activities when we are stable. We are usually good people and liked by others.

We are most often creative, and I feel we need creative outlets. I found Ikebana, writing, and painting. I take these seriously and have found great satisfaction in developing skill which also increases my ability to concentrate and focus. I have learned that building and maintaining an art skill contributes to self-esteem in a healthy way. I did well in my career because I made sure that I learned about the things that were important, when in doubt asked questions and then practiced doing that. And I have done well in Ikebana, as I practice and participate in doing things like having displays in shows that make me do better. Recently, I have discovered that I like to write. I am new at it and I take classes and attend a writer's group and practice. I try to write something every day. I have not been perfect at any of these things but enjoy doing them and strive to improve. These things make my life interesting and bring me satisfaction and pleasure. *I mention this because people with bipolar disorder tend to have certain talents the are important to pursue as it does help to bring meaning to life.*

I have heard people with bipolar disorder say they are more creative when manic. I believe this is most often not true. There are problems when creative things are done when actively manic. We usually do not follow through with things and seldom finish projects. *In addition, our judgment, especially regarding ourselves, is most often distorted. When manic we tend to think things we do are terrific when in reality our judgment is impaired because we are most often grandiose when manic.* And depression can interfere as well. It often is just difficult to move or concentrate. Because mood swings effect my ability to pursue these activities this is good reason for me to stay stable.

IN GRATITUDE FOR ACCEPTANCE

I HAVE NOT HAD AN EASY LIFE, BUT I have had a productive and satisfying life. *Because of my acceptance of my bipolar disorder and my alcoholism, I have learned how to be comfortable and basically happy.* Most often, I feel good about myself, and when I don't, I try to correct what I am doing wrong. I feel I am making progress in aging with some grace, though I am not always pleased that it is as much work as it is. I am still getting plenty of practice in acceptance.

I have known some wonderful and exceptional people and am thankful. I have worked to be kind to others and notice that most people return the favor. I continue to work hard in therapy and recovery as I still have plenty of room to grow. Once in a while I do have a bad day but not often. I truly enjoy my creative pursuits and feel they are important as the more I practice them, I get a little better, and that feels good.

I am generally comfortable with me, who I am, what I have done and am getting more comfortable with my age. Recently, I went to a movie, and the ticket person gave me a senior ticket without my asking. I told my friend Margi this and she looked at me, laughing, and said, "Well, duh." I came home and looked in the mirror and saw more wrinkles than I remembered. I just need to remember that I've earned them.

IN CLOSING

I HOPE SOME OF WHAT I HAVE SHARED will be helpful to others. *I am not glad that I am bipolar, but I am grateful I have learned to work with it. I am grateful that I am a sober woman and have received many rewards through recovery and the Program.* If you are bipolar, grab on and manage it well. If you are alcoholic or addicted, I hope you find recovery and that it will be a wonderful journey as my own recovery has been.

I celebrated the 50th anniversary of my career working with the mentally ill in January of 2018. On May 1, 2018 I celebrated my 20th anniversary in recovery from alcoholism. My 75th birthday was in February of 2018. I have also enjoyed the opportunity for growth and insight through many years in psychotherapy due partly to my own diagnosis and my understanding of treating it. Having worked in the mental health field, I am privileged to have had many colleagues and friends with the admirable qualities of compassion and realizing the rewards of service to others. I have known interesting and most often dear people as clients and have felt graced to witness improved quality of life for them due to work on their part as well as with talented professional therapists who have worked at my agency. The mentally ill are often capable of accomplishments which many others do not explore and do not give them the opportunity to attempt. Also, of great importance is the advocacy from others who care about this disenfranchised population and recognize their needs for respect, treatment and the opportunity to participate in their communities.

I am writing this legacy for several reasons. First, I will blame my psychiatrist. When a number of important people in my life died in a relatively short period of time, he suggested that I write my legacy. He felt it would help me deal with my own mortality, and I agree with him. I am also writing this for my nephew, whom I have only recently begun to know. He is interested in the history of our family, and this legacy may help; and I want him to know about me. Also, I want to do this aging thing with some dignity and grace, which has not always been easy. Writing this puts me in better touch with what my life has meant and serves as a reminder that I have had a life with good purpose. Finally, in sharing my experience, there is a chance it will be of help to others who also are bipolar and alcoholic.

I have been in therapy since I was twenty-four years old. *I will remain in therapy as I am bipolar which I must treat with medication in order to remain stable and function. I truly enjoy my therapy sessions that are to keep an eye out for symptoms that may indicate a need for a medication change, to keep a pulse on stress and to encourage me to increase my insight into my own behavior.* I have been blessed to have had quality psychotherapy from very well trained and supportive doctors. *My active participation in recovery from alcoholism contributes greatly to my stability* and keeps me aware of all I have for which to be grateful.

I have overcome some large obstacles and have had love and many friends. I have done service both professionally and privately. My life has been an interesting journey, and I am clear that I am not here by accident. I don't really fear death, as my higher power has always been kind, so why would that change? I am just not done yet.